95

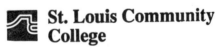

SCENE DESIGN
IN THE
THEATRE

Dennis J. Sporre

*University of North Carolina
at Wilmington*

Robert C. Burroughs

*Professor Emeritus
University of Arizona*

PRENTICE HALL
Englewood Cliffs, N.J. 07632

Library of Congress Cataloging-in-Publication Data

Sporre, Dennis J.
    Scene design in the theatre / by Dennis J. Sporre and Robert C.
Burroughs.
        p.   cm.
    Bibliography: p.
    Includes index.
    ISBN 0-13-791682-5
    1. Theaters--Stage-setting and scenery.   I. Burroughs, Robert C.,
1923-   . II. Title.
PN2091.S8S87 1990
792'.025--dc20   89-8505
                                                      CIP

Editorial/production supervision and
    interior design: Marianne Peters
Cover design: Lundgren Graphics
Manufacturing buyer: Carol Bystrom

Line art appearing on pp. 161–65 prepared by the Graphic Standards Board
of USITT's Education Commission. Used with permission of the United
States Institute for Theatre Technology.

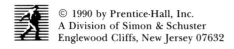

Printed in the United States of America
10 9 8 7 6 5 4 3 2 1

ISBN   0-13-791682-5

Prentice-Hall International (UK) Limited, *London*
Prentice-Hall of Australia Pty. Limited, *Sydney*
Prentice-Hall Canada Inc., *Toronto*
Prentice-Hall Hispanoamericana, S.A., *Mexico*
Prentice-Hall of India Private Limited, *New Delhi*
Prentice-Hall of Japan, Inc., *Tokyo*
Simon & Schuster Asia Pte. Ltd., *Singapore*
Editora Prentice-Hall do Brasil, Ltda., *Rio de Janeiro*

CONTENTS

PREFACE   *vii*

UNIT I THE FRAMEWORK

ONE   DESIGN THROUGH HISTORY   *1*

   Ancient and Classical Greece, 1
   The Hellenistic Period, 4
   The Greco-Roman Period, 6
   The Roman Theatre, 6
   The Medieval Theatre, 10
   The Italian Renaissance, 10
   Spain and Holland, 17
   The Elizabethan Theatre, 17
   The Baroque Period, 20
   The English Restoration, 23
   The Eighteenth-Century Georgian Playhouse, 23
   Nineteenth-Century Theatre, 25
   Early Twentieth-Century Design, 32
   Design since World War II, 39

TWO   *DESIGN AS VISUAL ART*   *47*

    Elements of Composition,   47
    Principles of Composition,   57
    Other Factors,   63

THREE   *PLAY ANALYSIS*   *68*

    Reading the Play,   68
    Determining the Facts of the Play,   70
    The Setting,   70
    Genre,   70
    Mood,   73
    Plot,   73
    Style,   75
    Utilizing Style,   82
    Production Demands,   82
    Research,   84

FOUR   *THEATRE FORMS AND ARCHITECTURE*   *87*

    General Considerations,   87
    General Requirements for Production Types,   93
    Theatre Forms,   96
    Aesthetics and Practicalities,   99
    Options within the Forms: Unit, Simultaneous, and Multiple Settings,   101
    Examining Some Possibilities,   105

FIVE   *WORKING IN THE THEATRE*   *106*

    Broadway Theatre,   107
    Work outside the Theatre,   109
    Union Exams,   109
    Production Organization,   110
    The Off-Broadway Theatre,   112
    The Equity Waiver and Showcase Theatres,   113
    The Regional Theatre,   114
    The Educational Theatre,   116
    The Community Theatre,   117
    The Design Portfolio,   118
    Composing a Résumé,   120

The Contract,   122
The Copyright,   122

UNIT II   PRINCIPLES AND PRACTICES OF SCENIC DESIGN

SIX   THE DESIGN CONCEPT AND PROCESS   *124*

Thumbnail Sketches,   125
Presentation Sketches,   126
Color Renderings,   128
Models,   133
Ground Plans,   135
Sightline Drawings,   135
Front Elevations,   135
Paint Details,   139

SEVEN   DRAFTING   *141*

Drafting Equipment,   141
Drafting Accessories,   151
Drawing Media,   152
Additional Materials,   154
Reproduction,   154
Drafting Techniques,   154
Mechanical Drafting Conventions,   156
Scale,   165
Types of Drawings,   166
Computer Drafting,   169
Perspective Drawing,   175

EIGHT   BUILDING THE DESIGN   *183*

Scenery Units,   183
Sculptured Effects and Textures,   192
Properties and Furniture,   193
Window Treatments,   196
Floor Coverings,   196
Exteriors,   196
Decor Items,   197
The Shop,   197
Materials,   212
Hardware,   219

NINE   *SCENE PAINTING*   *226*

    Design Transfer,   227
    Scene Paints and Pigments,   227
    Basic Procedures in Scene Painting,   233
    Paint Shop Organization,   242
    Drop Painting,   245
    Special-Effects Painting,   247

TEN   *RUNNING THE SHOW*   *253*

    Job Assignments,   254
    Property Head,   254
    Procedural Elements,   256

ELEVEN   *A DESIGN ANTHOLOGY*   *259*

    Summary,   259

GLOSSARY   *301*

BIBLIOGRAPHY   *305*

INDEX   *309*

PREFACE

This is a textbook written by two scenic designers who, between them, represent two-thirds of a century of experience teaching and practicing the art of scene design. This book reflects a deep concern for the quality of education and training given to those who, in whatever professional or other capacity, will involve their creative impulses in scenic design. Our expectation is to appeal to a wide audience comprising those who are approaching the art, formally, for the first time. We aim to go beyond the cookbook approach but intend to stop short of an opinionated epistle. Those who study this text will find in it a concern for disciplined training reflective of up-to-date technology, a sensitivity toward individual creativity, and a strong belief that what is designed for the stage tomorrow cannot ignore or be ignorant of what graced the stage yesterday. We do not apologize for presenting stage design

as an art whose heritage is fundamental to those who aspire to be its future artists. Good scenic design represents high artistry, not mere formularized craftsmanship. At the same time, we recognize that a career in scenic design today makes demands on the artist that go beyond "making pretty pictures." A scenic designer cannot drop the project after the rendering has been completed and return to find a constructed setting awaiting only his or her painting skills. Even at the Broadway level, the scenic designer is responsible for supervising the construction of the setting. At the off-Broadway, regional, educational, and community theatre levels, the designer is required to get even more closely involved with technology. With these realities in mind, we have included in this book material that some might argue is the realm of the technician. We suggest that a good designer must know all these details if he or she is to survive in the profession, at whatever level. Our experience has taught us that good scenic design, which includes successful execution of the setting, encompasses not only the art, but also the craft of theatre.

This book is designed primarily as a classroom text and is organized so that it follows a normal course outline. However, each chapter remains relatively self-contained. Therefore, those seeking source material in any circumstance will, we hope, be assisted. Stage design is a challenging and exciting enterprise; at least, we have found it so. We have tried to capture in our writing some of the excitement and pleasure the art has given us.

The illustrations for this book represent a school in and of themselves. The final chapter, in fact, contains no text at all; it comprises only scenic designs. We believe that the reader should gain as much from studying the designs presented here as from the text itself. We are deeply grateful to the staff of the New York Public Library Theatre Collection at Lincoln Center for their cooperation and assistance. We also are grateful to the Victoria and Albert Museum and the Theatre Museum in London, England and to the State Opera in Tbilisi, USSR for their cooperation.

We gratefully wish to acknowledge the many persons who have actively aided in the composition of this book. Among them are our wives, Hilda Sporre and Patricia Burroughs, and numerous friends and colleagues, including J. Robert Baker, Elaine E. Moe, Sydney Morrison, John Wareing, Gene Genematas, Jeffrey Warburton, Peter Wexler, Mary Ann Abosketes, Peggy Kellner, George Genematas, Dr. Mary Z. Maher, and John Wright Stevens. Special thanks are due Tom Macie for his time, advice, and drawings.

In addition, we are especially appreciative of A. S. Gillette, who instilled in us an honest respect for the art of scene design.

R. C. B.

D. J. S.

CHAPTER ONE

DESIGN
THROUGH HISTORY

The history of scene design is a fascinating one, dating back almost three thousand years. It had its beginnings in Greece and Rome, its Renaissance in Italy and England, a gaudy fling during the nineteenth century, and finally, a subdued fusion with the other theatrical arts in the early twentieth century. At times, it was little more than a collection of unimportant properties for the actor. In other times, its magnificence overshadowed both the plays and the actors. Its workers and artists comprised some of the greatest names and personalities in the theatre.

Most scenery, whether artistic design or mechanical device, developed directly from the structures that housed it, and a discussion of one is impossible without consideration of the other. So, to understand the evolution of scenery from the Greeks to the present, we need also to trace the development of the theatre building from the rude,

semicircular "bowl" of the Greeks, through the rectangular "peep-show" structures of the past 250 years, to some of the newer experimental forms.

ANCIENT AND CLASSICAL GREECE

Although theatre undoubtedly began in the dim, misty, and long-forgotten mystic rituals of early societies, the history of theatre architecture begins somewhere in the fifth century B.C. This period, referred to as the early Athenian, is subect to a good deal of conjecture; very little evidence exists concerning the actual architectural features of the early theatres. The plays of the period were predominantly religious and involved a large chorus, and so we can assume that the theatre required a large acting area. The religious nature of the plays appealed to large

1

masses of the population, and so we can assume further that the seating facilities of these theatres had to accommodate large audiences, providing them with a reasonably good view of the playing area. A brief contemporary reference to the collapse of wooden stands used for seating in 499 B.C. is about all the evidence we possess about the materials used in the early Greek theatre. From the shape of the theatre of later periods, we can deduce some characteristics of the early Athenian theatre prior to 450 B.C.: Probably the natural slope of a hillside comprised the first seating arrangement for the audience. More important personages undoubtedly sat on wooden seats or benches. At the bottom of the hillside a large circle, called the orchestra, provided performance space for the chorus. The wooden seats must have formed a semicircle around the orchestra, since they were arranged on a hillside. An altar, or *thymele,* occupied the center of the orchestra and served to honor the god of the particular festival (Fig. 1.1).

Excavations provide us with greater knowledge of the theatre later in this period. The theatre of Athens on the slope of the Acropolis was constructed on the site of an earlier theatre, built close to the old Temple of Dionysius (Fig. 1.2). This theatre consisted of a seating arrangement comprising an extended semicircle constructed of stone. It accommodated 17,000 spectators. The orchestra maintained the form of a circle, but behind it rose a scene building, probably constructed of wood and mounted on a stone foundation. The details of this building can only be assumed, but we believe it was a one-story edifice containing three doors facing the audience. It is possible that its practical roof could have been used as an additional acting area. A slightly raised platform may have run the length of the building, between the structure and the orchestra. The building itself was called the

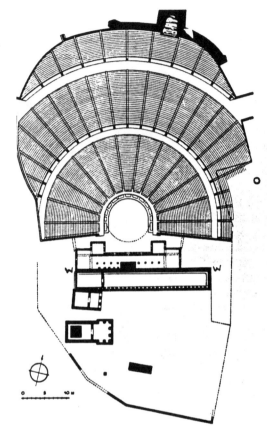

Figure 1.1 Plan of the classical Greek theatre. From Oscar G. Brockett, *History of the Theatre, 5th edition.* Copyright © 1987 by Allyn and Bacon, Inc. Reprinted with permission.

skene, and the narrow porch or colonnade attached to the front of the skene was called the *proskenion.* From these came our words scene and *proscenium.* Attached to the *skene* were projecting wings called *paraskena.* These contained openings allowing passage for both chorus and audience. The passageways themselves were called *paradoi* (parados). We do not know whether the theatres of this period enjoyed anything in the way of painted scenery, but some evidence from the Roman historian Vitruvius and from Aristotle suggests that possibility. Aristotle at-

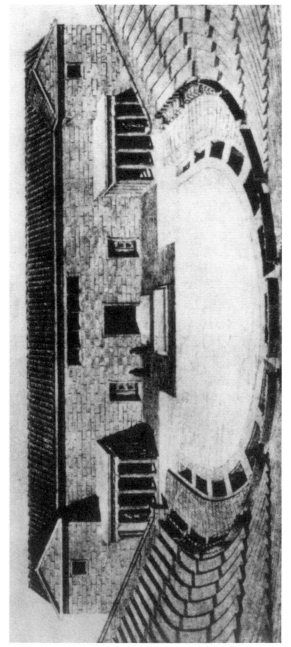

Figure 1.2 Model of the theatre at Athens. From Oscar G. Brockett, *History of the Theatre, 5th edition.* Copyright © 1987 by Allyn and Bacon, Inc. Reprinted with permission.

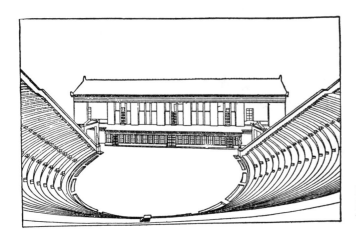

Figure 1.3 Reconstruction of the Hellenistic theatre at Ephesus, Turkey, c. 280 B.C., rebuilt c. 150 B.C.

tributes the use of painted scenery to Sophocles, and Vitruvius connects it to the tragedies of Aeschylus. However, the form of such scenery probably never will be known.

THE HELLENISTIC PERIOD

The period from roughly the fourth century B.C, to the Roman infiltration, about 250 B.C., is called the Hellenistic period. This was a time of great expansion for the theatre in Greece, and evidence exists of theatres at Epidaurus, Megalopolis, Thoricus at Attica, Eretria at Euboea, Piraeus, Syracuse at Sicily, as well as at Athens (Figs. 1.3 to 1.5). The general plan of the theatres did not change, but the skene frequently was two stories tall. Evidence also suggests a low stage connected by steps to the orchestra. After the chorus disappeared, in later Hellenistic times, a stage as high as twelve feet was not unusual.

According to Pollux, a Greek sophist and grammarian of the second century A.D., this period produced the first stage machinery and scenic units. Many of our modern stage devices can be traced back to these, and so it is important to discuss them briefly.

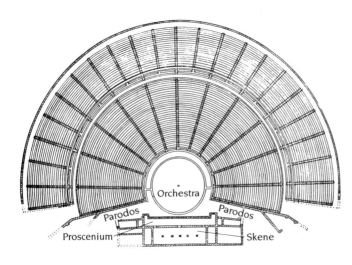

Figure 1.4 Plan of the theatre at Epidaurus.

Figure 1.5 Polykleitus the Younger, theatre at Epidaurus, Greece, c. 350 B.C. Diameter 373 ft., orchestra 66 ft. across.

Among the most interesting scenic units used by the Greeks were revolving, three-sided columns called *periaktoi*. These evidently were placed on each side of the stage and turned to present a different face when a change of scene was necessary. Probably the faces of the panels held nothing more than a decorative design, or perhaps certain symbols applicable to a particular scene. Use of these panels might be likened to our use of a revolving stage, although periaktoi themselves occasionally serve in the modern theatre as a scene-changing device.

Another shifting mechanism enjoyed by the Greeks was the *eccyclema*, meaning "that which is rolled out." The eccyclema was a low wagon on which a tableau was arranged. The Greeks declined to show violence on stage, and so this provided a bit of sensationalism in the form of gory scenes for tragedy. It also was used in comedy to great advantage. The eccyclema was hidden behind one of the three doors in the skene and rolled out at a specific time. Another type of wagon, of semicircular shape, revolved on a central pivot through a door onto the stage, and is sometimes referred to as the *exostra*. The eccyclema probably resembled our wagon stage and might very well be the forerunner of the jackknife stage.

The *machine,* also known as the *crane,* was used to raise or lower the actors. It could suspend them in the air, pick them up from the stage floor, and raise them to the top of the second-floor roof; it might even have been able to swing them from one side of the skene to the other. This device frequently lowered gods from the roof to the stage, as though they were descending from the heavens, and was called the *deus ex machina.* The deus ex machina bears a resemblance to the system of flying we use today.

We have some indication that painted panels, called *pinakes,* were used between the columns of the proskena. Possibly these panels may have had some realistic painting on them, but such a claim is unsubstantiated. Pinakes were undoubtedly portable and could be changed for different scenes. In addition to these machines and devices, Pollux mentions trapdoors and steps, called Charon's Steps; a celestial scaffold called the *theologeion,* used apparently as a platform for the gods; and a funeral-state-couch or *stroheion,* which was mounted on the eccyclema to carry the bodies of dead heroes. He also mentions such sound effects as thunder, created by pouring bags of pebbles into brass containers.

Unfortunately, Pollux is not always clear in his meaning, and he makes little reference to time sequences with regard to these scenic devices. Therefore, we do not know when these devices saw their first usage in the theatre. However, Pollux is still of great value, being the only source for much of our knowledge of the Greek theatre.

THE GRECO-ROMAN PERIOD

The Greco-Roman period followed the Hellenistic and was marked by a definite Roman influence in the Greek theatre. The orchestra was reduced to a semicircle. The scene building became an elaborate architectural façade two and sometimes three stories high, which still maintained three entrance doors. The stage itself was enlarged to a depth of twenty feet, effecting a definite change from the narrow stage of the Hellenistic period. Structures of this type were found at Termessos and Ephesus.

THE ROMAN THEATRE

Although the Roman theatre had its origins in the Greek theatre, it differed from the Greek in many ways. The Greek theatre was built into a hillside, but the Roman counterpart was always constructed on level ground. The outside of the Roman theatre buildings were covered with elaborate architectural detail. The shape of the auditorium, or *cavea*, was an exact semicircle, and it was connected to the scene building, thereby closing the passageway found in the Greek theatre (Fig. 1.6). Because of the shape of the auditorium, the orchestra became a semicircle as well, connecting with the front edge of the stage and providing space for additional seating for spectators. The stage itself was raised (although seldom over five feet), and its depth was increased even more than in the Greco-Roman period. The most impressive difference was in the façade of the scene building, or *frons scaenae*. Two and three stories high, this façade presented a series of elaborate porticoes, panels, niches, columns, capitals, and statues (Figs. 1.7–1.9). The Roman actor must have had to struggle to steal a scene from that wealth of detail. Probably a roof frequently covered the stage area, protecting it from inclement weather. The audience, too, was often protected by an enormous awning covering the auditorium.

Although the Roman theatre had a noble ancestor, it was not held in the same high esteem as was the Greek. The first permanent theatre, built by Pompey in Rome, did not appear until 55 B.C. Before that time, Roman theatres had been of a purely temporary nature, constructed of wood for a particular celebration and then demolished. One of these buildings was described by a Roman public official as having three stories of marble, glass, and gilded wood on 360 columns, and displaying 3,000 bronze statues. This amazing edifice could accommodate 80,000 spectators.

Roman theatre auditoriums were, as a rule, smaller than their Greek counterparts. This probably was due to government censure in the early days of the Empire, to the competition supplied by other forms of public entertainment, and to the weakness of the plays presented in these playhouses.

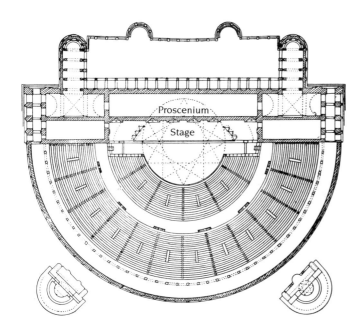

Figure 1.6 Plan of the Theatre of Marcellus, Rome, 23–13 B.C.

Figure 1.7 The theatre of Aspendos, 2d century A.D. From Dennis J. Sporre, *The Creative Impulse: An Introduction to the Arts,* © 1987, p. 140. Reprinted by permission of Prentice Hall, Englewood Cliffs, N.J. Also courtesy of The Victoria and Albert Museum, London.

Figure 1.8 Reconstruction of the stage of the theatre at Orange.

Figure 1.9 Reconstruction of the *scaenae frons* at Aspendos. From Dennis J. Sporre, *The Creative Impulse: An Introduction to the Arts,* © 1987, p. 141. Reprinted by permission of Prentice Hall, Englewood Cliffs, N.J. Also courtesy of the Victoria and Albert Museum, London.

The Romans made use of the scenic devices of the Greeks and added some of their own. The most interesting introduction was a curtain, or *auleum,* which was raised and lowered from a slot at the front of the stage. Vitruvius, with Pollux's lack of chronological identification, mentions three types of scenery. For tragedy he describes a background of columns and pediments used for nobles and kings; for comedy, rows of houses; and for satyric, natural hills, trees, and foliage. Undoubtedly this description did not apply to Greek Hellenistic theatre, although it might apply to the plays written in that period and revived in later times. Roman theatres, some of which are still standing, were found at Orange in France, in Djemila in North Africa, and at Aspendos, as well as in Rome and Athens.

THE MEDIEVAL THEATRE

After the fall of Rome around 476 A.D., the playhouse rapidly fell into disrepute, and by the end of the sixth century, organized theatrical performances seem mostly to have disappeared. For the next five centuries, the spark of theatre was kept alive by small groups of wandering minstrals, jugglers, acrobats, and actors. About the tenth century, the church began to allow certain dramatic elements to be included in the Mass in the form of tropes. This soon developed into dramatizations of Biblical stories and lives of the saints. In the twelfth century, church dramas moved outdoors, although some were presented in the church as late as the sixteenth century. Such religious plays used the front of the church for their setting and its doorways for entrances and exits. During this same time, medieval trade guilds began to produce and stage plays in the marketplace. The plays were frequently elaborate and costly productions involving seating

similar to modern bleachers for the audience and a series of "mansions" or stations that were used as backgrounds for individual scenes or episodes (Figs. 1.10 and 1.11). The most famous of these was a production of the Passion Play at Valenciennes, France in 1547 (Fig. 1.11), which consisted of a long stage with an enormous dragon's mouth spouting real fire and representing Hell at stage left, and heaven at stage right, with ships, lakes, and mansions in between. Another such production at Mons, France, in 1501, included fresh fruit on real trees, live birds, fishes, mechanical serpents, and elaborate sound and lighting effects.

THE ITALIAN RENAISSANCE

It is difficult to say exactly where and when the Renaissance began and the Middle Ages ended. Nor is the documentation regarding theatres terribly clear. One authority says that Alberti put a *theatrum* in the palace built in the Vatican for Nicholas V in 1452. However, no record exists of its use for dramatic performances. Unfortunately, *theatrum* also means a place for exhibition as well as a permanent playhouse. Another authority indicates that the Duke Ercole d'Este, in 1486, had an architect build a theatre based on the writings of Vitruvius. Someone else notes that this was the theatre that was built for the poet-playwright Ariosto in 1532, but the building burned a year later, and no plans or sketches of it were left. All of this confusion arises from the fact that many nobles and churchmen built temporary stages in their great halls for special occasions.

As for scenery, we are not any better informed. A Renaissance writer gives an account of a Cardinal Riario, who "first equipped the stage for tragedy beautifully" in an outdoor production between 1484 and 1486, and "first revealed to our age the ap-

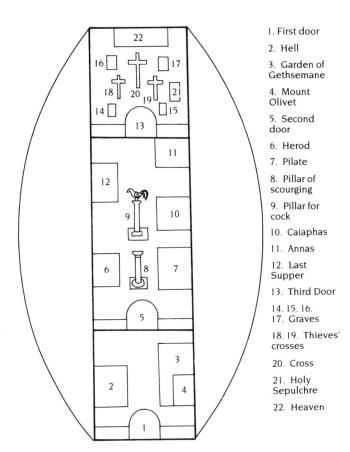

1. First door
2. Hell
3. Garden of Gethsemane
4. Mount Olivet
5. Second door
6. Herod
7. Pilate
8. Pillar of scourging
9. Pillar for cock
10. Caiaphas
11. Annas
12. Last Supper
13. Third Door
14. 15. 16. 17. Graves
18. 19. Thieves' crosses
20. Cross
21. Holy Sepulchre
22. Heaven

Figure 1.10   Plan of a medieval mansion stage showing the mansions in the Donaueschingen Mystery Play, Germany.

pearance of a painted scene." Whether this painting reflected a particular production or not, we cannot be certain; a great number of Renaissance artists, such as Mantegna, Raphael, and Michelangelo painted general backgrounds that had no relation to the plays that might be performed in front of them.

A contemporary account indicates that in 1486 the Roman comedy *The Menaechmi* was played in a courtyard upon "a wooden stage with five battlemented houses. There was a window and a door in each. Then a ship came in . . . and crossed the courtyard. It had ten persons in it and was fitted with oars and a sail in a most realistic manner." This was produced by the Duke Ercole d'Este. In

1487, he produced Plautus's *Amphitruo,* and, in 1491, the Duke revived the first show and had Nicollo del Cogo paint "a prospect of four castles." So we know that illusion was being employed as early as the 1480s. For the most part, Italian drama of the early and High Renaissance was theatre of the aristocracy and was produced with elaborate trappings, usually at court, and in a scenic style reflective of the visual art of the time (Fig. 1.12).

During this same time, the Roman Academy began producing Latin comedies and an occasional tragedy by Seneca. Other academies were formed in other towns and cities, the most noteworthy being the Olympic Academy in Vicenza. These academies soon

Figure 1.11 The Valenciennes Mystery Play, 1547. Contemporary drawing. Bibliotheque Nationale, Paris.

Figure 1.12 Baldessare Peruzzi, stage design, probably for *La Calendria*, 1514. From Dennis J. Sporre, *The Creative Impulse: An Introduction to the Arts*, © 1987, p. 270. Reprinted by permission of Prentice Hall, Englewood Cliffs, N. J. Also by courtesy of Scala/Art Resource, New York.

entered into competition with each other and most of them staged Roman plays. Vitruvius's works on architecture were discovered by the Italians in 1414 and published in the original Latin in 1486. Vitruvius described houses with painted columns and other architectural details but said nothing about how they were to be arranged on stage. Early scene designers solved the problems by using multiple stages with four or five curtained doorways under arches. Each character in the play had his own doorway with his name lettered over the door. A curtain took the place of the door, and when it was drawn back, the audience could see into a small room.

There is no record of Ariosto's theatre built in 1532 in Ferrara, but the next permanent theatre, the Teatro Olimpico in Vicenza, is still standing (Figs. 1.13 and 1.14). It was designed in 1580 for the Olympic Academy by the distinguished Renaissance architect Andrea Palladio. It was the first attempt to recreate a Roman theatre. It had thirteen rows of seats that followed the shape of an ellipse instead of a semicircle.

This provided better sightlines than had its Roman prototypes. It had a flat orchestra floor for the chorus and a raised stage backed by a long wall with three doorways. The long, back wall was flanked by two shorter walls. The center doorway took the form of a triumphal arch. Probably the other openings were intended to be covered with curtains. Palladio died the same year that the work was begun, and his successor, Vicenzo Scamozzi, made several radical changes to the design. Scamozzi slanted the stage floor and built short vistas of streets behind the five doorways. From the central arch, the vistas radiated out like the spokes of a wheel. The vistas were built of wood and plaster and were in violently forced perspective. The theatre was finished in 1584 and opened the following year with an enormous production of *Oedipus Rex* in Italian, with a cast of 108. The theatre held about one thousand persons, and is still used occasionally today for presentation of the classics.

Scamozzi designed another theatre that was even more modern by our standards. Constructed in the late 1580s in the tiny

Figure 1.13 Palladio, Teatro Olimpico, interior, Vicenza, 1580–1584.
Courtesy of Scala/Art Resource, New York.

town of Sabbioneta for the Academia dei Confidenti, this theatre seated only 250. Probably because of the small size of the theatre, Scamozzi was unable to build his multiple doorways, and instead constructed a single vista that began at the sides of the stage. This building doubtless influenced another architect, Giambattista Aleotti, who designed the Teatro Farnese only twenty miles away at Parma (Fig. 1.15). The auditorium held 3500 spectators and was in the shape of a horseshoe. The orchestra floor could be flooded with water for various kinds of spectacles. The stage, however, had a most modern touch—a wide proscenium arch framing a deep acting area. The Teatro Farnese opened in 1618 but, unfortunately, was destroyed during World War II. One scholar

wrote: "The Teatro Olimpico was a plausible imitation of the past, the Teatro Farnese, a startling preview of the future."

In 1545, Sebastiano Serlio, an architect and painter interpreted Vitruvius's description of scenery in his book *D'Architettura*. The book also included descriptions of how Serlio and his contemporaries built and painted their scenery. He published drawings of the three types of classic scenery: the tragic set with lofty palaces and temples for the great lords; the comic set with ordinary city houses on a public square (Fig. 1.16); and the satyr play with the landscape of trees, hills, and cottages. Scene designers in Serlio's time combined false perspective with certain three-dimensional elements. The backing was flat, but the wings were splayed at an

Figure 1.14   Palladio, Teatro Olimpico, stage, Vicenza, 1580–1584.

Figure 1.15   Giambattista Aleotti, Teatro Farnese. Rockefeller Collection, Yale School of Drama Library.

De M. Sebastian Serlio

Figure 1.16 Sebastian Serlio, stage setting from *D'Architettura,* 1540–1551.

angle and had cornices and architectural embellishments. "I made all my scenes of lathes covered with linen the cornice bearing out," Serlio writes. The retreating sides of the wings were cut and painted in false perspective. The wings further back were treated differently than those toward the front: "If you have any flat buildings, they must stand somewhat far inward, that you may not see them on the sides." These upstage wings had no cornices or three-dimensional ornamentation: "The painting work must supply the place by shadows without any bossing out." The first few feet of the stage floor were flat, but the rest of the floor receded at a gentle rake. This type of floor was used until the Victorian age and comprises the origin of our terms *upstage* and *downstage*. Such floors can still be found in some theatres in Europe and in the Asolo theatre in Florida.

Serlio also provided us details of effects, among which were thunder and lightning, moving mechanical figures and forms on wires, and colored and reflected light from candles using a "bright basin." From 1500 to 1650, Italian designers used other arrangements of the same idea, such as prisms, periaktoi, flat wings, and two giant screens for backings.

Another Italian designer, Sabbatini, wrote a book entitled *Pratica di fabricar scene e machine ne' teatri* in which he dealt with creating stage effects such as descending clouds and rolling waves. He also dealt with the problem of fast scene changes. He suggested extra flats that could be placed on the periaktoi on the sides away from the audience and two side wings that could be unfolded. Flat wings sometimes were made to slide on tracks, a device used until the nineteenth century.

The chariot and pole, invented by Torelli, also was a frequently used device (Fig. 1.17).

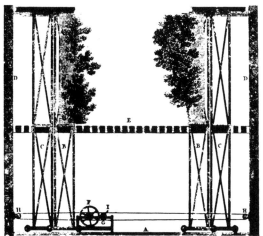

Figure 1.17 Chariot and pole scene-changing system. From Oscar G. Brockett, *History of the Theatre, 5th edition.* Copyright © 1987 by Allyn and Bacon, Inc. Reprinted with permission.

This was a modification of the grooved track.

Until the early nineteenth century, scene changing was done in full view of the audience. It was considered part of the entertainment. The Romans used the front curtain merely to open and close the play. No act curtain appeared in the theatre until 1800. The audience knew the scene was over when the actors left the stage. Illusion was the aim of the Renaissance designer. He depended upon the wonders of perspective to rival reality.

SPAIN AND HOLLAND

The Renaissance found its way northward into Holland and France and westward into Spain. Finally it reached England. In southern Spain, playhouses were erected in patios and courtyards. These were open to the sky; two or three galleries looked down on the stage on all four sides, and a covered entry-way led to the street. A playhouse such as this was constructed as early as 1520 in Malaga. Another appeared at Valencia by 1526, and a third, at Seville, by 1550. Northern Spanish cities did not have patios, and in their place, the Spaniards made theatres out of courtyards formed by the backs of several houses. These were called *corrales.* Valladolid had one of these by 1554; Barcelona, by 1560; and Cordoba, by 1565. Shortly after 1568, Madrid had five corrales. The name *corrale* was a term used for "theatre" in Spain until 1700.

In Holland, the theatre took a more elaborate form, such as the theatre at Ghent. This edifice, built in 1539, had an ornamental façade consisting of five doors on the lower level and three playing areas above. Structures such as this frequently presented *tableaux vivants,* that is, static scenes posed by living characters. The popularity of these scenes greatly influenced the theatre structures of the time.

THE ELIZABETHAN THEATRE

To examine the Elizabethan theatre, we must first give some attention to the builders. Carpenter-actor James Burbage is credited with constructing the first public playhouse in England, in 1576. Many authorities believe that he was definitely influenced by the theatre at Ghent. His first structure was called, simply, The Theatre. Burbage's theatre inspired the construction of the next theatre in a northeast section of London a year or so later. This was called The Curtain, because it was built on a piece of land known as Curten Close or Courtein. When the lease expired on the land, Burbage's sons tore down the building and used the lumber to build the famous Globe Theatre at Bankside, an area south of the Thames, in 1599.

Henslowe, a sixteenth-century speculator,

opened a theatre called the Rose in 1587, and in 1600 he built the Fortune, in northern London. The first Globe burned down in 1613, and Henslowe promptly turned his Bear Garden, in the same vicinity, into the Hope Theatre. By 1605, London had six public playhouses and one private one called the Blackfriars, a priory purchased by Burbage in 1599.

We know more about the theatres that Shakespeare played in than we do about his life, but that information is far from complete. Most authorities believe that the Elizabethan theatre took a unique form. The only previous theatres that approach it are the Spanish corrales, although the Elizabethan theatres may have some distant connections with the Dutch and the Italian. Our sources of information about the Elizabethan playhouse are (1) the great halls and inn yards where plays were given before the theatres were built; (2) the buildings used for bear-baiting and bullbaiting; (3) four sketches ranging in date from about 1596 to 1640, one of which is shown in Figure 1.18; (4) the wording of the contract for the building of the Fortune; and (5) evidence from the stage directions of Elizabethan plays.

The basic elements of the Elizabethan theatre comprise a stage with a door at each side, a balcony above to be used by the actors, a flat floor, and galleries at the sides and rear to hold the audience.

Only four pictures of theatre interiors of

Figure 1.18 Interior of the Swan Theatre, Bankside, London (opened 1598). Contemporary pen drawing.

the time have any reliability. The first is De-Witt's sketch (Fig. 1.18), of which only a copy remains. This sketch seems slightly inaccurate in view of its depiction of "stage business." The second is a picture on the title page of a play called *Roxana*, a tragedy written in Latin and printed in 1630. This picture seems inaccurate as well, and it is possible that the play may have been a university production at Cambridge. One of the best sketches is a drawing reproduced in a play called *Messalina*, in 1640, but this shows only a portion of the stage. The last source is a drawing printed in 1672, which might very well be a performance in a private hall.

The contract for the Fortune, between Henslowe and his carpenter in 1600, required a building resembling the old Globe in all but one respect: it was to be square instead of octagonal. The building was to be eighty feet on all sides and fifty-five feet within. There were to be three stories with galleries providing convenient divisions for gentlemen's rooms and two-penny rooms. The first story was twelve feet high, the second, eleven, and the third, nine. The stage was to be forty-three feet wide, and it was to extend halfway across the open yard, making it twenty-seven and one-half feet deep. Also included were rooms in which the actors could change their attire, a "shadow," or cover, over the stage, and a "tiring house," which may have included an inner and an upper stage. The contract specified convenient windows in the tiring house, probably used for balcony scenes.

The actual structure of the stage has troubled scholars for years; some claim that there was no permanent "inner" stage, inasmuch as important scenes would be lost to the audience if performed there. It is possible that a special structure could have been built out from the back wall. Certainly there were "upper" stages; such a contention is borne out by sketches and stage directions

such as occur in *Richard III* and *Antony and Cleopatra*. Most authorities believe that there were two additional stages on the gallery level that had windows as specified in the Fortune contract. Therefore, the Elizabethan theatre appears to have had seven acting areas: (1) the main stage, (2) an inner stage on the same level, (3) the gallery, (4) an inner stage on the gallery level, (5, 6), the two windowed stages at the sides, and (7) the high place for the musicians. Stairways served the various levels, including the hut and also the cellarage under the main stage.

The hut was the top of the tiring house and had room for cannons and other sound machines. From here, the actors could enter the "shadow," or heavens, which was the roof over the stage, and they could be let down into the scene through a trapdoor. The main stage also contained a number of traps.

The forestage, or apron, was very prominent. In most cases it was wedge shaped and extended well into the open pit or yard. Above this there may or may not have been a porchlike structure supported by two columns. The inner-above and the inner-below probably were equipped with traverse curtains that could be opened or closed to divide the propertied inner stage from the unpropertied forestage.

When we examine the Elizabethan play, we soon realize how flexible the stage must have been. *Antony and Cleopatra*, for example, has forty-three scenes. The public playhouse in Elizabethan times comprised what we call theatre of convention. That is, the *mise en scène* did not rely on illusionistic scenery. On the other hand, plays done at court and in the inns appear to have used a great amount of scenery. Money was spent for "a citie and a battlement, for canvass to cover divers towns and howes and other divesses and clowds, for clowdes and curteynes, for one great city, one senate house for seven cities, one villadge, one Country howes, one battlement for great cloths and greate curteynes." In the public theatres, as we noted previously, little in the way of scenery was used. There were some suggestions of settings on the inner stage—for example, hangings or set pieces for rooms, and trees for a wood. Henslowe's records list only properties:

1 rock, 1 cage, 1 Hell mouth
1 tomb of Guido, 1 tomb of Dido, 1 bedstead
1 wooden hatchet, 1 leather hatchet
Iris head and rainbow; 1 little altar
1 copper target, 17 foils
3 timbrels, 1 dragon in Faustus
1 pope's miter
3 Imperial crowns, 1 plain crown

Some scholars believe that lettered signs or locality boards were used over the side doors of the stage to identify location.

By the time of James I, Italianate scenery and scenic devices definitely began to invade court performances. Beginning in 1605, Italianate scenery was employed in the masques staged by Inigo Jones. Toward the end of the reign of Charles I, scenery seems to have spread from the court masques to performances in private theatres. The chief distinction of the masque was that it introduced to England Italianate scenery, stage machines, and the proscenium. Inigo Jones designed a new frame of symbolic figures and ornament for each of his productions (Fig. 1.19). At first he used the multiple stage with its mansions and also the single stage set of Serlio. However, because he liked startling changes of scene, he began to use the revolving prisms (periaktoi) together with the bent or angled flats and groups of wings which moved in grooves. Rather than use a front curtain drawn to each side to reveal the first scene, a practice followed since approximately 1565, Jones introduced a drop curtain painted with designs. At first this curtain was designed to fall into a slot, as did

the Roman curtain, but it was later changed to move up and down through the use of ropes and pulleys. However, the curtain still was used only at the beginning of a show: Jones delighted in making magical transformations in full view of the audience.

THE BAROQUE PERIOD

After 1650 the new trends and directions in theatre centered themselves in France and Italy, where experimentation in theatrical structures and scenic design took on new meanings. Palladio and Serlio were out of date, and every production was rendered in a more spectacular and ostentatious fashion. In France, around 1655, the Salle des Machines was constructed in the Tuileries. This edifice consisted of a stage that was 32-ft. wide at the proscenium arch and 132-ft. in depth. It could accommodate enormous machines as large as 40-ft. wide by 60-ft. long.

The Italians were not idle during this period either. In the second half of the seventeenth century, the rage for Italian opera spread all over Europe, and every noble wanted to make it a part of his court festivities. Italian scenic designers and painters migrated to other countries. They traveled to Vienna, Munich, and Dresden. The first great family of Italian scenic artists was the Mauri family, consisting of five brothers; three were decorators and two were machinists. They originally came from Venice but moved to Parma and then to Germany. In Parma they had a young assistant who was to found another and more famous family of designers: Ferdinando Galli da Bibiena (1657–1743). He designed for the opera house at Parma in his early years, and later he was summoned to Barcelona to design the fetes for the wedding of Charles and Elizabeth, later Emperor and Emperess. He then moved to Vienna, where he remained for the

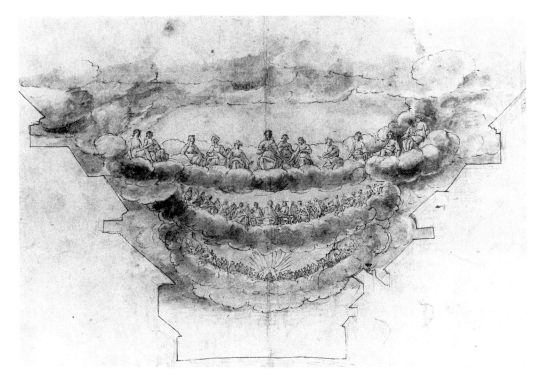

Figure 1.19 Inigo Jones, "The Whole Heaven" in *Salmacida Spolia.*
1640. Collection the Duke of Devonshire, Chatsworth, England.

greater part of his life. Many of his original drawings have been preserved, and he is credited with the revolutionary departure in design that involved the use of diagonal perspective drawing (Fig. 1.20).

His brother, Francesco Galli da Bibiena (1659–1739), worked at Rome, Mantua, Genoa, and Naples. He built theatres in Vienna, Verona, and Rome, and ended his days, as did his brother, teaching scene design at Bologna. Two of Ferdinando's sons, Giuseppe and Antonio, also became scene designers. Giuseppe was the more important and prolific of the two. He worked with his father in Barcelona and Vienna, decorated his first opera in 1716, worked at Prague, Dresden, Munich, Breslau, and Graz, and around 1750 decorated the opera house at

Bayreuth in connection with his son Carlo. Carlo later worked in Italy, France, Holland, Flanders, England (about 1763), and perhaps even in Russia. This famous family, in three generations, spread the practice and principles of Baroque theatre decor across the entire continent.

Another family of designers was the Gallari family from Piedmontese, who worked in such places as Turin, Milan, Innsbruck, and, finally, Berlin, at the Royal Opera House as protégés of Frederick the Great. Italy led the world in design of theatre structures during this period. Some artists worked toward the elaboration of the setting, while others devoted themselves to the development of machinery, and still others worked to construct seating arrangements

Figure 1.20 Giuseppe Galli da Bibiena, design for an opera, 1719. Contemporary engraving. The Metropolitan Museum of Art, The Elisha Wittelsey Collection. The Elisha Wittelsey Fund, 1951.

that would best aid the spectator in viewing the magnificent spectacles behind the proscenium arch.

Since the Greeks, the tendency in auditoriums was toward greater length, with the precise shape taking different forms in the hands of different architects. There were straight galleries running at right angles to the stage front; ovoid galleries; horseshoe-shaped galleries. The ovoid gallery could be seen in the Teatro di Torino and the Teatro d'Imola. The straight galleried type was found in the Teatro di Fano. The horseshoe shape could be found in the La Scala at Milan.

Three styles of proscenium arches graced this period. In one, the proscenium pillars stand at the extreme corners of the stage; a false façade recedes obliquely back to them to draw the eye directly into the scenes. In another, the simple proscenium arch, with no recesses, is very similar to our present proscenium. In the third, the proscenium pillars appear in front; the arch is carried around in a semicircle and supported on two other pillars farther backstage, providing not one, but three, arches. The chief setting appeared in the center arch, and drapes, backclothes, or flats, appeared behind the other two. Also at this time on the European continent, the proscenium arch began to move forward to the apron, placing the actors behind it instead of in front of it. However, England retained the apron stage for almost another 150 years.

THE ENGLISH RESTORATION

During the English Restoration period, the theatre building became a link between the earlier Elizabethan playhouse and the modern proscenium. The Restoration theatre borrowed, not directly from its immediate predecessor, but from a combination of two Renaissance forms: the proscenium arch from the Italians and the French, probably through the work of Inigo Jones, and the enormous apron or forestage and a form of the inner-above from the Elizabethan public theatres.

Four theatres were built in rapid succession in London after 1660. The first was the Duke's House in Lincoln's Inn Fields (1661); then came the Theatre Royal in Bridges Street (1663); the Duke's House in Dorset Garden (1671); and the Theatre Royal in Drury Lane (1674). Nothing further was constructed until Betterton reconstructed Lincoln's Inn Fields in 1695. In 1705, Vanbrugh opened an opera house in Haymarket, and the theatres that followed fall under the heading of Georgian or eighteenth century, even though they still contained features of the Restoration.

In general, the Restoration playhouse included the following: a proscenium and a stage with movable flats and backdrops; a deep apron or forestage for most of the acting; entrances for the actors in the walls of the proscenium; chandeliers in the auditorium and over the forestage; footlights consisting of candles; a raked stage slanting upward from the footlights; a pit, or main floor, with benches (price of admission was two shillings and six pence). The floor of the auditorium was raked, and one row of boxes rose above the pit (four shillings). Two large galleries were above the boxes (one, a shilling and six pence, and the other, one shilling). The pit was usually sunk below ground level and treated as a basement. It has been described as an amphitheatre and took various forms, including a near semicircle, a magnet shape, a broad fan shape, and a rectangle. It was entered by doors in the side walls near the stage. The boxes ran on all three sides of the pit, and some contained as many as seven rows of seats.

Production techniques were comparatively simple. Backdrops could be raised or lowered, and a front curtain often was painted with a scene. Between the backdrops and the front curtain stood rectangular painted flats or wings arranged in groups of four or five, which ran in grooves. The outer flat in each group could be pulled back to reveal a new one. A flat on one side and a flat on the other could be pushed to the middle of the stage to form the back wall of a set. These flats were called shutters when they were used in place of a backdrop. This arrangement did not produce much in the way of illusion, but the method was simple and quite economical and did not require the raising or lowering of the front curtain to change a scene.

Only one designer was outstanding during this period and that was a student of Inigo Jones, John Webb, who drew heavily on the Italian influence and on the decor of the court masques.

THE EIGHTEENTH-CENTURY GEORGIAN PLAYHOUSE

Theatre structure did not change radically during the early part of the eighteenth century. Several new theatres were built, and the old ones were altered. Even on the continent, examples of the forestage-façade style could be found well into the century (Fig. 1.21). The first theatre of the period to be built in London was the Potter's Little Theatre in Haymarket in 1720. Covent Garden, Drury Lane, and Vanbrugh's Opera House were altered around midcentury. At that time, such theatres as Astley's, the Pantheon, The King's Concert Rooms, the Royal Circus, and the Royalty were constructed. Several characteristics differentiated the Georgian theatre from that of the Restoration. Seating capacity increased in many cases. Architectural treatment of the side boxes was simplified, creating a lighter building style and a greater relation of structural elements. A number of spiked railings were placed around the stage and auditorium to prevent members of the audience from climbing on stage or into more expensive seats. The number of boxes or galleries increased. Some had as many as five tiers of boxes towering above the pit. Eventually, a definite division existed between the side boxes and the front boxes, and during this period the private box appeared. Private boxes were frequently called lattices or lettices, because of the presence of a lattice across the front. At this time came the box lobby, a corridor or promenade behind the boxes. Pay boxes also came into use. These were small cubicles for the taking of money, situated in the vicinity of each entrance.

The stage itself showed little change until the next century, but scenery witnessed some

Figure 1.21 Interior of the Hotel de Bourgogne, c. 1765. Bibliotheque Nationale, Paris.

interesting developments. Drifting away from the heavy Baroque, artists turned toward a more classical style, and also began creating what is known as the "landscape style." Ferdinando and Giuseppi Galli receive credit for introducing the romantic, naturalistic landscape to the stage. A further new theory championed by Philippe Jacques de Loutherbourg (1735–1810), suggested that a stage setting did not have to be architectural. De Loutherbourg came to England in 1771 and later designed scenery for Drury Lane. Most of his work was done for pantomimes and various entertainments under David Garrick's direction. His invention of transparent scenery, moonshine, fire, volcanoes, and cutout scenery produced spectacular effects. Near the end of the century, William Capon provided what are known as "romantic architectural settings" for J. P. Kemble's revivals of Shakespeare. These designs were based on authentic documents and constitute the first attempts to emphasize research and historical accuracy. Prior to the eighteenth century (ostensibly the discovery of the ruins of Herculanaeum and Pompeii), history was considered irrelevant to art.

NINETEENTH-CENTURY THEATRE

England

In the nineteenth century, theatres increased in number and decreased in size. Lighting moved slowly through the era of the candle, gaslight, limelight, and finally to the incandescent lamp. In scenery, a change appeared not only in a move toward historical accuracy and realism, but also in its physical arrangement. The wing and drop set, so popular in the eighteenth century, gave way to the box set with its three realistic walls. Definite and imaginative theories of staging were developed and used. With the increase in the number of theatres in England, a new and bourgeois type of program emerged. Theatre programs, in the main, centered on pantomimic and musical shows, a forerunner of vaudeville of the 1920s. Melodramas, burlettas, and reviews became popular. Such productions required elaborate scenic devices and effects. Horses, fire engines, ships, and wild animals were among the props used. Burnings, floods, and snowstorms could be seen every season. These effects were not limited to the minor and less dignified theatres. Drury Lane spent £5000 on the *Cataract of the Ganges.* The Old Vic installed a curtain of mirrors.

For two centuries, the pit or ground floor of the auditorium had provided the cheapest admission price. Until 1660, there were no benches in this area, only "standing room." Benches, hard, uncomfortable, and without backs, were finally introduced in the eighteenth century, but this entire part of the theatre had no aisles or reserved seats. Finally, at the beginning of the nineteenth century, new or rebuilt theatres began to reduce the size of the apron, and theatre managers filled the extra space with a row of "stalls" with backs and, eventually, upholstery and armrests. Since these seats could bring as much as six times the amount for ordinary "pit" benches, managers began adding more and more "orchestra" seats, and the pit was pushed farther and farther back until it was eliminated altogether in most theatres. Next, the four or five rows of large boxes on the side walls and at the back of the theatres were raised and the pit extended under them. This changed the boxes into balconies (Fig. 1.22) and increased the seating capacity of the particular house, although such changes decreased advantageous sight lines somewhat. In addition, the proscenium

Figure 1.22 Interior of the State Opera House, Tbilisi, Georgia, USSR. 19th century, restored.

doors, which opened onto the apron, were eliminated in spite of objections from the actors, who found it necessary to revise many of their techniques and simple stage rules.

A trend toward historical accuracy in settings and costumes began in Germany around 1810 and is attributed to Josef Schreyvogel, director of the Brugtheater in Vienna. In England, J. R. Planche persuaded Kemble and Macready to mount *King John* and *Coriolanus* in reasonably accurate costumes and sets. Accuracy began with Shakespearean productions and carried over into most theatrical presentations. This trend, called antiquarianism, peaked in the mid-nineteenth century in the spectacular pro-

ductions of Charles Kean. Charles Kean dominated the London stage of the 1850s. His trademark (some of Kean's critics used the term "abomination") was the spectacular and antiquarian Shakespearean "revival." In every Kean revival, the settings took focus. His focus on scenery was an outgrowth of the previous century and the influence of landscape painting in the theatre. Kean's spectacular climax scenes followed the trend toward a "sensation scene," which was the chief attraction of every melodrama. Kean thought that "historical accuracy might be so blended with pictorial effect that instruction and amusement would go hand in hand." He was a fellow of the Society of Antiquaries, and in pursuit of archeological exactness employed the most distinguished specialists of his day. Kean brought centrality of mise en scène to productions of legitimate drama, in contrast to its previous relegation to the pantomimes (Figs. 1.23 and 1.24). The graphic clarity, straightforward simplicity, and realism of Kean's and Grieve's settings lack the subjective atmosphere and fragmented composition of the earlier Romantic style, which also carried into the second half of the century and might be applied to William Telbin's designs for Charles Fechter's controversial revival of Shakespeare's *Hamlet* in 1864 (Fig. 1.25).

The onset of realism as a standard for production led to three-dimensionality in settings and away from drop and wing scenery to the box set. The stage floor was leveled. New methods of shifting and rigging were devised to meet specific staging problems. Over a period of years, all elements of the production became more and more integrated in a total aesthetic unity, much in the spirit of Wagner's *Gesamtkunstwerk*. As we said, the distraction of scene changes was alleviated by closing the curtain to hide stage hands.

Stage space itself became clearly defined

Figure 1.23   Charles Kean's production of William Shakespeare's *Richard II*, London, 1857. Act 3, scene 3, Flint Castle (restored). Contemporary watercolor by Thomas Grieve. Courtesy of the Victoria and Albert Museum, London.

Figure 1.24 Charles Kean's production of William Shakespeare's *Richard II,* 1857. Interpolated between acts 3 and 4. The entry of Bolingbroke into London with Richard II as captive. Contemporary watercolor by Thomas Grieve. Courtesy of the Victoria and Albert Museum, London.

and separated from the audience. Rather than playing on the forestage between audience-occupied stage boxes, the actors moved upstage, within the confines of the scenery.

It is difficult to ascertain exactly when the box set came into being. Some eighteenth-century plans show wings hinged to allow them to be aligned from the proscenium to the backdrop. In 1804, joined pairs of wings that contained practical doors and windows appeared at the Court Theatre at Mann-

heim, in Germany. In 1811, Goethe criticized the French theatre for attempting to set up real walls on the side of the stage. However, the person who receives the most credit for popularizing the box set is Mme. Vestris. In 1832, a critic wrote of one of her productions "the stage's more perfect enclosure fits the appearance of a private chamber infinitely better than the old contrivance of wings." In 1834, when Drury Lane produced a new play, a reviewer wrote "the stage was entirely enclosed," and even suggested that

Figure 1.25 William Telbin's designs for Charles Fechter's revival of Shakespeare's *Hamlet*, London, 1867. The Castle. Contemporary watercolor. Courtesy of the Victoria and Albert Museum, London.

there was a ceiling instead of a row of hanging borders. In 1841, Mme. Vestris produced Dion Boucicault's comedy *London Assurance* in Covent Garden, and the critics noted the realism of its rooms with their heavy moldings, real door, doorknobs, and ample and correct furniture. Many scholars give credit for the popularity of the box set to Tom Robertson, playwright and director, and to his leading acting couple, the Bancrofts. However, their use of the box set was not noted until 1865.

Before development of the box set, scene changes were made in full view of the audi-ence. The front curtain did not mark the ends of the acts in England until 1800; some sources suggest that scene curtains were not used until 1881, in a production by Henry Irving. In an additional development, Mme. Vestris and her co-worker Planche, became the first to make use of traps in the stage floor to raise and lower sections of the stage. During the last quarter of the century, entire stages were divided into traps through which sections of settings could be raised from the basement.

In 1817, gaslight was introduced to the London stage. Whether or not this was an improvement is debatable. Nearly four hundred theatres burned in America and Europe between 1800 and the coming of electricity. Gas did have two advantages, however: The flow could be controlled and, consequently, dimmed, and it could even be extinguished and relit. So, for the first time, the auditorium could be darkened and all light concentrated on the stage, thereby creating an isolated and self-contained stage world (Fig. 1.26). Gaslight was exceedingly brilliant and made it possible to do away, for the most part, with border lights. In 1816 limelight came into being. It was an intense, white light formed by heating a piece of limestone with a very hot combination of gases. When it was used with a curved mirror, it became a spotlight of unusual brightness. In 1846 the arc light, produced by arcing an electric current between two carbon rods was first introduced at the Paris Opera House.

Another interesting development in scenic practice, the simultaneous set, began in the early part of the century. This simultaneous set was not like the simultaneous stages of medieval times; rather, it usually consisted of the cross section of a house. In London in 1817, the setting for *The Actor of All Work; or First and Second Floor* showed two rooms at

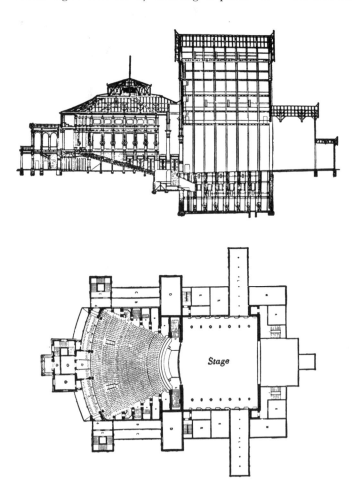

Figure 1.26 Gottfried Semper in collaboration with Richard Wagner, the Bayreuth Festspielhaus, opened 1876. Section and plan.

the same time, one above the other. *On the Ground Floor and in the Second Storey* (1830) by Johann Nestroy, a Viennese playwright, used the same device. Modern designers rely frequently on this novelty—for example, in *Desire Under the Elms, A Streetcar Named Desire, The Remarkable Mr. Pennypacker, Death of a Salesman, The Desperate Hours, Brighton Beach Memoirs,* and *Broadway Bound.*

In 1866, "the Theatre Duke" took the leadership of the Saxe-Meiningen players and became the first director to practice ensemble playing, foreshadowing Stanislavski and the Moscow Art Theatre. In addition to being a very careful director with a visual imagination, the Duke was a gifted artist and scene designer. He promoted the use of various playing levels on stage and saw to it that his settings, costumes, and properties were illusionistic as well as accurate. The Saxe-Meiningen Players eventually toured Europe and England and greatly influenced all who saw them, including Sir Henry Irving, who spared no expense to employ the greatest historians, painters, and musicians for his productions.

Although obscured by the rush to historical realism, the German theatre became intrigued with adopting a simple unit setting for Shakespeare. As early as 1840, Karl Immerman created an excellent design for a Shakespearean unit setting superimposed on a proscenium stage. With only one exception, in 1844, England made no other attempts to stage Shakespeare in anything but multiset productions until 1881, when William Poel produced *Hamlet* with only curtains for a background; in 1900, he constructed an Elizabethan stage within a conventional one.

France and America

In France in 1887, the naturalistic movement under Andre Antoine gained impetus by his use of ultrarealistic scenery and props. He borrowed or rented everyday furniture, and in one play he used as props real legs of lamb and carcasses of beef. Naturalism was carried to an almost ridiculous extreme by David Belasco in America at the turn of the century.

The nineteenth-century theatre in America had a slow beginning. In 1800, only a handful of houses existed and barely more than 150 actors, all on the Atlantic coast. By 1885, America had more than 5,000 playhouses in at least 3,500 cities, as well as 50,000 to 70,000 players. In keeping with this growth, America soon developed new ways of lighting the stage, changing scenery, and making theatregoing more pleasant.

In 1869, Booth excavated under his new theatre and installed hydraulic machinery that raised and lowered sets through slots and traps in the floor. In 1880, Steele MacKaye built an elevator stage in the rebuilt Madison Square Theatre. One stage could be lowered into the basement and changed, and the other could be raised to a second floor and changed there. In the same theatre he also installed gas footlights in 1874 and became the first to use indirect lighting for the auditorium. Another innovative practice placed the orchestra above the proscenium arch, similar to the Elizabethan theatre. Other devices used by MacKaye for the first time in America included illuminating the stage with electricity, air-cooling the theatre and using an elevator in the orchestra pit to lower musicians out of sight during a performance. He also invented steel wire frames placed under theatre seats to hold hats of the spectators. He pivoted the folding chairs in the orchestra so the entire floor could become a mass of aisles.

For the Chicago World's Fair of 1893, MacKaye designed a 12,000-seat theatre called the Spectatorium. He planned a huge sky cyclorama made of linoleum instead of canvas, which was framed with an adjustable proscenium. This cyc was to be a concave area 500 feet wide on a stage 150 feet deep. MacKaye also invented the first "cloud machine" to fill the sky with moving mists. On his stage he planned six miles of railroad tracks to carry twenty-five motor-driven wagons, anticipating slip stages by some twenty years. As if this were not enough, he planned to be able to flood the stage in order to float the three ships of Columbus and have them sail across the stage by means of the wagons. Unfortunately, these plans were not realized because of financial problems in America in 1892, and MacKaye had to content himself with a structure cut down to one-fifth of his projected size.

EARLY TWENTIETH-CENTURY DESIGN

The naturalistic movement inspired by Andre Antoine and his Theatre Libre found an ardent advocate in Konstantin Stanislavsky (1856–1938) and Vladimir Nemiravich-Danchenko (1859–1943) in their famous Moscow Art Theatre. Best known for their productions of Chekhov's plays, such as *Three Sisters* (1901) and *The Cherry Orchard* (1904), and Maxim Gorky's *The Lower Depths* (1902), their settings became the epitome of theatrical naturalism.

In the meantime, England was discovering Ibsen and working with the realistic writing of Oscar Wilde, George Bernard Shaw, John Galsworthy, and Arthur Wing Pinero and, with only occasional exceptions, allowing designers such as Charles Ricketts (1866–1931; Fig. 1.27) and Norman Wilkinson (1882–1934) to produce some magnificently painted stage pictures. The English theatre seemed to resist being influenced by any European and American developments for almost half a century. However, in Germany, Otto Brahm (1856–1912) founded an inde-

pendent company called Die Freie Buhne, based on Antoine's Theatre Libre and dedicated to performing the plays of Ibsen and Hauptman in the realistic mode.

The early part of the 1900s found the American stage still dominated by the director-manager, the most successful of which was David Belasco (1859–1931). His passion for exact reproductions of reality were carried to extremes. In *The Governor's Lady* (1912), Belasco faithfully reproduced New York's well-known Child's Restaurant on stage, complete with frying pancakes. His production of *The Easiest Way* (1909) used materials taken from tenement buildings in lower Manhattan, including the wallpaper. He heightened his realistic productions with elaborate electrical effects calculated to intrigue and fascinate his audiences, as well as to reinforce the mood of the melodramatic plots.

Although the realistic school of stage scenery was to dominate the English-speaking stages for the first half of the century, there were substantial revolts against the box setting and the two-dimensional painted wing and drop presentation.

Adolphe Appia (1862–1928), a Swiss, was the first to formulate the ideas fundamental to The New Stagecraft. He found the divergent elements of moving three-dimensional actors and two-dimensional vertical scenery incongruous to the concept of artistic unity. He advocated changing production standards by insisting on three-dimensional structures illuminated from various angles. He believed that light must change as action and mood change in order to create an organic whole.

In England, an outspoken theatre theorist, E. Gordon Craig (1872–1966), produced writings that had a strong influence on designers in both Europe and America. Originally an actor and designer, Craig created a sustained impact through creative ideas

Figure 1.27 Charles Ricketts, scene design for Aeschylus's *The Eumenides,* c. 1922. Courtesy of the Victoria and Albert Museum, London.

voiced in numerous inspirational publications. His philosophies involved the development of a single superindividual or master artist who would control the creative unity of a production; this individual would be producer, playwright, and designer of scenery, costumes, and lighting. The actor, then, would become a type of marionette useful only as an instrument to represent the other, more artistic areas. In actual practice in the theatre, Craig's philosophies involved large scenic screens, simple platforms, and steps with creative lighting, all of which directly opposed the realistic school of design.

However, Craig's few designs proved to be more controversial than his writings. In the 1912 production of *Hamlet* at the Moscow Art Theatre, his 30-ft.-high flats completely dwarfed the actors and defied the scene shifters.

William Poel (1852–1934) was another English actor-producer and founder of the Elizabethan Stage Society who pleaded for a return to the simple and minimal scenery of the Shakespearean stage, which would produce a maximum poetic effect. Like Craig, Poel was overlooked in England until the second half of the century, but he proved to be strongly influential in Germany, and eventually, in America.

Craig's description of theatre's superartist found embodiment in Germany's Max Reinhardt (1873–1943), a man who became one of the most influential production geniuses of the early twentieth century. As a director-producer or *regisseur,* he controlled the setting, lighting, costumes, music, playwriting, and choreography and produced in spectacular outdoor locations as well as in intimate productions in small theatres. He created such monumental works as *Oedipus Rex* (1910) in Vienna and *The Miracle* (1911) in London. He is credited with initiating highly stylized backgrounds with strong vertical lines balanced by equally strong horizontal emphasis, which accommodated huge casts. He continued to be one of the strongest theatrical influences in Western Europe, with his range of exciting productions, until 1933, when he fled to America to escape Nazism. He worked in Hollywood films, directed an outstanding touring stage production of *A Midsummer Night's Dream* (1934), and opened a school for actors and directors in Los Angeles.

Another German producer and a follower of Reinhardt was Erwin Piscator (1893–1966), whose famous production *The Good Soldier Schweik* (1927) made use of large cartoonlike drawings, projections, moving treadmills, and solitary pieces of scenery. Piscator followed Reinhardt to the United States in 1938, and founded and directed the New School for Social Research in New York; he directed many outstanding productions before returning to Germany in 1951.

In Russia, another director-producer had a strong influence on the art of scene design. Although three-dimensional scenery was the trademark of the realistic Moscow Art Theatre productions, a new development, inspired by contemporary movements in the European art world, began to appear under the leadership of Sergei Diaghilev (1872–1929), the noted Russian impresario. Russian ballet, traditionally staged in nineteenth-century drop and wing settings, began, in Diaghilev's Ballet Russes, to reflect current Parisian movements such as impressionism, cubism, and fauvism. The most impressive set designers to work for Diaghilev

were Leon Bakst (1870–1960) and Alexander Benois (1870–1960). This new development in the age-old art of scene painting was not so much a beginning as a brilliant phase of the craft, which eventually involved such artists as Picasso, Derain, Naguchi, and Dufy.

By 1920, the New Stagecraft, as it was termed, had gained wide acceptance. The expressionist movement began to affect scenery, which resulted in designs carrying a definite statement. Simplification and distortion created strong images of chaotic realities and fantasies. Originating in Germany with playwrights such as Kaiser, Wedekind, and Toller, expressionism in the theatre concerned the inner life of humankind rather than outward appearances. American designers also were influenced by the expressionist movement, but only a few American playwrights, such as Elmer Rice and Eugene O'Neill, Marc Connelly and George S. Kaufman, briefly involved themselves in the movement. However, designers began to realize that scenery could be more than just a background and could carry a message equal to that of the playwright's.

Another European influence was constructivism, which had its origin in the Moscow Art Theatre under the auspices of Vsevolod Meyerhold (1874–1942). Purely theatrical, the setting was reduced to structural forms, using steps, platforms, and a skeletal framework that provided the actor and the director with almost unlimited space for movement and action. Elements of constructivism are still seen in contemporary theatres, but mostly because of production economics rather than aesthetic statements.

Exciting developments in French scene design were brought about by actor-director Jacques Copeau (1878–1949) with his Theatre du Vieux-Columbier. He advocated performing Shakespeare's and Moliere's classics on a simple unit setting that could adapt to any desired locale. His very successful residence at New York's Garrick Theatre from 1917 to 1919 had a profound effect on American staging techniques.

By 1920, America was producing a new generation of scene designers who were inspired by the progressive movements taking place in Europe and were willing to harmonize with the exciting work of playwrights such as Eugene O'Neill (1880–1953), Elmer Rice (1892–1967), Maxwell Anderson (1888–1959), and John Howard Lawson (1895–1977). The three top designers were Robert Edmond Jones (1887–1954; Fig. 1.28), Lee Simonson (1888–1967; Fig. 1.29), and Norman Bel Geddes (1893–1958; Fig. 1.30), who brought visual artistry to a theatre that had been influenced by Belasco and his realistic dramas for several decades.

Jones, a native of America who studied in Berlin before World War I, startled Broadway with his striking setting for Anatole France's medieval farce *The Man Who Married a Dumb Wife* (1915). He followed with brilliant designs for *Redemption* (1918), *The Jest* (1919), *Richard III* (1920), and *Hamlet* (1922). Later works included *Mourning Becomes Electra* (1931), *Mary of Scotland* (1933), and *Lute Song* (1946).

Concurrently, Lee Simonson began working with the Washington Square Players and quickly moved up to designing some of the new and innovative Theatre Guild's best-known productions, such as *He Who Gets Slapped* (1922), *Marco Millions* (1928), *Amphitryon 38* (1937), and the Ring Cycle for the Metropolitan Opera in 1947.

The third member of this American triumvirate, Norman Bel Geddes, began de-

Figure 1.28 Robert Edmond Jones, *original design for Macbeth.* Courtesy of The New York Public Library.

Figure 1.29   Lee Simonson, constructivist set for Eugene O'Neill's
Dynamo, 1929. Courtesy of The New York Public Library.

signing on the West Coast but moved to New York to create scenery for the Metropolitan Opera in 1918. Perhaps his most outstanding work was for Max Reinhardt's *The Miracle* in 1924, when he transformed a Broadway theatre to resemble a cathedral. His stark space stage with steps, platform, levels, and corners for Raymond Massey's production of *Hamlet* (1931) set the staging pattern for classical dramas for the next thirty years. With the advent of the Great Depression, Bel Geddes moved from designing for the theatre to the more secure area of industrial design, in which he was equally successful.

The growth of the professional theatre in the middle 1920s created an atmosphere that encouraged talented design students to seek apprentice positions in the studios headed by the leading designers of the New Stagecraft. Two of the most talented and brilliant of these were Jo Mielziner (1901–1976; Fig. 1.31) and Donald Oenslager (1902–1975; Fig. 1.32), who proceeded to dominate the professional design field for the next forty years.

Mielziner designed more than three hundred settings for some of the most successful plays produced in the American theatre. Nor was he limited to set designing. He frequently designed lighting as well. He was involved with the architectural design of more than fifteen theatre plants, including the Vivian Beaumont and the Forum theatres at Lincoln Center in New York. His most outstanding productions have been since 1940 and include *The Glass Menagerie* (1945), *Death*

Figure 1.30   Norman Bel Geddes, scene design for *The Patriot*.
Courtesy of The New York Public Library.

of a Salesman (1949), *A Streetcar Named Desire* (1947), *The Lark* (1955), *Gypsy* (1959), and *After the Fall* (1964). His designs were characterized by a strong poetic feeling emphasized by his lighting, skeletal scenic forms, and a liberal use of scrim and gauze. Mielziner, in his early years, was an apprentice with Lee Simonson and later with Robert Edmond Jones, which provided him with an exceptional background in the profession.

Donald Oenslager designed his first Broadway production in 1925, the same year he joined the faculty of the new Yale Drama School. For the next forty-five years, he commuted weekly between New York and New Haven. He is credited with establishing the first professional course in stage design to be taught at a university. He was responsible for the training for several generations of exceptional Broadway designers, and he influenced the formation of visual theatre courses in American colleges and universities for the next four decades. Designing both settings and lighting, he worked with opera, ballet, musicals, and straight dramas. Some of his most important projects include *Anything Goes* (1934), *You Can't Take It with You* (1936), *Born Yesterday* (1945), *Coriolanus* (1954), *Tosca* (1960), and *Antigone* (1967).

His designs always reflected his philosophy of the theatre—that is, the designer is "essentially an artist/craftsman." He believed that the designer's knowledge must include a history of architecture, painting, and engineering. The designer must always be extremely flexible, allowing the freedom of his

Figure 1.31   Jo Mielziner, original design rendering for *The Gay Divorce* (1932). Courtesy of The New York Public Library.

or her imagination to guide the design development. The wonderful visual details of his designs reflect his academic dedication to historical accuracy and research. Oenslager was also a consultant on many noted theatre structures including Avery Fisher Hall and the State Theatre at Lincoln Center, as well as the John F. Kennedy Center for the Performing Arts in Washington, D.C.

England, meanwhile, remained relatively uninfluenced by the early twentieth-century developments in design that were taking place on the continent and later in America. The British theatre continued on the conservative and uninspired paths of realism and the nineteenth-century box set. Only a few of the established actor-managers were affected by the innovative philosophies of Craig and Poel.

Two of the more outstanding British scenic artists of the 1920s were Rex Whistler (1905–1944) and Oliver Messel (b. 1904). Whistler, whose career was cut short by his untimely death in 1944 at the age of thirty-nine, designed beautifully rendered sets and drops for several reviews and plays including *An Ideal Husband* (1943) and *Love for Love.* His detailed delicacy and use of color made him one of the most brilliant theatre craftsmen of the modern British theatre.

Oliver Messel began by designing settings and costumes for British master-showman C. B. Cochran (1872–1951). Beginning with reviews, Messel quickly moved into classics, ballet, and musicals. He eventually worked on both sides of the Atlantic, including designing for motion picture operas. He continued as a strong force in international scenic design into the 1970s. His designs reflected his background and training as an artist-decorator and were characterized by wit, suggestion, and delicacy.

Figure 1.32   Donald Oenslager, scene designs for *Uncle Tom's Cabin* (1933). Courtesy of The New York Public Library.

By the end of 1930, the progressive cultural scene in Europe, Britain, and America slowly came to a standstill as World War II made its devastating impression on the Western World.

DESIGN SINCE WORLD WAR II

Although the 1930s were marked by notable experimentation in scene design, the economic depression and the succeeding war years slowed development in the commercial theatre. With the advent of the 1950s, the American theatre saw the many experimental and progressive activities disappear, and a more mature and established style of design began to emerge. The profession was reinforced by strong unions and the con-

struction of new theatre buildings at educational institutions as well as in most major metropolitan communities in America. New audiences were created, many of whom would never view a Broadway show, and regional theatre became as important to the urban cultural scene as parks and museums.

Television began to provide visual staging, which had not been necessary in the radio industry. In addition, colleges and universities began creating theatre training programs designed to graduate professionally oriented designers. Experimentation in design was encouraged by the new theatre buildings themselves, with their multiform stages and electronic equipment. Plastic materials now available for the designer-technician also allowed for new solutions to old problems. The proscenium arch no longer separated the actor from the audience, and the two now became more integrated into a "theatrical experience."

The Broadway theatre was graced with the vitality and talents of such designers as Lemuel Ayers (Fig. 1.33), Oliver Smith (Fig. 1.34), Ralph Alswang (Fig. 1.35), and William and Jean Eckart (Fig. 1.36), all products of university and professional school training. Ayers (1915–1955) designed the delightful, stylized *The Pirate* (1942), *Oklahoma* (1943), *Bloomer Girl* (1944), *Kiss Me Kate* (1948), and *Kismet* (1954). All displayed his fresh, colorful approach to musical comedies. He was equally at home with poetic realism in *Journey's End* (1939), *The Willow and I* (1942), and *Harriet* (1942).

Award-winning Oliver Smith (b. 1918) has been one of the most active of contemporary designers, with over three hundred productions to his credit, including *On the Town* (1944), *Brigadoon* (1947), *My Fair Lady* (1957), *Becket* (1960), *The Night of the Iguana* (1961), *The Odd Couple* (1965), and *All Over Town* (1974). Smith moved easily among genres, designing for musical comedy, drama, ballet, and opera, as well as film. Originally a student of architecture, he quickly moved into the professional design field, where his versatility as well as his colorful palette made him the top American designer of the fifties and sixties.

The husband-and-wife team of William (b. 1920) and Jean (b. 1921) Eckart also divided their time among musical comedy, drama, and films until moving to university teaching at the decline of the Broadway theatre in the 1970s. Their best-known works were *The*

Figure 1.33 Lemuel Ayers, scene design for *Cyrano de Bergerac*. The New York Public Library.

Figure 1.34   Oliver Smith, scene design for *Brigadoon;* chapel scene.
The New York Public Library.

Golden Apple (1954), a delightfully stylized turn-of-the-century musical *Mame* (1966), and *She Loves Me* (1962), all of which displayed a strong sense of delicacy and color.

Ralph Alswang (b. 1916) concerned himself with more realistic dramas, but his execution was meticulous and extremely functional. Examples are *The Rain-Maker* (1954), *Sunrise at Campobello* (1958), *A Raisin in the Sun* (1959), and *Hostile Witness* (1966).

In England, Tanya Moiseiwitch (b. 1914), after several years of designing for repertory companies outside of London, moved to London's theatre scene, bringing her wonderful adaptability to the Royal Opera and the Royal Shakespeare Company. Her most notable work, however, can be seen in the architecture of the theatre in Stratford, Canada, and the Guthrie theatre in Minneapolis.

Among other British designers who brought ingenuity and interest to postwar theatrical efforts was Loundon Sainthill (b. 1919), a talented artist from Australia. His unusual designs for *The Tempest* at Stratford-on-Avon in 1951 called for more than one hundred lighted candles on stage for one of the more striking scenic effects. Peter Brook (b. 1925), director and designer whose individual style contributed greatly to the success of *Love's Labor's Lost* (1964) and *King Lear* (1962) at the Memorial Theatre at Stratford, also designed as well as directed *The Visit* (1958), *The Balcony* (1960), and *The Persecution and Assassination of Marat as Performed by the Inmates of the Asylum of Charenton Under the Direction of the Marquis de Sade* (1964).

James Bailey (b. 1922) first drew the attention of the theatregoing public in 1948 with

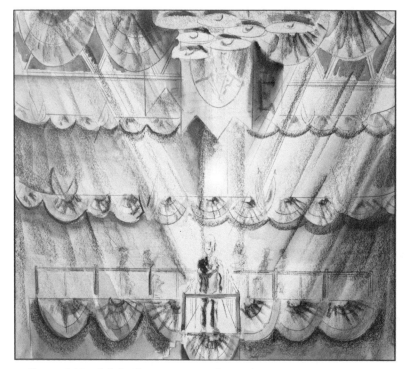

Figure 1.35 Ralph Alswang, scene design for *Sunrise at Campobello,* act 3, scene 3. The New York Public Library.

his romanticized nineteenth-century production of *Hamlet* for the Royal Shakespeare Company. He continued to design the classics with *The Way of the World* (1953) and *A Midsummer Night's Dream* (1958).

A most interesting and prolific group of designers named Motley comprised three very talented women: Elizabeth Montgomery (b. 1904) and Audrey and Margaret F. Harris. Designing both costumes and settings, these skilled artists produced, inspired, and created work for over forty years on both sides of the Atlantic.

By 1960, rising costs due to increased salary and material expenses began to create problems for live performances. Electronic shifting devices, required to eliminate backstage salaries, added to initial production design costs. Designers with graduate de-

grees in theatre began to establish themselves in television, film, and theatre. With the advent of the new regional theatres throughout America, young scene designers no longer were confined to Broadway productions, but accepted assignments in Dallas, San Francisco, Minneapolis, Atlanta, and Washington. Veteran designers such as Mielziner, Oenslager, and Alswang took on the additional chores of theatre consulting, assuring that new theatre buildings would be functional as well as architecturally inspirational.

Two established designers achieved new and well-deserved success in the sixties. Ben Edwards (b. 1916) designed *Purlie Victorious* (1961), *The Ballad of the Sad Cafe* (1963), *Purlie* (1970), and *Moon for the Misbegotten* (1973). Howard Bay (1912–1987; Fig. 1.37) is recog-

Figure 1.36 William and Jean Eckart, scene design for *Reuben Reuben*. The New York Public Library.

nized for *Toys in the Attic* (1960) and *Man of La Mancha* (1965), which he designed for the ANTA Washington Square Theatre. The setting consisted of a breathtaking, floating thrust stage with suspended stairs. The design dramatically changed the old-fashioned concept of pictorial design so long associated with commercial postwar musicals. He taught scene design at Brandeis University for fourteen years and was noted for using many innovative materials in his productions.

Boris B. Aronson (1900–1980) began designing on Broadway in the early 1930s, after some years of work with New York Yiddish Theatre. He spent the next forty years as one of the American theatre's most prolific and respected scenic designers. He was the designer for some of Broadway's most success-

ful productions, including *Awake and Sing* (1935), *Cabin in the Sky* (1940), *Detective Story* (1949), *The Diary of Anne Frank* (1955), and *Do Re Mi* (1960), but he truly hit his stride starting in the middle sixties with his wonderful and imaginative setting for the musicals *Fiddler on the Roof* (1964), *Cabaret* (1966), *Zorba* (1968), *Company* (1970), *Follies* (1971), and *A Little Night Music* (1975). He was the recipient of many prestigious awards and grants, including New York Critics Awards, Maharam Awards, an American Theatre Wing Award, a Guggenheim fellowship, five Tonys, and a Ford Grant.

A former apprentice of Mielziner's, Ming Cho Lee (b. 1930) began his noteworthy career designing for Joseph Papp's Delecorte Theatre in 1962 and soon became a leading American designer; he succeeded Oenslager

Figure 1.37 Howard Bay, scene design for *Carmen,* act 2. The New York Public Library.

as Professor of Stage Design at the Yale School of Drama, and worked consistently in regional theatres, on Broadway, in opera, and ballet. His outstanding work on *Peer Gynt* (1967), *Roberto Devereux* (1970), and *Much Ado about Nothing* (1970) firmly established him as a most successful professional designer.

Peter Wexler (b. 1936; Fig. 1.38) drew the attention of audiences with his inventive organic setting for APA's (Association of Producing Artists) production of *War and Peace* (1962). He quickly moved to become resident designer for Los Angeles' new Mark Tabor Theatre after designing their initial offering of *The Devils* (1967). He followed this with an extraordinary design for revolving stages for the Broadway musical *The Happy Time* (1968), the settings and film design for

The Trial of the Catonsville Nine (1971), and *The Matter of J. Robert Oppenheimer* (1969).

In 1973, he designed the scenery, costumes, and visual effects for the Metropolitan Opera's huge production of *Les Troyens.* Wexler was one of the designers who responded to the appeal of new advances in materials and mechanics in the 1960s. His work captured the atmosphere essential to an environment for the play, rather than being limited to time and space aspects alone.

Another designer who looked for challenges in the profession is Santo Loquasto (b. 1944), who became associated with the Public Theatre in the early 1970s with *Sticks and Bones* (1972), *The Championship Season* (1972), and with *King Lear* for the New York Shakespeare Festival. He designed for the Arena Stage, Hartford Stage Company, and

Figure 1.38 Peter Wexler, scene design for *Les Troyens*. Metropolitan Opera, New York.

the Yale Repertory Theatre, as well as many other regional theatres. Other designers who began in the 1960s include Robin Wagner (b. 1933), Douglas Schmidt (b. 1942), and Karl Eigsti (b. 1938).

The 1980s held a definite decline in commercial Broadway productions but a distinct rise in regional theatre production and an increase in working artists in the field of design. The training in education centers such as Yale, Carnegie Tech, University of Iowa, Boston University, University of Indiana, Lester Polakov School of Design, and others have resulted in increased strength in the level of creativity, experimentation, technical skills, imagination, and sheer artistry on the part of the American designer. No longer is the design just the environment of the play; now it is frequently the essence of the play, insinuating a mood or suggesting an atmosphere coupled with a rhythm inherent in the script and the total production. In musicals such as *Starlight Express* and *Phantom of the Opera*, one can argue that the de-

sign *is* the production. Today's designers work easily among the various media of theatre, opera, ballet, and television, and strive for flexibility in adapting to various theatre locations and stage requirements.

England in the 1980s enjoyed a renaissance with the National Theatre Company and the Royal Shakespeare Company, subsidized by the British government. The historic West End, equal to America's Broadway, enjoyed almost four times the number of commercial productions as its American counterpart. Musical productions such as *Cats, Starlight Express, Les Miserables, Time,* and *The Phantom of the Opera* all were graced by designers' lavish settings, which challenged audience imagination. Productions ranged from revivals to new plays, American imports, and the classics. The most innovative British designers are Ralph Koltoi, John Napier, Farrah, Terry Parsons, John Bury, and Alan Tagg.

Our treatment of contemporary designers must also mention Josef Svoboda, the Czekoslovakian designer whose experiments and teaching grew out of his association with Prague's Laterna Magica in the 1950s. Svoboda has undertaken frequent workshops and design assignments in Europe and North America up to the present time.

Today's designers are aware of their era, especially its technological developments and the need to design for the specific area of space dictated by the production. Flexibility is the key word, and modern designers know there are many ways to approach a play's design. They are adaptable to budgets, facilities, and labor issues involved in production. Talent and enthusiasm are not enough; contemporary designers are disciplined as well as dedicated.

CHAPTER TWO

DESIGN
AS
VISUAL ART

However else we may view stage design, it is, first and foremost, a visual art. Although stage design serves the theatre and conforms to the aims and necessities of theatre art, we cannot escape the fact that its roots and guiding principles are those that underride the visual arts—that is, the two-dimensional arts of painting, drawing, printmaking, and photography and the three-dimensional arts of sculpture and architecture. Therefore, our first step in understanding stage design must lead us not into things theatrical, but, rather, into the basic rubrics that govern visual art. These rubrics are called the elements and principles of composition. They are the devices that organize a visual design so that it speaks what the artist intends in a language the audience can comprehend.

ELEMENTS OF COMPOSITION

Line

The basic building block of a visual design is line. To most of us, a line is a thin mark such as this: ——————————. We find that connotation in visual art as well. In Figure 2.1 we find amorphous shapes. Some of these shapes are like cartoon figures; that is, they are identifiable from the background because of their outline. In these instances, line identifies form and illustrates the second sentence of this paragraph. However, the other shapes in Figure 2.1 also exemplify line. These shapes appear black or white against the background. If we put our finger on the edges of these shapes, we have inden-

Figure 2.1   Joan Miró, *Painting* (1933). Oil on canvas, 68 1/2″ × 77 1/4″. Collection, The Museum of Modern Art, New York. Gift of the Advisory Committee (by exchange).

tified a second aspect of line—the boundary between areas of color and between shapes or forms. There is one further aspect of line, which is implied rather than physical. The three rectangles in Figure 2.2 create a horizontal "line" that extends across the design. There is no physical line between the tops of the forms, but their spatial arrangement creates one by implication. A similar use of line occurs in Figure 2.3, in which we can see a definite linear movement from the upper left border through a series of swirls to the right border. That "line" is quite clear, even though it is composed not of a form edge or outline but of a carefully developed relationship of brush stroke and numerous color

areas. This treatment of line is also seen in Figure 2.4, although here it is much more subtle and sophisticated. By dripping paint onto his canvas (a task not as easily executed, simplistic, or accidental as it might appear), the artist was able to subordinate form, in the sense of recognizable and distinct areas, and thereby focal areas, to a dynamic network of complex lines. The effect of this technique of execution has a very strong relationship to the actual force and speed with which the pigment was applied.

Line is used by the designer to control the vision of the audience, to create unity and emotional value, and ultimately to develop meaning. In pursuing those ends, and by em-

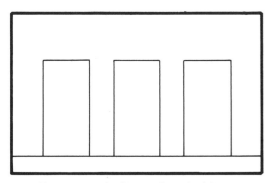

Figure 2.2 Outline and implied line.

ploying the three aspects of line noted earlier, the designer finds that line has two characteristics: It is curved or it is straight. Whether it is expressed as an outline, an area edge, or by implication, and whether it is simple or in combination, a line is some derivative of the characteristics of straightness or curvedness. We can speculate, as some do, whether line can also be thick or thin. Certainly that quality is helpful in describing some designs or other works of art. Those who deny line that quality, however, have a point difficult to refute in asking, If line can be thick or thin, at what point does it cease to be a line and become a form?

Figure 2.3 Vincent Van Gogh, *The Starry Night* (1889). Oil on canvas, 29″ × 36 1/4″. Collection, The Museum of Modern Art, New York. Acquired through the Lillie P. Bliss Bequest.

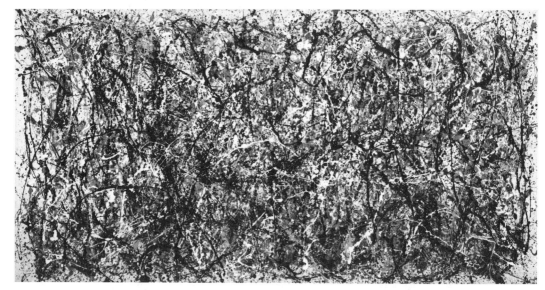

Figure 2.4 Jackson Pollock, *One (Number 31, 1950)* (1950). Oil and enamel paint on canvas, 8′ 10″ × 17′ 5 5/8″. Collection, The Museum of Modern Art, New York. Gift of Sidney and Harriet Janis Collection Fund (by exchange).

The use of line affects an audience's response to the setting. Figure 2.5 illustrates how use of curved line can elicit a sense of ease and relaxation. On the other hand, the broken line in Figure 2.6 creates a much more dynamic and violent sensation. We also can feel that the upright triangle in Figure 2.7, although solid and stable, is more dynamic than the horizontals of Figure 2.8, because it uses stronger diagonal line, which tends to stimulate a sense of movement. Precision of linear execution also can create sharply defined forms or soft, fuzzy images. Vertical lines can signify life and grandeur; horizontal lines can signify tranquility and death. Of course, it is best not to try to get too specific in the symbolic qualities of any compositional quality. We need to remember that our purpose is to create meaning for the audience and not an arcane presentation of our own sophistication.

Form

Form and line are closely related both in definition and in effect. Form is the shape of an object within the composition, and *shape* is often used as a synonym for form. Literally, form is that space described by line. A building is a form. So is a tree. We perceive

Figure 2.5 Curved line.

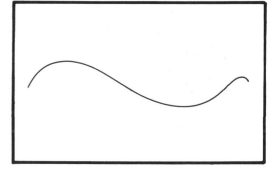

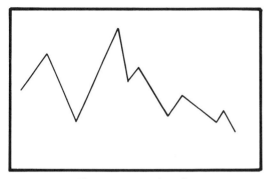

Figure 2.6 Broken line.

them as buildings or trees, and we also perceive their individual details because of the line by which they are composed; form cannot be separated from line.

Color

Color is a complex phenomenon, and no less than three theories exist as to its nature. At this point, it probably is not important for our purposes to understand these theories or how they differ. But knowing that they exist helps us understand why some sources use different terms to describe the same color characteristics, and other sources use the same terms to describe different characteristics. Although the treatment that follows may not be entirely satisfactory to

Figure 2.7 Upright triangular composition.

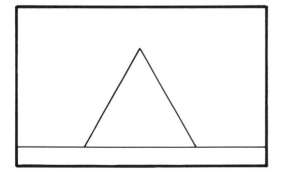

those who learned color theory from one or another of these sources, we think it is a fair way to introduce color to the beginning designer.

To begin, color characteristics differ, depending upon whether we are discussing color in light or color in pigment. For example, in light the primary hues (those hues which cannot be achieved by mixing other hues) are red, green, and blue; in pigment they are red, yellow, and blue. Inasmuch as this is a scenic design book, the discussion that follows concerns color in pigment. Color in light, although it definitely affects color in the scenic design, is left to texts on stage lighting.

HUE. Hue is the spectrum notation of color; a hue is a specific pure color with a measurable wavelength. The visible range of the color spectrum extends from violet on one end to red on the other. The color spectrum consists of the three primaries—blue, yellow, and red—and three additional hues that are direct derivatives of them—green, orange, and violet. These six hues are the basic hues of the spectrum, and each has a specific, measurable wavelength (Fig. 2.9). In all there are (depending upon which theory one follows) from ten to twenty-four perceivably different hues, including these six. These perceptible hues are the composite hues of the color spectrum.

For the sake of clarity and illustration, let us assume that there are twelve basic hues. Arranged in a series, they would look like Figure 2.10. However, since combinations of these hues are possible beyond the straight-line configuration of the spectrum, it is helpful to visualize color by turning the color spectrum into a color wheel (Figure 2.11). With this visualization, we now can discuss what we can do to and with color. First, we can take the primary hues of the spectrum, mix them two at a time in varying propor-

Figure 2.8 Piet Mondrian, *Composition in White, Black and Red* (1936). Oil on canvas, 40 1/4″ × 41″. Collection, Museum of Modern Art, New York. Gift of the Advisory Committee.

tions, and create the other hues of the spectrum. For example, red and yellow in equal proportions make orange, a *secondary* hue. Varying the proportions—adding more red or more yellow—makes yellow-orange or red-orange, which are *tertiary* hues. Yellow and blue make green, and also blue-green and yellow-green; red and blue give us violet, blue-violet, and red-violet. Hues directly opposite each other on the color wheel are *complementary*. When they are mixed together in equal proportions, they produce gray (see "Intensity"). First, therefore, we can vary hue.

VALUE. Value is the relationship of black to white and gray. The range of possibilities from black to white forms the value scale, which has black at one end, white at the other, and medium gray in the middle. The perceivable tones between black and white are designated light or dark (Fig. 2.12).

The application of the effects of value on color is treated in different ways by different sources. Providing an overview or a nondebatable description is difficult. However, it appears most helpful if we approach the subject less from a theoretical or definitional point of view and more from a practical one.

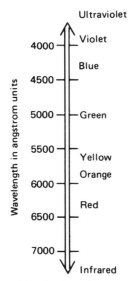

Figure 2.9 Basic color spectrum.

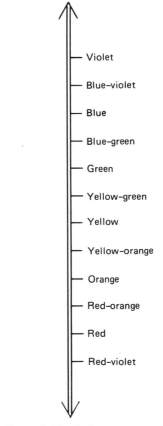

Figure 2.10 Color spectrum, including composite hues.

That is, what can a designer do to change color in order to create a design that gives the effect we desire? As we indicated, we may mix primaries to create secondary and tertiary hues. We thereby change hue. Every hue has its own value; that is, in its pure state each hue falls somewhere on the value scale in Figure 2.13.

In practical terms, the application of this concept causes different sources to travel different roads. How does one change a hue to a different value on the value scale? Many authorities say that value is changed by adding black or white. White raises value; black lowers it. However, the actual mixing of paints to achieve different values is not quite that simple. For example, if we take primary red, whose value is medium dark, and add various amounts of pure white, the changes that occur are perceivably different from the changes that occur when medium gray, medium-light gray, and high-light gray are added to the same pure red. Identical ranges of color do not result from the two proc-

esses. Let's take it from another direction. Suppose we wish to create a gray-pink color for our design. We take primary red and add white. The result is a *tint*, pink. To subdue the pink, we add just a bit of black or green. Have we both raised and lowered the value of the original red? Of course not. We have merely raised the red to a lighter value.

There is a broad range of color possibilities between high-light gray and pure white, or between a pure hue and white, which seems not to fall on the traditional value scale. That range of possibilities can be described by the term *saturation*. A saturated

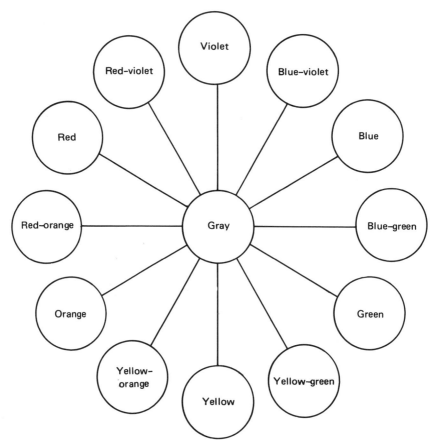

Figure 2.11 Color wheel.

hue is a pure hue. An unsaturated hue is a hue to which some quantity of white alone has been added. Unsaturated hues, such as pink, are known as tints. What is not entirely clear is whether saturation is part of or separate from value—that is, whether the two terms should be considered as separate properties of color change or whether value includes saturation. More on this momentarily.

We can easily see that some colors are brighter than others. As we noted, the perceivable difference in brightness between primary yellow and primary blue is due to their difference in value. However, it is possible to have a bright yellow and a dull yellow. The difference in brightness between the two may be a matter of surface *brilliance,* or reflectance, a factor of considerable importance to the stage designer and to all visual artists. A highly reflective surface creates a brighter color, and therefore a different response from the observer, than does a surface of lesser reflection, although all other color factors may be the same. This is the difference between high-gloss, semigloss, and flat paints, for example. Surface reflectance is probably more a property of

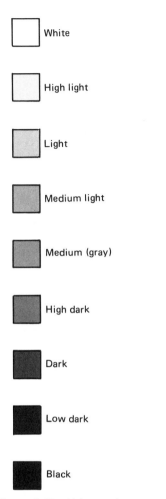

White

High light

Light

Medium light

Medium (gray)

High dark

Dark

Low dark

Black

Figure 2.12 Value scale.

texture than of color. However, the term *brilliance* is often used to describe not only surface gloss but also characteristics synonymous with value. Some sources also use *brilliance* as a synonym for *saturation,* while still others use *saturation* as a synonym for an additional color-change possibility, *intensity.*

INTENSITY. Intensity is the degree of purity of a hue. It also is sometimes called *chroma.* Returning to the color wheel (Fig. 2.11), we note that movement around the

wheel creates a change in hue. Movement across the wheel creates a change in intensity. If we add green to red, we alter its intensity. When, as in this case, hues are directly opposite each other on the color wheel, such mixing has the practical effect of graying the original hue. Therefore, since graying a hue is a value change, one occasionally finds *intensity* and *value* used interchangeably. Some sources use the terms independently but state that changing a color's value *automatically* changes its intensity. We are well advised to ponder the implications of these concepts. There is a difference between graying a hue by using its complement and graying a hue by adding black (or gray derived from black and white). A gray derived from complementaries, because it has color, is far livelier than a gray derived from black and white, which are not colors.

All of this discussion and divergence may be academic, but it illustrates the problem of attempting to describe complex phenomena.

The point to be made here is not that definitions are illogical, hopeless, or incomprehensible, but rather that one can use proper descriptive terminology as an aid to understanding what is happening in a design. Some individuals never will admit the viability of someone else's usage if it in any way differs from their own. But divergences are not necessarily matters of correctness or incorrectness. Often they are simply attempts to describe the indescribable so as to promote a clearer understanding and experience. The difficulties we have noted regarding color terminology essentially stem from differences in theory and the application of theory to practice. Attempts to create color wheels, three-dimensional color models, and all-inclusive terminology are our attempts to explain a marvelously complex natural phenomenon—color perception—that we still do not comprehend in its entirety.

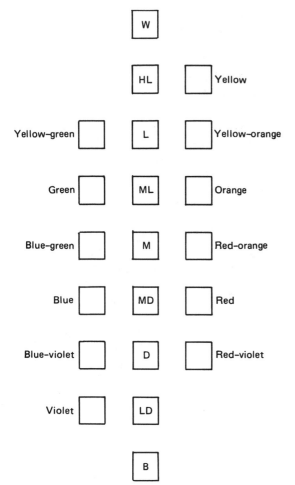

Figure 2.13 Color-value equivalents.

The composite, or overall, use of color by the designer is termed *palette.* A designer's palette can be broad, restricted, or somewhere in between, depending on whether the designer has utilized the full range of the color spectrum and on whether he or she explores the full range of tonalities—brights and dulls, lights and darks.

The colors of a designer's palette are referred to as *warm* or *cool,* depending upon which end of the color spectrum they fall on. Reds, oranges, and yellows are said to be warm colors. Those are the colors of the sun and therefore call to mind our primary source of heat. So they carry strong implications of warmth. Colors falling on the opposite end of the spectrum—blues and greens—are cool colors because they imply shade, or lack of light and warmth. Tonality and color contrasts also affect an audience's response. Stark value contrasts, for example, contribute significantly to harshness and dynamic senses.

The response our design achieves is highly dependent upon our sensitivity to color usage and our sophistication in manipulating, for the proper effect, the properties we have just discussed. Each hue has hundreds of possibilities, and only the poorest of designers is content to accept a color straight from the tube without careful analysis of what comprises just the right tone for the specific effect desired.

Mass

Three-dimensional objects take up space and have density. They have *mass*. On stage, objects have literal mass; in the two-dimensional rendering, objects have relative mass. However, even onstage, the mass (that is, the volume and density of objects) is relative to one factor (that is, the actor). Much of what we have to say to an audience through the design is affected by the mass of the elements we place in the *mise en scène* and their relationship to the actors. The *scale,* then, as well as the mass of objects, can place the human condition in a juxtaposition to the environment that can make some very specific statements about the meaning of the play.

PRINCIPLES OF COMPOSITION

Repetition

Probably the essence of any design is repetition: how the basic elements in the design are repeated or alternated. Central to repetition are three concepts: rhythm, harmony, and variation.

RHYTHM. Rhythm is the ordered recurrence of elements in a composition. Recurrences may be regular or irregular. If the relationships between the elements are equal, the rhythm is regular (Fig. 2.2). If not, the rhythm is irregular. A rhythmic pattern emerges from the nearly exact repetition in Andy Warhol's *Green Coca Cola Bottles* (Fig. 2.14). Each bottle receives equal emphasis,

resulting in an unvaried and endless succession of beats. Such strictly regular rhythms form only one of our design choices. In *Interior of a Dutch House* by Pieter de Hooch (Fig. 2.15), the definite rhythm established by the rectilinear pattern of the floor and windows is relieved by the larger rectangles of the map, painting, fireplace, and table. Decisions about such choices require justification based upon the script and the goals of the production.

HARMONY. Harmony is the logic of the repetition. Harmonious relationships are those whose components appear to join naturally and comfortably. If we choose to use forms, colors, or other elements that appear incongruous, illogical, or "out of sync" with each other, then we create the visual equivalent of musical dissonance; the constituents simply do not go together in the way our cultural conditioning would describe as natural. Consonant and dissonant relationships or harmony have their place in scenic designs as they do in musical compositions. However, it is up to us to be sure that there is a reason for whichever form of harmony we choose to use.

VARIATION. Variation is the relationship of repeated items to each other; it is similar to theme and variation in music. Can we take a basic element and use it again with slight or major changes? By using variation, we keep the design unified and organized and thereby increase the possibility that the audience will understand what we are trying to say.

Balance

The concept of balance is vital. It is not difficult to look at a design and almost intuitively respond that it does or does not appear balanced. Every artist has this "second

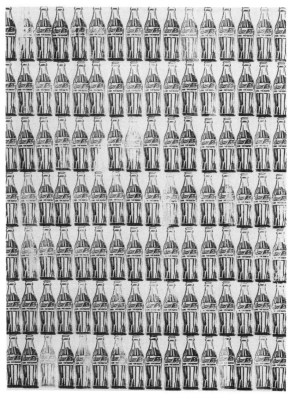

Figure 2.14 Andy Warhol, *Green Coca Cola Bottles.* (1962). Oil on canvas. 82 1/2″ × 57″. Collection of Whitney Museum of American Art, New York. Purchase, with funds from the Friends of the Whitney Museum of American Art. 68.25

sense." How we achieve balance significantly affects the message of the design.

SYMMETRY. The most mechanical method of achieving balance is symmetry, or, specifically, *bilateral symmetry,* the balancing of like forms, mass, and colors on opposite sides of the centerline or vertical axis of the design (Figs. 2.16 and 2.17). Symmetry is so precise that we can measure it. Designs employing symmetry tend to be stable, formal, and without much sense of motion. Designs in which elements radiate from or converge on an actual or implied central point exhibit *radial balance* (Fig. 2.18).

ASYMMETRICAL BALANCE. Asymmetrical balance is achieved by careful placement of unlike items. It is sometimes referred to as psychological balance. It is inherently more subtle and dynamic than symmetry. It might seem that asymmetrical balance is a matter of opinion. However, intrinsic or intuitive response to what is balanced or unbalanced is relatively uniform. Asymmetrical balance can be achieved in a myriad of ways and with divergent factors, for example, Figure 2.19. A practical test to determine whether your design is balanced or not consists of looking at the design in a mirror. If it appears balanced in the mirror, you can be relatively confident that it is.

Focal Area

When an audience perceives a design for the first time, the eyes move around it, paus-

Figure 2.15   Pieter de Hooch, *Interior of a Dutch House.* 1658. Oil on canvas, 29″ × 25″ (schematic). The National Gallery, London.

ing briefly at the areas that have the greatest visual appeal. These are focal areas. A design may have a single focal area to which the eye is drawn immediately and from which it will stray only with conscious effort. Or it may have an infinite number of focal points. Such a design would be described as "busy"; that is, the eye bounces at will from one point to another in the design, without any attraction at all.

Figure 2.16   Symmetrical balance; closed composition; composition kept within the frame.

Figure 2.17   Symmetrical balance; open composition; composition allowed to escape the frame.

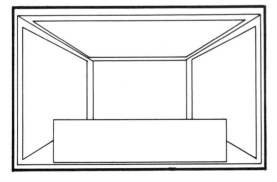

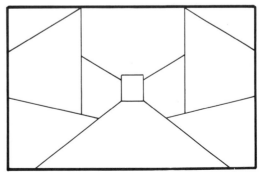

Figure 2.18 Radial balance.

Figure 2.19 Asymmetry.

Focal areas are achieved in a number of ways: through *confluence of line* (Fig. 2.20), by *encirclement* (Fig. 2.21), and by color, to name three. To draw attention to a particular point in the design, we may make all lines lead to that point. We may place the focal object or area in the center of a ring of objects, or we may give the object a color that demands attention more than the other colors in the picture. For example, bright yellows attract the eye more readily than do dark blues. In the theatre, focal areas in the design must be carefully coordinated to work in concert with the foci of the director and the actors during every scene. It is vital that a scene design stand on its own as a carefully composed picture with specific focal areas, but it must cause focus to fall properly with regard to the dramatic rhythm of the production and the composition achieved by groupings of actors.

Proportion

Proportion is a principle of composition that deals with the *relative* size of the various parts of the design. *Scale* is a term often used as a synonym for proportion. Relationships in a design are never absolute, only relative. A part of a design, whether a tree, a sofa, a moulding, or a stair unit, is never too large or too small in itself, but only in relation to other parts of the design. For example, a heavy baroque cornice might be perfect for a palace but not for a studio apartment. A plaid wallpaper pattern is only a number of straight lines crossing each other, but the proper proportion of the lines and spaces created by those crossings depends on numerous factors such as the distance they must carry in the theatre, the style of the room in which they occur, the character of the people who live in that room, and so on.

Figure 2.20 Confluence.

Figure 2.21 Encirclement.

Paintings chosen to decorate a wall in a setting may be too large, too small, or just right only in relation to the overall space around them.

What then comprises good and bad proportion? Like balance, good proportion seems to be a matter of intuition or of taste. Good proportion seems to be whatever we find pleasing.

Proportion in the design helps to relate design elements to indicate style, focus, power, position, and so on. The designer must recognize that proportion has been applied differently in different cultures, for example, Greek classicism, Renaissance, and Mannerism. In the twentieth century no one porportion has dominated. Our emphasis on pluralism has left the use of proportion to the discretion of the artist. The stage designer must match the use of proportion to the overall dictates of the production.

Unity

With a few exceptions, we can say that artists strive for a sense of self-contained completeness in their artworks. That is to say that an important characteristic in a work of art is the creation of unity and the means by which unity is achieved. All of the elements and principles of composition should work together to provide a design that hangs together to work toward meaning. Often, compositional elements are juxtaposed in an unusual or uncustomary fashion to achieve a particular effect (Fig. 2.22). Nonetheless, that effect usually comprises a conscious attempt at maintaining or completing a unified statement—that is, the total picture. Every element we have discussed in this chapter may be utilized in such a manner that it works with the other elements to give a picture that is unified. Our mastery of compositional de-

Figure 2.22 Euripides, *The Bacchae.* University of Illinois at Chicago Circle. Dennis J. Sporre, designer.

vices is not complete until we can discern how a composition works as a totality.

OPEN COMPOSITION. In achieving unity, we have the choice of allowing the composition to escape the frame. This is called open composition (Fig. 2.17). It is a stylistic and philosophical device that can suggest a world or universe outside the design. Open composition in painting and music was common during the baroque age and represented an overwhelming cosmos. Understanding the philosophical and compositional devices of particular periods is critical to the design of historical plays.

CLOSED COMPOSITION. Composition in which use of line and form always directs the eye into the design is called closed composition (Fig. 2.16). Painting, sculpture, and music in the classical style used closed composition predominantly. This illustrates a concern for the self-containment of the design

and for precise structuring. Unity does not depend on one or the other of these forms, but our use of open and closed composition reflects the purpose and meaning of our design and relates to the way we choose to unify it.

OTHER FACTORS

Texture

Texture in a design is the apparent roughness or smoothness of whatever surfaces comprise the design. Texture in the color rendering, or course, is strictly illusory. In the finished design, texture may be illusory or real, depending upon your choice regarding whether painted detail or actual three-dimensional texture is needed to convey your images to the audience. Beyond such considerations, however, texture is a design

Figure 2.23 Kevin Cavender, *The Greeks.* Hillberry Repertory Theatre. Scene design by John Wade; light design by Gary M. Witt.

tool quite apart from its intrinsic illusions of bricks or wood grain, for example. Surface textures comprise one of the designer's most effective tools for creating variety and interest. Whether the setting is realistic or not, texture needs to be explored thoroughly as a design choice.

Style

Sooner or later in every production meeting, the question of style arises. Style is fundamental to the theatre production, to the scene design, and to the scenic designer as a visual artist, whose personal style of designing must mesh somehow with that of the production as a whole. So before we go any further, we need to understand some of the things the term *style* implies. A standard dictionary definition would indicate that style comprises those characteristics of an artwork that identify it with a period of history, a nation, a school of artists, or a particular artist. We might say that style is the individual personality of the artwork. That definition is fairly concise, but how does it affect us? How do we use it? When we look at a painting, for example, or listen to a piece of music, we respond to a complex combina-

Figure 2.24 Robert C. Burroughs, scene design for realistic setting— *Arsenic and Old Lace.* University of Arizona, Tucson.

Figure 2.25 James T. Singelis, scene design for stylized setting for film *Christmas When*. New York City.

tion of all the elements that make up the work—elements of form and content. In the painting we see, among other things, colors, lines, and even perhaps the marks made by the brush as the paint was applied. In the musical piece we hear melodies, rhythms, harmonies, and so on. No two artists use these elements of their medium identically. Each artist has individual preferences and techniques. So when an expert compares several paintings by more than one artist, the expert can tell which paintings were painted by which artists. The expert extracts clues from the artwork itself: Are the colors bright, dull, or some combination? Are the lines hard or fuzzy, the contrasts soft or hard? Are the rhythms simple or complex? Those individual clues, those applications of elements, help to indicate the artist's style, a style that may or may not be a reflection of society or philosophy, of biography or artistic considerations. Groups of artists often work together closely. They may study with the same teacher, or they may share ideas about how their medium of expression can overcome technical limitations or more adequately convey the messages or concerns they all share. As a result, artworks of these artists may show characteristics of such similarity that the trained individual can isolate their works. I recently interviewed a design candidate whose style was so similar to mine that I knew he had studied with someone from the same school and teacher as had I. It turned out that his graduate work had been done under one of my graduate classmates of twenty years ago. The similarities that allow for such identification comprise the style of the group. Further expert examination can also isolate the works of individuals

Figure 2.26   Gary English, scene design for unit setting—*The Roar of the Greasepaint, The Smell of the Crowd.* University of Arizona Repertory Theatre, Tucson, Arizona.

within the group. This same process of isolation and identification can be applied to artworks coming from certain nations, and even to rather large slices of history.

We must be careful, however, when we use the labels by which we commonly refer to artworks. Occasionally such labels imply stylistic characteristics; occasionally they identify broad attitudes or tendencies that are not really stylistic. Often debate exists as to which is which. For example, *romanticism* has stylistic characteristics in some art disciplines, but the term connotes a broad philosophy toward life in general. Often a style label is really a composite of several styles whose characteristics may be dissimilar but whose objectives are the same—for example, *classicism*. Terminology is convenient but not always agreed upon in fine detail. Experts

occasionally disagree as to whether certain artworks fall within the descriptive boundaries of one style or another, even while agreeing on the definition of the style itself.

In a question directly related to theatre artworks, which include elements of several arts, we can ask how the same label might identify stylistic characteristics of two or more unrelated art disciplines, such as theatre, painting, and music. Is there an aural equivalent to visual characteristics, or vice versa? These are difficult questions, and potential answers can be troublesome as well as debatable. More often than not, similarity of objectives and date, as opposed to directly transferable technical characteristics, result in the same stylistic label being used for works in quite different disciplines.

For the designer, questions of style have

personal, historical, and production ramifications, as we discuss in chapter 3. Before setting pencil to paper in any production, we must carefully analyze how we are going to deal with the style of the literary script, place it in a historic framework (contemporary or historic style), translate the result into a visual style, and render it in the personal style that each of us will develop (Figs. 2.23–2.26). Above it all hangs the rather ephemeral combination of acting, literary, costume, lighting, property, sound, and setting characteristics, which, taken in total, comprise the overall style of the production.

CHAPTER THREE

PLAY ANALYSIS

READING THE PLAY

To assimilate all of the information you will need in order to make all of the decisions you will need to make, you will need to read the play a minimum of three times. As we discuss in this chapter, you will approach the play in order to find everything from your immediate "gut" reactions to technical requirements, mood, time, place, and such seemingly esoteric matters as an understanding of structure, genre, and style. The material in this chapter is designed to assist you, first, in knowing what you must look for in the play to prepare yourself for preproduction meetings with the director and staff as well as for the design itself. Second, the material in this chapter is designed to serve you as a resource so that you can have at your fingertips some of the potential answers to the questions you must address.

First Reading

Probably the most important reaction we have to a play occurs when we read it for the first time. In that first experience, what the play is and what we are combine into a unique set of first impressions. Anything that occurs after this important first meeting alters both our reaction and the play itself. Whenever we set about consciously to ask questions about the play and to attempt to answer those questions, we modify our natural response (which is the one the audience will have), and begin the process of analysis.

Certainly, however, natural response and conscious analysis are not totally separate processes. An individual with great breadth of background and experience and years of probing play after play undoubtedly begins the process of analysis, even if he or she consciously tries to avoid it at first reading. So, in a very real sense, the inexperienced designer may be better equipped to find in the play the sense and tone the audience will find, and thereby be better equipped to capture the proper style and atmosphere for the design than is the experienced and sophisticated designer. The neophyte tends passively to allow the first reading of the play to act upon him or her and, therefore, will perceive a level of understanding of the play that the trained and experienced designer may miss. So, it is vital for the design that we approach the play on first reading with a virgin mindset, putting aside until later, if we can, any analytical thoughts. It is vitally important to capture fresh, first impressions of the play and to hold them for use in creating the broad strokes and colors of the design.

As soon as you have completed your first reading, take time to examine what you *feel* about it. Did you like the play? Did you find it dull or exciting, or just so-so? Why did you feel that way? Were you amused or depressed? Were you truly interested in the outcome, or was that less important than the credibility of the characters of the personages? Did you react by thinking that you know people like these, or did you find the people larger than life, types rather than individuals? Were the actions and issues outside your range of experiences?

Asking questions like these and understanding your responses will put you in touch with the range of your first impressions. Since, as we said, your first impressions probably will be much like those of the audience (which will not have time, while watching the production, to analyze it), you, as a designer, will then be able to assist in making the play work for the audience. You will be able to assist the director in working out the problems in the script that led, for example, to any negative first impressions you may have had, and to capitalize on those

elements that gave you your positive impressions.

Nonetheless, the first reading is just that—the *first* reading. It must be followed by more readings and by analysis, as opposed to first impressions, as vital as they may be. When we begin to apply analytical method, we modify our natural response, and we find a more complex meaning in the play. We also begin to find all details from which the backbone of the design will emerge. Remember, both first impressions and analysis are important for the designer; you must learn how to capture both, to store each as you deal with the other, and to recall them vividly as you create the design.

Beyond the First Reading

Our natural response to the script usually involves our attitude toward the people of the play, most likely to a single person upon which we are led to focus. Do we like that person? Do we like other persons in the play? (We are using the word *person* here, rather than *character,* because, as we shall see, *character* has a more technical meaning. A more formal and correct designation of *person* would be *personage,* one of the dramatis personae.) The important question for us is, Do we like the personage in the play more or less significantly than his or her credibility warrants? Some of the best drawn and most important personages in plays are villains—for example, Iago in *Othello.* We may dislike him on a moral level but appreciate him artistically as a fully realized character. Our analysis will help us fine-tune the focus of the play by balancing our sympathies for one personage against the development of another. These conclusions are essential for the designer, whose understanding of the play and its workings must be every bit as detailed as are the director's. If the designer is to function as an artistic member of the production team, he or she must fully understand the play he or she is called upon to *design*. Otherwise, the designer is merely a "go-fer," doing nothing more artistic than executing someone else's conceptions.

DETERMINING THE FACTS OF THE PLAY

Our analysis needs to bring forward the facts of the play—that is, the literal facts from which the play was constructed. We can call the facts of the play, its story. Facts are not the plot. We will see how plot, in the Aristotelian sense, comprises the structure of the play. The facts, or story, are just that:

In 1889, Annie, a schoolteacher with romantic notions about the sea, married Captain Keeney, the most successful whaling-boat skipper of Homeport. After four years, and as yet, childless, she imagines her husband's life at sea as free and adventuresome compared to her life in Homeport. So, she convinces her reluctant husband to allow her to accompany him on a voyage that began in June, 1893 . . . and so on.

These are facts. Now, what does the playwright make of them? What will an audience make of them?

THE SETTING

Playwrights normally give careful attention to *time* and *place,* the two elements of setting. Our job is to be sure that we understand all of the ramifications of what may seem, at first glance, like a straightforward extension of what we have just described as the facts of the play. Setting is more than that. Time and place create important, although sometimes subtle, nuances important to what the play means and to transmitting that meaning to an audience. Some playwrights are explicit about setting. Others are noncommittal, leaving it entirely up to the ingenuity of the designer or director. We cannot be noncommittal. We must know. Is the setting what it is because of the personages and their characters, or are the people the way they are because of the setting? Our design will tell the audience the answers to these important questions.

We will need to determine several specifics about time and place; for example, what is the time of day? Light and atmosphere are different at different times of day. The same may be said for the month or season. Do windows and doors need to be open or closed; what type of foliage is appropriate? Does the set need to be dressed to accommodate a holiday? When and where does the action take place? Norway in 1900 is obviously different from China in 1600.

GENRE

Next, we must come to grips with the genre of the play; that is, what kind of play is it? Designing an appropriate setting requires a careful answer to this question, and it is a question that may have important historical overtones to it. To cope with the question of genre and to apply it to any given play requires a familiarity with the genres of theatre history. Here are a few of the more important. Some we hardly see anymore. They are products of a specific time and context. Nonetheless, when we attempt to design a play from a historical era, we cannot try to fit it into a generic mold that is inappropriate just because the original genre may no longer be used.

Autos Sacramentales

The *autos sacramentales* was a form of religious drama from the last half of the sixteenth century in Spain. These plays were associated with the festival of Corpus Christi, which emphasized the power of the church's sacraments. The auto sacramentale combined the characteristics of the morality and cycle plays and depended heavily on allegory, using characters such as Sin, Greed, Pleasure, Beauty, and Grace.

Burlesque

This genre appeared in the early part of the eighteenth century and comprised satirical treatments of political issues and other art forms. It was very similar to ballad opera, with the exception of its omission of sung dialogue. Henry Fielding was the best example of writers of this genre. In the nineteenth century, the *burlesque-extravaganza* parodied well-known subjects with broad comedy and song and dance spectacle. Later in the century in the United States, it assumed the form of the combination of short comedy and musical sketches by which it is known today. The style can also be seen in such contemporary favorites as *Little Mary Sunshine* and *Dracula*.

Burletta

Burletta is a form of comic opera popular in England during the eighteenth and early nineteenth centuries. It was introduced as a device for altering dramas in order to escape the requirements of the English Licensing Act of 1737; it consisted of a balance between music, spectacle, dumb show (pantomime), and dialogue.

Comedy

Comedy is a dramatic form whose aim is to amuse and whose outcomes are usually happy. Its concerns are wide ranging, and it comprises several subgenres that are categorized by their use of appeals to the intellect or their dependence upon physical buffoonery. *Classical* or *Greek comedy* interspersed beautiful lyrics with obscenity, slang, and broad verbal humor. *Roman comedy* presented social types in stylized intrigues of stratagems and conspiracy. *Medieval comedy* applied not only to plays but also to nondramatic literary compositions that had happy endings and were written in the vernacular. *Renaissance comedy* utilized Roman comedy as its model. Plays fitting the criteria for *Elizabethan comedy* were seen as comedies as long as their outcomes for the major characters were happy. *Comedy of humors* occurred at the same time as Elizabethan comedy and focused on idiosyncracies of unpleasant characters. The *French comedy* of Molière is a genre of its own and focuses on major flaws in the human character. *Restoration comedy* and *comedy of manners* are part of the English tradition, and rely heavily on the devices of high comedy in their depictions of the social scene. *Sentimental comedy* flourished in England in the seventeenth and eighteenth centuries. Another eighteenth-century comic genre was *comedie larmoyante,* or "weeping comedy," which had pathos as its source of humor. *Farce,* sometimes described as a separate genre, is comedy that depends on broad physical pratfalls for its humor. It is the opposite of high comedy and also is called low comedy. *Dark comedy* treats the humorous situation in a different manner and uses gallows humor and satire.

Cycle Plays

The cycle plays were groups of vernacular, medieval religious plays. They flourished in the fourteenth century.

Drame

The drame was a domestic tragedy popular in the eighteenth century.

Farce

See "Comedy."

History Plays

History plays were a genre popular in the Elizabethan Renaissance. These were plays that used history as source material and that found their roots in medieval saint plays. Shakespeare's *Julius Caesar* is an example of this genre.

Melodrama

Melodrama, a combination of the terms *melo* (Greek, meaning "music") and *drama,* is characterized by characters involved in serious situations and arousing suspense, pathos, terror, and, occasionally, hatred. Melodrama employs stereotyped characters and issues of good and evil battling in exaggerated circumstances. All issues are either black or white; there are no shades of gray. It is intended for a popular audience and is concerned primarily with situation and plot. Melodrama is conventional in its morality and tends to be sentimental and optimistic. Good always triumphs in the end. Elaborate scenic devices form a major part of its appeal. Melodrama reached its height as a dramatic genre in the nineteenth century, but it can still be found today in many popular movie and television portrayals.

Miracle Plays

Miracle plays were medieval religious plays, usually performed in cycles, whose subject matter dealt with the lives of the saints, apocryphal visions of the Virgin, and so on.

Morality Plays

The morality play was a type of medieval religious drama in which the personages take the form of allegorical abstractions such as Everyman, Good Deeds, Faith, and Mercy. The genre developed in the last quarter of the fourteenth century. Its themes portray the conflict between good and evil powers over people's souls, and the journey or pilgrimage of life with its choice of eternal destinations.

Mystery Plays

This genre takes its name from the Latin word meaning "service" or "occupation" rather than from the word for "mystery." Probably the designation refers to the production of religious plays by the occupational guilds of the Middle Ages rather than the "mysteries" of revelation. The name was given to any of the Biblical plays performed, usually in cycles, during the late Middle Ages and early Renaissance.

Pastoral

Pastoral was a sixteenth-century Italian genre imported to England in the early seventeenth century. It was supposedly based on the Greek satyr play and had part of its roots in the English court masques. Its characters were goddesses, naiads, and shepherds, along with mortals set in idealized landscapes where danger and death threatened but were not allowed to strike. Reason prevailed in causing the triumph of order over chaos.

Tragedy

Tragedy is a genre in which the protagonist undergoes a morally significant struggle that ends disastrously. The word itself means "goat song," and the genre began in ancient Greece. In Greek classical tragedy, the hero is a type, larger than life, who gains a moral victory amid a physical defeat. The hero usually suffers from a tragic flaw,—that is, some defect that causes him to participate in his own downfall. In the Middle Ages, *tragedy* referred to any narrative in which a person of high rank fell from high state to low. Renaissance tragedy looked to classical tragedy as its theoretical base. In Elizabethan England, the genre often was combined with comedy, but tragedies such as Shakespeare's *King Lear* nonetheless maintained true tragic spirit. French neoclassical tragedy observed what scholars of the time believed were the classical "rules" for the genre, following such strictures as the "unities" and Alexandrine verse form. Modern tragedy has followed diverse paths relative to characters, diction, and the meaning of tragic theme. Its heroes often are ordinary people in the dilemmas of ordinary situations.

Tragicomedy

As the name suggests, this genre is a mixture of the genres tragedy and comedy. It contains elements of both and meets the definition of neither. Tragicomedy is often associated with melodrama, and its history goes back to ancient Greece.

MOOD

Knowing the genre of the play will help you come to grips with the overall *mood* of the play. Each scene will probably have its own tone or atmosphere—that is, its mood—but there must be a prevailing sense of mood for the entire production, and the genre establishes this to a large degree.

PLOT

The next step in our analysis is to determine the plot (or the structure) of the play and how and why the play works. Plot, as we will describe it, is an Aristotelian concept, and for plays that are of classical derivation in style, it is the most important element of the play. For anticlassical styles, plot is of lesser importance; nonetheless, it remains a critical key to understanding the play and the relationship of the design to it. Aristotle, writing in the fourth century B.C., was the first to develop a theory of drama. He used for his models primarily the tragedies of Sophocles, who wrote nearly a century earlier. Aristotle's concepts shaped and still shape the way we analyze plays. His analysis of tragedy lists six parts (in order of importance): plot, character, thought, diction, music, and spectacle. It will not be necessary for us to discuss all of these in any great detail. We assume that anyone who has need of this book will be familiar with basic theatre principles. What we will discuss is a brief application to design, more as a reminder or review than as an introduction to new material.

For our purposes, we will need to define and apply the parts of plot that are the major building blocks of the play. These are *exposition, complication,* and *denouement.*

Exposition

Exposition is the part of a play's structure in which the playwright provides background information necessary for the audience to follow the subsequent action. The exposition introduces the personages of the play, their characters, relationships, backgrounds, and the present situation. Different playwrights use different devices for providing expositional material, but the exposition is usually a definable section at the first of the play. The set can be an important contributor to expositional material by providing information for the audience about who the personages are, where they are, and why they are there. As an expositional device, the set also can indicate expectations and conventions involved in the theatrical message.

Complication

According to the French critic Ferdinand Brunetière, drama is conflict. Perhaps not every play fits that definition, but the fact remains that in order to interest an audience, conflict of some sort is a fundamental and effective dramatic device. At some point in the play, the status quo needs to be upset, and the normally expected course of events needs to be frustrated. The upset and frustration cause the audience to have some reason to be interested in what is to transpire. Such conflict is that reason. At a specific moment, the playwright causes an action to take place or a decision to be made that upsets the *stasis,* or status quo. That moment is called the point of attack, and it introduces the second structural part of plot, the complication. The complication is the meat of the play, and it comprises a series of conflicts that rise higher and higher in intensity until they reach the point where they must achieve some resolution. That high point is the *climax,* and it constitutes the end of the complication section. It is absolutely critical for the designer to know when these crises occur. The set must allow the action at these important times to have the necessary focus and compositional intensity it requires. For example, if the climax focuses on the entrance of a character, then the designer must be sure to design, in form and position, an appropriate portal of entry for that character. Quite simply, the set must be designed with the critical crises of the complication section in mind. Often these moments make specific demands on the set designer, such as the disappearance scene in *The Foreigner* by Larry Shue. In this scene, an actor, covered by a sheet, must appear to "melt" into the floor. Even when nothing so specific is called for, the design must enhance the crises by giving the director the relationships, tone, and foci appropriate to each, and, especially, to the climax.

Denouement

The denouement is the final resolution of the plot. It can take various forms and occupy various lengths of time. In Aristotle's analysis, the denouement is the period of time in which the audience is allowed to sense that the action is ending; it is a necessary period of adjustment, downward in intensity, from the climax. The denouement brings about a clear and ordered resolution. How the designer effects the requirements of the denouement in the setting is a matter determined by the needs of each production. However, unless we know where the denouement is and how the playwright and director are utilizing it, our design cannot be effective.

Plot, then, gives the play its structure, without which the audience cannot comprehend its meaning. The designer must shape the setting to the plot and the demands that the plot lays out.

The remaining five parts of Aristotle's analysis also must be attended to, and our close examination of each of them will give us vital information upon which our design will build. **Character,** the driving psychological force of the people of the play tells us what kind of environment we will need to develop. Whose character is dominant? Whose play is it? As we noted earlier, is the environment shaped by the character of one person or another, or vice versa? **Thought,** the playwright's ideas, or the intellectual content of the play, has important impact on the setting. If we do not understand what the playwright is trying to say, then we cannot design a setting that will give any help whatsoever to the production. **Diction** is the language the playwright writes. A play written in poetic diction may suggest a totally different set of stylistic demands for the designer than will one written in normal conversational style. **Music** is all of the aural components of the play, including the clash of swords and the inflectional and volume considerations given by the actors to the playwright's diction. Understanding this aspect of the play may have an important impact on what you wish to do with your design. Finally, **spectacle,** for Aristotle, is what we as designer's are about. Spectacle is the totality of the visual elements of the play, including settings, costumes, and the physical actions of the actors. We must have a point of view about where spectacle fits into this production in terms of importance, and how, within that priority, the set relates to the other visual elements. Grandiose physical gestures and action by the actors in a set with fussy detail and miniature scale might be totally wrong for a particular production.

STYLE

Part of our analysis of the play focuses on its style (see chapter 2, "Design as Visual Art"). Most plays are reflections of a cultural and historical context, and establishing their foci depends partly upon our understanding the characteristics of style that were prevalent when the play was written, whether or not we choose to produce the play in its original style. Understanding the style of the playwright's work can help us choose how best to produce the play so as to transmit the playwright's intentions, his or her viewpoint or perceptions of reality, to our audience.

According to Curt Sachs (in *A Commonwealth of Art*), the entire history of Western arts has been shifting back and forth between classical and anticlassical styles. Whether or not that assertion is true is not the subject for discussion here. However, understanding style for production (beyond the definition given in chapter 2) requires a functional knowledge of the styles of Western theatre history. What follows is a summary of some major styles, classical and otherwise, that have occurred in the past twenty-five hundred years. Every play in the Western tradition has its roots in at least one of these styles. So historical style, like historical genres, needs to become a part of our working knowledge as designers.

Absurdism

Absurdism is a rather vague and undefined twentieth-century movement that took its name from the 1961 book *The Theatre of the Absurd* by Martin Esslin. The movement can be traced to an early phase involving the playwright Pirandello, in the first third of the twentieth century. However, the later phase is one into which various playwrights of the post–World War II *avant-garde* have been cast. The style gains its name from the nonsensical behavior of characters in many post-war plays, which depict a cruel and morally destructive world in which people are condemned to failure by their inability to communicate with each other.

Aestheticism

Aestheticism is a style of the late nineteenth century that departed from the realistic style of production and rejected the idea that drama should be utilitarian or that the popular audience was a proper judge of merit. The style and its principal proponent, Oscar Wilde, advocated "art for art's sake." Wilde suggested that society should seek to turn life into a work of art, rather than to have art imitate life.

Baroque

Baroque, which originally meant "a large, asymmetrically shaped pearl," is a term that designates a style and period in Western arts occurring between 1600 and 1750. Essentially, baroque is a seventeenth-century style; the overlap into the eighteenth century is primarily in deference to J. S. Bach and G. F. Handel, important musical composers, both of whom lived and composed until that time. The style is one of large-scale, dramatic, emotional tendencies, utilizing profuse and elaborate ornamentation. Its base is in the systematic rationalism of seventeenth-century philosophy. In the visual arts, composition that escapes the frame predominates. Baroque style is anticlassical in tone.

Classicism

Classicism can be both a style and a point of view. It originated with the application of the word *classical* to the arts of ancient Greece and Rome. It has been expanded, however, to include any similar literary or artistic style or point of view. For example, as we will note momentarily, a style called neoclassicism appeared in the visual and performing arts in the seventeenth century, and a style called *classical* occurred in music in the eighteenth century. A strangely titled style in architecture, called romantic classicism, occurred in the nineteenth century. Classicism concentrates on the intellect rather than on emotion and considers elements of structure and form to be more im-

portant than other characteristics such as feelings. In the theatre, plays of classical tendencies exhibit, in production, more formality than do anticlassical plays, and character development is likely to emphasize type rather than individuality. We must recognize, however, that, although classicism focuses on intellect, and anticlassical styles, such as baroque, focus on emotion, this does not mean that form and structure are lacking in the anticlassical or that emotion is lacking in the classical. Focus is a matter of degree and emphasis. Emotion is a part of classicism, just as structure is always present in the anticlassical. However, emotion in classicism is consciously controlled and subordinated.

Constructivism

Associated with Russia and the director Meyerhold in the early twentieth century, constructivism, also called formalism, sought to remove all decorative luxury from the theatre. Meyerhold regarded the theatre as a "machine for actors." Acting, costumes, and settings, thereby, assumed a stylization of nearly abstract proportions.

Cubism

Cubism is principally a style of visual art whose experiments with planes and shapes (Fig. 3.1) found their way into the theatre in the early twentieth century through experiments by E. Gordon Craig. Although Craig's designs do not look at all like the paintings of Picasso and Bracque, who exemplify this style of painting, Craig adapted cubist thinking by replacing pictorially realistic scenery with arrangements of shapes that suggest the character and atmosphere of the theatrical environment, rather than depicting a location literally. Cubism also found an expression in the theatre in scenery, which mir-

Figure 3.1 Pablo Picasso, *Les Demoiselles d'Avignon*, 1907. Oil on canvas, 8' × 7' 8". Collection, The Museum of Modern Art, New York. Acquired through the Lillie P. Bliss Bequest.

rored its characteristic fragmentation of shapes and planes.

Eclecticism

Traditionally, eclecticism is a style that combines elements of various styles. In the theatre, it is a production style whose base is flexibility and whose innovator was Max Reinhardt. The style is sometimes called theatrical realism, sometimes theatricalism, and it presupposes that each play requires a different style, applicable to and stemming from the play itself. Coming, historically, from the very late nineteenth and early twentieth centuries, it opposed the then-prevalent practice of producing all plays in the current style. In eclecticism, each production becomes a problem whose solutions included finding situations, including the form of the theatre plant itself, that are applicable to the specific play.

Expressionism

Expressionism is a movement that attempts to express the underlying or subconscious reality of its subjects rather than to reproduce the mere surface appearance. Essentially, expressionism, which arose primarily in Germany in the first quarter of the twentieth century, was a revolt against the then-current art and civilization, which the expressionists believed were superfi-

cially attractive but rotten at the core. Expressionism relies heavily on distortion of salient features, by which the artist hopes to draw the respondent into feelings about a particular part of the work that are similar to the artist's (Fig. 3.2).

Fauvism

Fauvism is a style in painting and sculture that originated in the early twentieth century. Its name means "wild beasts," and the word represents the reaction of a critic to an exhibition of artists of the time, including Henri Matisse. The style was applied to theatre scenery in an attempt to liberate color from its representational usage, and, thereby, to create fantastic and exotic con-

Figure 3.2 Max Beckman, *Christ and the Woman Taken in Adultery,* 1917. Oil on Canvas, 58 3/4″ × 49 7/8″. The Saint Louis Art Museum, Bequest of Curt Valentin.

trasts in stage costume. The style further awakened a new sense of design for purely decorative purposes in both costumes and settings.

Formalism

See "Constructivism."

Futurism

Futurism was a movement centered in Italy between the years 1915 and 1950. Its manifesto argued for the transformation of humanity through destruction of the past. Futurists sought to rescue theatre art from a museum-like atmosphere, to force audience and performers into confrontation, to use technology to create multimedia productions, and, thereby, to create interdisciplinary artworks.

Hyperrealism

See "Realism."

Impressionism

The impressionists, whether in literature, painting, theatre, or music, sought to force the respondent to participate in recreating the experience of the artist. Their method was to suggest the "impression" or effect on the artist rather than to make precise and explicit the objective characteristics of things or events. The movement had its center in France in the latter half of the nineteenth century. In painting, which is the best-known representation of the style, the impressionists achieved their effects by using color, sketchy lines, and obvious brush strokes (Fig. 3.3). They sought to achieve the effect or rapid vision of a scene and its resultant spontaneity, as opposed to graphic details, which they found to be outside the workings of natural vision.

Naturalism

Naturalism is a style of the late nineteenth century, stemming from the works of Balzac and developed by Zola, among others. It was particularly important in literature and drama, and its purpose was to dispel superstition and idealization. Its method applied scientific objectivity to the observation of its subjects and made the range of subjects for artistic vision unrestricted, something previously forbidden by convention. Proponents of naturalism sought to be more widely inclusive of details than were the realists. They sought to "tell everything," to show reality exactly the way it was, by the technique of "brutal photography." Naturalism was a "slice-of-life" reality that experimented with its characters so as to trace their development as it was dictated by heredity and environment. Underlying naturalism was a pessimistic determinism in which free will became virtually nonexistent. The individual is a pawn of nature, without responsibility. Naturalistic theory rules out entirely any tragedy of classical nature.

Neoclassicism

Neoclassicism occurred during the seventeenth and eighteenth centuries. It was a conscious attempt to attain the restraint, polish, and objectivity which its proponents (sometimes erroneously) saw in classicism of the Greek and Roman eras. Perhaps because of a decline in individualism and a tendency toward conformity occurring toward the end of the Renaissance, theoretical remarks, intended as observations about literature and drama (most notably the observations of Aristotle in the *Poetics*), increasingly came to be seen as rules. The result, in drama, was *the*

Figure 3.3   Claude Monet, *On the Seine at Bennecourt (Au Bord de l'eau, Bennecourt)*, 1868. Oil on canvas, 81.5 × 100.7 cm. Potter Palmer Collection, © 1988 The Art Institute of Chicago, All Rights Reserved.

unities of time, place, and action, which playwrights abhorred, but which institutional pressures enforced.

Neoclassicism is classical in spirit but is not a slavish imitation of classicism. For example, the most conspicuous feature of classical tragedy is the chorus, which neoclassicism ignores. So, neoclassicism may be described as a new style inspired by an ancient one, but not directly an imitation of it. Two aims of neoclassicism originally were (1) to produce the illusion of reality, and (2) to follow the dictates of decorum. Like classicism, neoclassicism tends toward character types rather than individuals and features mythical characters and stories.

Neorealism

Neorealism (see "Realism") is a style adhering to the precepts of realism, with an added indebtedness to the psychologists

Freud and Jung. The style is characterized by sensitive psychological character studies of social misfits and is of American derivation. This style is exemplified by the playwrights Arthur Miller and Tennessee Williams.

Realism

Realism holds to the purpose that art should depict life with complete and objective honesty. It focuses on verifiable details rather than on sweeping generalizations, and on impersonal accuracy rather than on artistic interpretation. Realism began in the eighteenth century and flourished in the late nineteenth and early twentieth centuries, with the growth of science, philosophical rationalism, and the revolt against the emotional excesses of the romantic movement. In attempting to avoid idealism and romantic "prettifying," realists often stress the commonplace, trivial, sordid, and brutal aspects of life. However, unlike naturalism, which is an extreme form of realism, realism does employ aspects of artistic selection to shape its vision. Thereby, it falls short of the nonselective "slice-of-life" presentation of the naturalists. The term *hyperrealism* has been applied to those adherents of nineteenth-century realism, such as Charles Kean, who introduced "antiquarianism" or "historical accuracy" into stage production, and who applied those principles to such revivals as Shakespeare, in which each scene was invested with full-stage, fully realistic and historically accurate settings. Designs for such productions employed archaeologists as design consultants, if not as scene designers.

Romanticism

Romanticism is the antithesis of classicism. It focuses on unbridled emotion, feeling, and an escape to the exotic: the faraway and long ago. Romanticism grew from roots in the sturm und drang ("storm and stress") movement in German literature of the late eighteenth century and flourished in the early half of the nineteenth century. It was a revolt against neoclassicism. In contrast to the neoclassicists, who portrayed heroic, typical characters, the romantics sought out lowly and eccentric ones. Rather than cultivating high poetry, they used the everyday speech of actual people. They experimented with form and language and often brought to the fore subjects such as incest, which previously were taboo. Romanticism glorified the individual, especially the outcast and the downtrodden. Goethe's sorrowful hero, Werther, became the romantic, ideal, anti-hero hero. The romantic movement centered in France, Germany, and England but also spread throughout Europe and the Western Hemisphere. In many respects, the romantic movement never ended. Other styles have come to the fore, but the basic tenets of romanticism continue to be found in every art form.

Surrealism

Surrealism, or "superrealism," began in France between World War I and World War II. The surrealist manifesto of Andre Breton calls it "pure psychic automatism . . . free from the exercise of reason and exempt from any aesthetic or moral purpose," a mysticism seeking total liberation of the unconscious, in the magic of art, to "create an evocation freed from time and space and movement." In combining dadaism with Freud, the surrealists insisted that automatic, illogical, uncontrolled fantasies and associations of the mind represented a higher reality than the realistic and deliberately manipulated world of the external senses. The surrealists present a dream world in which the interpretation of the dream is left totally to the audience. The illogical and the inexplicable predominate.

Symbolism

Symbolism is a conscious and deliberate employment of symbols as a technique. The movement began in the late nineteenth century in France, and is best illustrated by the plays of Maurice Maeterlinck (1862–1949), especially *Pelléus and Mélisande* (1892). Fundamental to symbolism is the belief that the normal, transient, objective world is not true reality, but only a reflection of an invisible absolute. Symbolism, therefore, became an antithesis to realism and naturalism, both of which seek to capture transient reality. For the symbolist, however, reality could only be suggested. Symbolists group condensed syntax and minor images around one central metaphor. The result is deliberately esoteric. Any subject is acceptable, as long as it captures the artist's subtle intuitions and contributes to a total design. Art exists for its own sake.

UTILIZING STYLE

A play from one of these stylistic traditions would be appropriately at home when produced in that style. However, your artistic sense may suggest that a play would be equally at home in a related style. The actual goals for the production may suggest that a style other than the historically accurate one would be more conducive to those goals. Ultimately, you need to do what seems best for the work, but do keep your artistic and scholarly integrity. Some reasons for choosing a style—for example, "just to be differ-

ent"—probably will not yield a worthwhile production.

PRODUCTION DEMANDS

Actor Movement

At this early stage in your planning, you will need to find in the script clues to the kinds of movements and spatial relationships required for the actors. The director has the ultimate responsibility for determining actor movement, but the scene designer needs to be prepared to point out practical factors you find in the script. For example, does the script imply the presence of a high level for one character to speak down to another character? Does, for example, the text of Shakespeare's *King John* (Fig. 3.4) require the young prince actually to jump from a parapet in full view of the audience? How do you intend to handle that issue in the set design? Does the play call for active movement by large groups of actors? Does your concept allow for getting the body of Juliet from her bedchamber to the tomb?

As a designer, you must pick up on what you perceive to be problems as well as potentials for the actors. If your visualization for a scene from *Gideon* includes the Angel perched above Gideon on an outcrop of rock, can you sell that idea to the director as a means for establishing a dynamic relationship among the characters and the setting? Your attention must always be on creating spaces in which positive things can happen with actor movement. At the same time, you must be acutely aware of potentially harmful traffic patterns you may be laying for the director and the actors. Empty corners, recessed areas, and certain step unit placement can create situations into and out of which movement may be restricted or im-

Figure 3.4 William Shakespeare's *King John.* Dennis J. Sporre, designer, University of Illinois at Chicago.

possible. As you imagine the visual impact of your setting in this early preparation period, rethink every level, angle, space, and entrance for its effect on the actors. In some cases, your design may be dependent upon the physical size of the actor who is cast in a particular role.

Furniture also must be considered at this point. You must plot its quantity, placement, and the need for it to accommodate actor movement and relationships. Familiarity with furniture styles from various periods will assist you greatly in your early reading— that is, before you have a chance to do your research. Some periods have delicate, smallish pieces, and other periods have large,

cumbersome pieces. Available space on stage can be affected considerably by what style is required.

Properties also must be closely examined. Some hand and set props are required by the action, and you will need to read carefully to find them. You should never depend upon prop lists or italicized stage directions in modern play scripts for determining what is required.

Set props are items that are part of the visual picture of your design, and they contribute significantly to the finished look of your design. How thorough and careful you are in the selection and placement of set props can make the difference between the setting seeming incomplete or fully appropriate. *Hand props* are objects the actors actually use as part of their stage business. Some of these may be set props as well.

Scene Changes

We will discuss in detail in the next chapter the options available relative to physical necessities of the setting and the performance space. However, as we read and analyze the play in our initial approach, we need to make some rudimentary notes regarding the progress of the play and its scenic changes. The style of the play may make some accommodation to the need for set changes relative to scene changes. For example, Shakespearean plays, whether comedies, history plays, or tragedies, all require numerous *scene* changes, and we need to be alert to these as we analyze the play. However, a scene change may or may not require a *set* change, depending upon whether you envision the production in a conventional atmosphere such as the seventeenth-century Globe Theatre or in a historically illusionistic atmosphere such as a Charles Kean revival from the nineteenth century (Fig. 3.5). As you prepare for production meetings, the implications of scene change requirements need to be well thought out. A play such as *The Amorous Flea* is written so that the scene changes must be done in full view of the audience while the actors sing (Fig. 3.6). You must find such requirements when you read the play.

RESEARCH

At some time after you have read the play at least once and before you put pencil to paper, you will need to research any number of details. Your research may entail further reading about the play or the author. You

may wish to research critical reviews of the play from previous productions. Anything you can do to broaden your options will probably lead to a better design. Certainly you will need to turn to source material for your design, especially if it is historical and realistic in style. Where you turn will depend to a large degree on who you are and where you work. The broader your background in the arts, especially in painting, architecture, landscape architecture, literature, and interior design, the more options you will create for yourself in knowing where to turn for your research. As we stated before, one of the reasons we have included as much history as we have in this text is our belief that, in order to be a competent designer, you need to have these kinds of information as part of your working knowledge. The more you can call upon immediately, the more time you will have to search out unique details and to think about the essences that will make your design superior rather than ordinary.

Your research needs, then, to be premised on three things: (1) the broadest functional knowledge of art, literature, and cultural history you can muster; (2) a thorough knowledge of your local library and its collections; and (3) your own personal morgue of resource materials. Slides and photos of architectural details are invaluable. If you are working in an educational theatre, do everything you can to make input into library purchases; constantly scan publishers' catalogues for books, slides, and tapes to suggest for library purchase. Visit historical places and photograph authentic interiors. Take photographs of tree trunks and rock forms.

You cannot reproduce on stage what you cannot accurately remember. However, do not fall victim to the urge merely to recreate details on stage. Anyone who has ever taken a beginning painting or drawing class knows that there is a difference between the out-

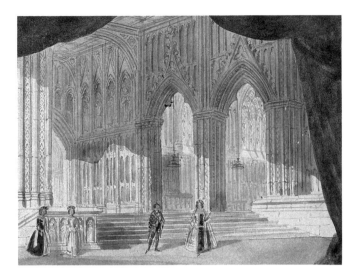

Figure 3.5 William Shakespeare's *Richard II.* Charles Kean's production, London, 1867. Act 3, scene 2, entrance into St. Stephen's Chapel. Contemporary watercolor by Thomas Grieve. *Courtesy of the Victoria and Albert Museum, London. Reprinted from Dennis J. Sporre, The Creative Impulse: An Introduction to the Arts, © 1987, p. 396. Reprinted by permission of Prentice Hall, Englewood Cliffs, N.J.*

Figure 3.6 Jerry Devine and Bruce Montgomery's *The Amorous Flea.* Dennis J. Sporre, designer. The University of Iowa.

ward appearance of an object and its essence. Theatre is concerned with essences. A Greek column on stage must say more than "Here is an accurate copy of a Greek column." It must say something about the relationship of the style of the Greek column and its essence to the meaning and impact of the play. Your setting is not just a place; it is a symbol of a reality that extends beyond the stage and touches the human condition and experience of the audience. Your research will give you details; your creativity and sensitivity will transform those details into art.

CHAPTER FOUR

THEATRE FORMS AND ARCHITECTURE

THE ACTOR-AUDIENCE RELATIONSHIP

Whatever idealism you carry with you into the real world of the scene designer, you will quickly learn, as did E. Gordon Craig (see chapter 1) that your creative imagination can proceed only as far as the limitations of time, budget, staff, and physical space will allow. As men and women of the theatre, we designers are limited by the theatres in which we are asked to work. This chapter treats the physical theatre, its types, potentials, and limitations, both practical and aesthetic. As you read what follows, you must use your common sense to avoid drawing sweeping generalizations about our specific observations. Every theatre plant is different and must be treated as an individual. Probably greater physical and aesthetic differences exist among examples of each general type of theatre form than exist among the forms themselves. Both the Purdue Music Hall, which seats 6,402, and Thalian Hall

(Fig. 4.1), which seats just over 600, are examples of the proscenium form. They are, however, incomparable in terms of aesthetics and practicalities. All of this must be kept in mind as you digest the general comments in the next few pages.

GENERAL CONSIDERATIONS

Every theatre needs to come as close as possible to meeting certain general standards. As a designer, you need to begin your thinking with the entire theatrical ambiance "on the drawing board," so to speak. Often, a minimum of effort can transform a problematic theatre into an ideal production environment. Your design should not begin at the edge of the preestablished stage; it should begin at the edge of the street outside the theatre. You may or may not be able to

Figure 4.1   Thalian Hall, Wilmington, North Carolina.

change the auditorium in which you are required to work; nonetheless, you need to
know the qualities toward which the production environment should strive. You may be
able to change more than you think, initially,
if you know the ideals to pursue. On the
other hand, you also need to know these
ideals, or conditions to be maintained,
should you be able to make wide-ranging
changes in an existing facility. The first basic

requirement for any production is the audience's need to see and hear.

Vision

In describing the ideals or basic requirements for the performing space, we have drawn freely from Harold Burris-Meyer and Edward Cole's classic on theatre architecture, *Theatres and Auditoriums,* and refer the reader to that work for more detailed information. Our purpose in this book, of course, is not to instruct you in designing an auditorium; however, some of the same principles must be attended to when undertaking a set design within any existing theatre. The designer's purpose is to try to design a setting that will meet desirable characteristics for audience ease of vision. Even within a form so seemingly arbitrary as a proscenium form, there often is much that we can do to be sure that our design is not limited by unfavorable conditions forced upon us by a poorly designed auditorium.

As we discuss in chapter 6, sightline planning is an essential part of scenic design, but planning the angles and sightlines of the set also requires attention to the relationship of the stage to the critical seats of the auditorium. These critical seats may have to be adjusted as part of the design process. Many auditoriums, especially school auditoriums, were designed more as lecture halls than as theatres, and sightlines from the critical seats in the front rows and on the sides simply cannot be accommodated. In situations such as these, an acquiescence to sightlines as you find them can destroy the aesthetics and perhaps the practicalities of a design. You cannot allow more than a handful of seats to have untenable sightlines. You are better off taking out or roping off several rows of seats than you are having a score of unhappy patrons at each performance. The following principles regarding visibility are basic.

First, the audience member should be able to take in the full action on the stage without eye movement (polychromatic vision). To meet this need, the width of the stage action should not exceed 40 degrees of horizontal angle from any seat in the house (Fig. 4.2). Second, in order for objects and actors on stage to be perceived in the intended relationship to each other, no seat in the house should exceed 60 degrees of horizontal angle from the centerline (Fig. 4.3). Third, audiences will not choose seats beyond a line approximately 100 degrees to the curtain at the proscenium. The shaded areas of Figure 4.4 contain undesirable seats. Fourth, audience ability to recognize standard shapes is reduced significantly if the vertical angle of observation exceeds 30 degrees (Fig. 4.5).

Figure 4.2 Maximum angle for polychromatic vision.

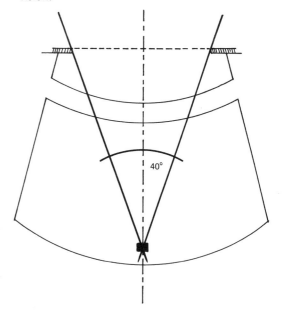

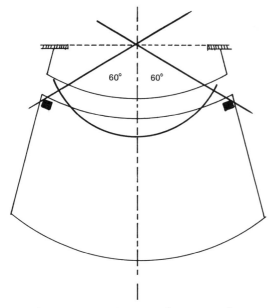

Figure 4.3   Maximum angle to centerline.

In addition, Burris-Meyer and Cole further suggest that one should attend to audience angles of vision in terms of visual significance in scenes of conflict. In other words, in terms of angles of vision, actors placed face to face in confrontation will not be face to face for a certain percentage of the audience. This is especially true for arena and thrust stages. The question facing the designer is, how can the set design assist in minimizing the number of seats wherein one actor will actually block another?

Next, in determining a new seating arrangement for a production, the designer should be sure that no patron sits directly behind another. Seats should be staggered as much as space will allow.

Finally, we need to remember one other architectural principle relating to audience vision. An audience member cannot perceive facial expressions plainly at any distance exceeding fifty feet. Any distance exceeding seventy-five feet for legitimate theatre is intolerable.

Acoustics

Acoustics vary from theatre to theatre, and some auditoriums require no extra effort on the part of the designer. Other auditoriums will take agonizing thought to create in the design a shell that will enhance the actor's projection, and, thereby, the audience's ability to hear. One reason why ceilings on realistic interiors became popular was the sound reflection they give in proscenium theatres, in which sound is likely to be sucked up the chimney of the stage house or prohibited from crossing the footlights because of sound-absorbing teasers. So, the auditorium space needs to be carefully considered in the design-planning process so that sound can be enhanced in those houses in which its transmission is a problem. Whether the result of poor auditorium de-

Figure 4.4   Audience choice for desirable seats.

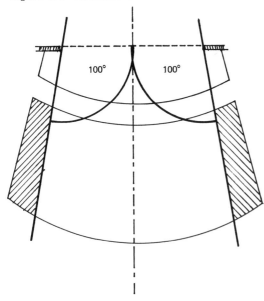

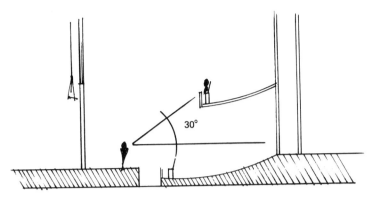

Figure 4.5   Audience ability to recognize standard shapes.

sign, poor actor training, something else, or some combination, the aggravating fact of contemporary theatre is that it more and more is losing the qualities of the live performance—qualities that lie at its heart as an art. The perceived need to amplify everything and everyone exists everywhere. Wireless microphones seem to be a staple product in theatre productions of the closing years of the twentieth century. If the auditorium can be enhanced for hearing by the set design, then, for the sake of the live art of theatre, the designer should make every effort to do so.

Distractions

Your design considerations must further accommodate an audience's need to see and hear the show without distraction. This requirement includes everything from noisy air conditioners and exhaust fans to scene shifting, actor entrances and exists in "blackouts," and noisy plumbing in adjacent restrooms. Every theatre facility has its legendary problems with regard to physical idiosyncracies extrinsic to what we normally call production problems. However, insofar as a facility's idiosyncracies affect an audience's attention, it is, nonetheless, a design problem.

Perhaps more to the design point are aesthetic considerations involving theatre forms in which act and scene curtains cannot be used to mask actors who must "appear" in place at the beginning of a scene or be removed from view before the house lights rise. Contemporary audiences have become accustomed to any number of distractions in the guise of conventions. Nevertheless, good design can and should relieve the audience of distractions rather than straining its suspension of disbelief. A highly problematic distraction precipitated by careless design, especially in the open, thrust, and arena forms, is the half-blackout. Here, stage lights must be left on dimly so that actors, still visible, can get off and on stage without running into various obstacles. The result is a ludicrous situation in which the mood and rhythm of the production are suspended. Few distractions supercede this one in disrupting production aesthetics. Simply put, your design must accommodate a means by which actors can negotiate on and off stage movement in a manner appropriate to the demands of the play, with the physical circumstances of the physical theatre accounted for. When, as is usually the case, a blackout is necessary, your accommodation to the physical theatre must allow it. Failure to meet this need can disrupt the flow and plausibility in many plays.

Safety

It seems obvious, but it must be stated, that audience and actor safety are vital considerations in design considerations of house and stage. In their zeal to create a production ambiance that is novel and creative, many designers are guilty of disregarding safety. Such oversight inhabits the educational and community theatre, especially. Care and discretion are the designer's watchwords in this regard. No theatrical effect or condition is worth even the slightest injury or risk. Injury to an audience member will undoubtedly result in a lawsuit, which may end your career and ruin your life. Failure to maintain safe practices and equipment cannot be tolerated.

Seating Comfort

Finally, your considerations for the audience must allow its members to sit in comfort. Part of audience comfort relates to the angles of visual perception just noted. In addition come solutions for audience seating in novel actor-audience arrangements or in flexible theatre plants. Such solutions as benches, folding chairs, and portable bleachers often seem brilliant. However, you must remember that the audience will contain the elderly, the infirm, and, often, the handicapped. These, as well as young and healthy audience members, cannot tolerate two or more hours on a flat slab with no back support, or even on a folding chair with no padding or arms. In the long run, solutions to

	Subject Matter	Visual Components	Auditory Components
Pageant	Incidents from history or local folklore having historical or religious appeal assembled into a plow boy's epic. Story oversimplified, direct, romanticized, salutes a glorious past, promises paradise as a just reward for something or other. No controversial matter included.	Realistic dramatic episodes acted or mimed. Period costumes. Mass movement. Ballet, folk dances. Marches. Permanent decorative backgrounds with movable scenic pieces. Scenery simple, suggestive rather than closely representational. Local geographic features included. Stage machinery in operation. Elaborate lighting. Steam and water curtains. Pyrotechnics. Display of technical virtuosity. Individual performer counts for little.	Music: symphonic, organ, choral. Synthesized descriptive score. Speech: narrator's, principals. Speech dubbed on pantomime scenes. Incidental sounds, descriptive effects. All sound amplified. Level often too high for comfort. Reproduction often less natural than in motion pictures.
Grand Opera	Classic tragedy, folklore, sagas, mythological tales, superheated passion, men vs gods. As currently produced, subject and story are of little importance.	Elaborate conventionalized pantomime by principals. Elaborate costumes, symbolic color. Occasional mass movement by chorus and ballet. Monumental settings (Valhalla, the bottom of the Rhine). Elaborate lighting. Technical tricks: appearances, magic fire, etc.	The world's best music sung by most accomplished artists, accompanied by thoroughly competent orchestra and chorus. Soloists sing everything at relatively high intensity to achieve audibility and dominate orchestra.
Vaudeville Revue	Vaudeville: Assorted songs, dances, dramatic episodes, blackouts, trained animals, acrobats, bell ringers, jugglers, magicians, ventriloquists, mind-readers, musicians, clowns; in fact any feat or phenomenon of man or	Performers principal visual element. Costumes bright. Scenic background unimportant except as it contributes necessary paraphernalia or adds flash to act. Lighting conventional; follow spots on principals; no illusion	Speech and music. Not subtle, high in intensity, aimed at the gallery. Popular and classical songs, instrumental and orchestral numbers. Revue has musical unity and balance.

design problems that leave even a part of the audience in discomfort cannot be deemed acceptable. An audience member in discomfort cannot and will not give the production due attention. As a designer, you are partially, if not totally, responsible for the success or failure of a production when such auditorium/audience basics are at stake.

GENERAL REQUIREMENTS FOR PRODUCTION TYPES

A major consideration that the theatre building forces upon the design is the general appropriateness of that theatre form for a particular type of production. Although we may fail in a scholastic sense to recognize it, when we face the real world, we quickly recognize that every design is a product of the specific theatre in which it will be executed, and that not all theatres are appropriate for all shows. So, in a very real sense, the design process begins with the choice of the production itself. If the production is inappropriate for the theatre form in which it must be produced, then very little can be done by the designer to extricate himself or herself from a morass of shortcomings caused by this inappropriate linkage.

Here are some general descriptions for various types of productions regarding the theatre space and other factors required.

Routine	Audience	Comment	Theatre Required
e or two a day, generally long. Sunday shows where permitted. Realistic episodes connected by spoken narrative. Dance, march, choral, orchestral interludes. Single intermission. Closely integrated, carefully timed performance. High production costs.	Same as country fair. Pageant is the only type of live show many ever see. Best mannered audience in the show business. Subject matter principal attraction: production next. Ball-park system of seating. Considerable advance sale. Admission low.	Always good for a season when there is an event or institution which can generate enough interest to draw an audience. More truly the people's theatre than any other dramatic form.	Large open-air amphitheatre, stadium, or ball park.
week in repertory. Show, 2 to 5 acts or two short operas on one bill. Long performance. Long intermissions to shift scenes usually set full stage. Despite repertory organization, rehearsals slighted to save costs which are excessive. Performance often slipshod in all save rendition of songs. Names in cast count.	Gallery and standing room: Music lovers. Boxes: The guests of patrons. Sometimes patrons. Orchestra: Average theatre goers with a special liking for music, averaging about 62 years of age. Large potential audiences alienated by shabby productions and high prices. Boxholders' manners worst in show business. Admission high.	Democratization of opera under way in America. Dramatization of plot started by Herbert Graf. Mass attendance at conventional repertoire questionable, since the subject matter of most operas is so far removed from American cultural heritage. Present efforts to revitalize opera are handicapped by stuffy tradition and record of dullness.	In cities: A large theatre needed to pay high production and operating costs. Comfortable seats and lounges—the performance is often long. Opera houses being built into municipal arts centers. Summer opera can often do with a tent or shed.
udeville: Two-a-day to five-a-day (continuous cycle: noon to midnight). 8 to 15 acts per performance. Each act 10 to 15 minutes long. Acts arranged in ascending entertainment value with preferred	Vaudeville: The late George V, Judy O'Grady, and a large coterie of people who prefer vaudeville to any other type of theatrical performance. Vaudeville addicts had attendance habits more thoroughly	Vaudeville is too ancient a form and has survived too many vicissitudes to justify fear that its present eclipse is permanent. Simple motion picture routine and low film costs have induced managers to ab-	Large enough to pay operating costs with ticket price below opera. Small enough so facial expression counts. Equipped for fast changes of simple scenes.

	Subject Matter	*Visual Components*	*Auditory Components*
	beast (not excluding elephants) which can be gotten onto a stage and which is calculated to have sufficient audience appeal through uniqueness, novelty, skill, virtuosity, renown, or notoriety. Revue: same material assembled about a central theme, produced for a run, trouped as a unit.	of time or place. All scenic elements combine to center attention on performer. Revue: Design unity sometimes runs through whole production. Much more elaborate and effective setting than in vaudeville.	
Musical *Folk Opera* *Operetta* *Musical Comedy*	Line of demarcation between types not clear. Often the best in musical theatre. Reasonably simple story. Framework garnished with music and dancing. Book generally satirizes some current situation of general interest. Boy meets girls in fanciful rather than realistic surroundings.	Actor's business realistic or appropriate to script: conventionalized for musical numbers and dancing. Elaborate costumes harmoniously keyed to color scheme of the production. Scenery usually functional, decorative, stylized rather than realistic. Machinery for quick change and for effect. Lighting arbitrary and for novelty and visibility rather than for conformity with dramatic necessities. New production forms and techniques readily adopted. Pleasant eye entertainment.	Auditory component given appropriate importance relative to visual as dictated by necessity for achieving maximum total effect. Semiclassical and popular music (sweet, hot, and blue), sung by principals, occasionally with chorus and usually with pit orchestra accompaniment. Subject matter and personality of singer often more important than musical excellence. Noisy entr'acte, overture, and covering pieces played by pit orchestra (about 20 pieces). Spoken dialogue between songs. Ear entertainment.
Legitimate Drama	Plays. Live shows employing all dramaturgical, artistic, and technical devices to persuade the audience to suspend disbelief and credit the characters and the story as presented.	The actor. Human scale used for all elements of production. Business realistic or in conformity with any other stylistic idiom. Costume appropriate to the character, situation, and production style. Visual elements of the production coordinated to achieve maximum dramatic impact. Lighting in conformity with style of production; provides visibility sometimes greater than that in nature.	Human voice in speech. Incidental sound to indicate locale, advance plot, create and sustain mosphere and mood. Overture and entr'acte music from orchestra (by no means universal). Vocal, instrumental, or reproduced music as required within the play.
Concert	Music. From Beethoven to boogie woogie, from a solo (with piano accompaniment) to an augmented symphony orchestra with cannon for the *1812 Overture.*	White tie and tails or any other costume that seems appropriate.	Music, requiring optimum acoustics, varying with the music, if possible, but not with the size the audience.
Night Club Cabaret	Personalities with topical or sentimental songs and patter (Sophie Tucker, Edith Piaf, Judy Garland) alternating with dance, tableau, slapstick, juggling.	Bright lights, spangles, bare skin, some effects—waterfall, the suspended glass runway. Period or national decor.	High-intensity amplified song. Orchestra appropriate to atmosphere. Soloists, choruses.

Routine	Audience	Comment	Theatre Required
spot next to closing. Acts alternate full stage and shallow to facilitate changes. Changes fast, covered by music from pit orchestra, and patter by a master of ceremonies. vue: Eight a week, otherwise similar to vaudeville. Production costs vary widely from peanuts up.	ingrained than any other audience. Admission prices moderate. Revue: Audience and admission same as for musical comedy.	andon it. Ominously falling motion picture attendance now apparent, may bring it back. Revue: Similar in genre to vaudeville. Overworking of the principals constitutes a severe handicap and makes for a dull final half-hour.	
ght-a-week. Six evenings. Matinees Wednesday or Thursday and Saturday. Combination production. Running time about two and a half hours. Conventionally two, at most three, acts. Few but elaborate sets. Stage machinery used in view of audience for novelty. All changes except act change covered by music or singles in one. Star often more important than show. Production costs high.	Operetta: The whole family, particularly in the case of Gilbert and Sullivan. Musical comedy: downstairs, the tired business man, the hostess and her party, the deb and her boy friend. Upstairs: The clerk and his date, the suburbanite and his wife, Tilly and the girls (with chocolates at matinees). The holiday spirit is to be found in the audience at the musical show more than in any other audience except at circuses. Admission high: only slightly below opera.	Folk opera (*Porgy and Bess, Oklahoma*) and Operetta: Operetta very durable, good for revival as long as grand opera. Popularity of chamber opera with components similar to those of operetta, increasing. Musical comedy perishable but source of songs with lasting popularity. Both forms good all-season entertainment.	High production costs necessitate a large theatre, though the importance of the individual performer and the required subtlety of effect rule out the grand opera house. Equipment similar to, but more than in, a good legitimate house. Large orchestra pit.
me as operetta and musical comedy. Considerable variation in structure from no intermission (HOTEL UNIVERSE) to 52 scenes (GÖTZ VON BERLICHINGEN). Performance length varies from one hour (THE EMPEROR JONES), usually played with a curtain raiser, to three evenings (MOURNING BECOMES ELECTRA). Production combines generally most skillful planning and direction and most painstaking rehearsals of any popular entertainment form—resulting generally in most finished performance and best obtainable interpretation of playwright's script.	People with sufficient culture to appreciate a conventionalized and aesthetic form of entertainment. As the general cultural level rises, audiences for legitimate drama increase. Small house and high production costs keep admission scale above that of motion pictures.	Legitimate drama is best dramatic medium for revealing character or constructing plot. It is the freest and most flexible form in the theatre, and therefore the tryout ground for new ideas, concepts, and techniques. The legitimate theatre is always reported to be on the verge of total and final collapse, and probably will be for another twenty-five centuries or so.	Most varied requirements of any theatrical type. Small enough so facial expression is significant, equipped for fast changes and effects. Specialized theatres (Shakespearian, Arena) limited in usefulness.
ɔloist or orchestra seldom repeats the same program at successive performances or performs more than 6 times per week.	More people attend concerts than major-league baseball games.	Concert popularity is growing rapidly. Concert halls appear in plans for most new art centers. The visual aspects of concert are too often neglected.	Acoustics are the prime consideration. Given good acoustics, a forestage or a wide proscenium and a concert set will make any house a concert hall.
vice nightly for large shows, oftener for singles. Last show ends by 2 A.M. Acts arranged as in (and may be the same as) vaudeville. Show changed as often as necessary to keep the customers coming. Elaborate shows once a season.	Out-of-towners who like to dine, drink, and dance. Expense account patrons. Some regulars.	This symbol of the affluent society has absorbed the best of the talent which once graced the vaudeville and presentation stages. Found where money flows freely: Las Vegas, Paris, New York, Miami Beach.	Audiences at tables in tiers around 3 sides of the stage. No stage depth required.

	Subject Matter	*Visual Components*	*Auditory Components*
Motion Pictures	Original screenplays. Adaptations from plays, musicals, short stories, novels, comic strips, and television plays to the celluloid medium, changed in conformity with intellectual and artistic limitations of the producers to what they think is palatable to an audience. Boy meets girl, etc., ad infinitum. Current events and animated cartoons.	Rectangular screen on which are projected moving images in black and white or in color of anything which can be photographed. The 18 × 24 face that launched (or sank) a thousand ships. Infinite variety (giants to dwarfs, planets to microorganisms, moving glacier to humming-bird's wing). The wide screen and the A-O optical system make film the most flexible medium in the theatre.	Reproduced sound of anything t can be got onto a sound track and off through a loud-speake Multi-channel systems with wide-screen picture make poss ble superb exploitation of the auditory element of the show.
Dance	Dance, for many years confined to playing in any available hall, has now demonstrated enough popular app to warrant building theatres especially for it. A dance theatre should provide flexibility in stage levels an backgrounds, sufficient rise for audience seats so that the routine may exploit its three-dimensional chara ter, and an orchestra location.		
Burlesque	Burlesque can use almost any theatre which can accommodate legitimate dramas. Routine like musical with emphasis on individual performer. New theatres are not built for burlesque—old ones are adapted if necessary.		

THEATRE FORMS

Throughout theatre history, the actor-audience spatial relationship has witnessed every conceivable arrangement. In our time, the overriding pluralism of artistic styles and performance aesthetics leaves open so many options, again, that the auditorium space becomes a critical factor in the design process. We are not restrained much by the shell of the auditorium because, following the considerations previously discussed in this chapter, just about any auditorium form can be modified into at least the basic semblance of another form. However, each theatre form has its own characteristics and aesthetics, advantages, and limitations. Not all will work well for every production format; likewise, not all theatre forms will work well for every play. Auditorium form, then, inescapably inserts itself into design considerations. In general, theatres may be divided into the following forms.

Arena

The arena form or theatre-in-the-round (Fig. 4.6) surrounds the action with audience seating. This format of actor-audience relationship perhaps is the oldest and most natural arrangement for viewing an event. Its devotees argue that the arena form (whether circular, ovoid, square, rectangular, or some other configuration) provides the most intimate kind of theatrical experience possible.

Thrust

A second actor-audience arrangement is the thrust or three-quarter stage (Fig. 4.7). Occasionally the term *open stage* is applied to this form. In the three-quarter circumstance, the audience surrounds the stage on all but one side. Perhaps the most familiar illustration of this form of theatre is what we assume to be the theatre of the Elizabethan public theatre noted in Figure 1.18.

Routine	Audience	Comment	Theatre Required
s many shows per day as can be run profitably. Picture Palace: Feature, shorts (travel, cartoon, one-reel dramatic sketch, etc.), news, trailers. Total show time two hours. Ten A.M. to midnight seven days a week. Five-minute intermission between shows covered by recorded music or the mighty organ. Neighborhood: 1:30 to midnight or three a day. Show changed twice or three times weekly. Second feature takes place of news and shorts. Intimate: Single feature plus news. Newsreel: One-hour show, news, shorts, and cartoons.	The American people. Frequency of individual attendance ranges from habitual addiction to occasional patronage of selected programs. Little attention given to announced starting times; hence, continuous flow of audience with some concentration in early afternoon, late afternoon, early evening, and late evening. Admission low.	Once the most popular type of theatrical production; television has superseded it as purveyor of horse opera and the machine-made plot. Quality improves with declining quantity. Potentially the most significant form of theatre.	Neighborhood: Comfortable seats and popcorn. Metropolitan: The old presentation house or motion picture palace (no more of these will be built). Drive-in: Pictures in the parking lot. Easy access, roads from many directions requisite. Intimate: Small, luxurious, in a metropolitan location.
resentation	A form once very popular, now limited to a few metropolitan locations. Prime example: Radio City Music Hall. New theatres will not be built for this form. The ground in the appropriate location can earn more money with another type of structure.		
uppets	Puppet shows have played successfully in everything from Radio City Music Hall to the living room at home, to the trailer in the park. Whatever will accommodate an audience is suitable for puppets.		

Harold Burris-Meyer and Edward Cole, *Theatres and Auditoriums,* 2nd ed. (New York: Van Nostrand Reinhold Company; 1964), pp. 2–5. Used y permission.

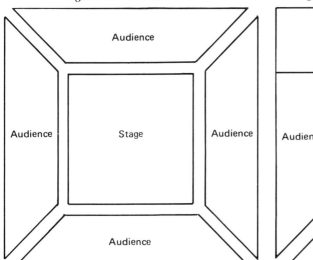

Figure 4.6 Arena form.

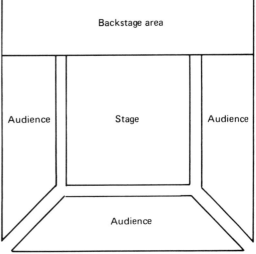

Figure 4.7 Thrust or three-quarter form.

Proscenium

The proscenium stage has dominated the-atrical production since the Renaissance. It consists of the audience seated on one side of the stage while viewing the action through an architectural opening called a proscen-ium arch (Fig. 4.8). Because of the framing effect of the proscenium arch, this form of stage arrangement is often called a picture-frame stage. Its development followed the development of rational perspective in vi-sual art in the Italian Renaissance and was the theatre's attempt to make the mise en scène look like a framed painting.

Open Stage

The term *open stage* is sometimes used syn-onymously with the term *thrust.* We use the term here to refer to additional actor-au-dience relationships which the three-quarter arrangement does not accurately describe (Figs. 4.9 and 4.10). In the diagram shown in Figure 4.9, the audience arrangement is simi-lar to that in the thrust form. The extension

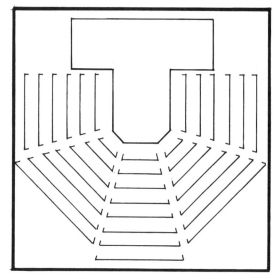

Figure 4.9   Open stage 1.

of the acting areas to the left and right of the stage extension changes the actor-audience relationship and, therefore, the aesthetics from that of the true thrust form. In the ar-rangement seen in Figure 4.10, the actor-audience arrangement is identical to that of the proscenium. However, in the open stage,

Figure 4.8   Proscenium form.

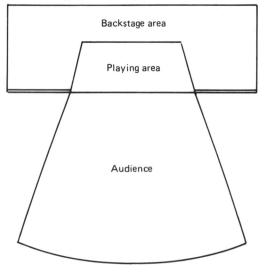

Figure 4.10   Open stage 2.

no barrier exists between the audience and the stage, and the scenic and aesthetic possibilities are quite different from those of the proscenium theatre.

Extended Stage

In the format known as the extended stage, the action wraps around the audience (Fig. 4.11). Here, again, we have what is in essence a variation of the proscenium or open stage arrangement, except in this case, the stage wraps around the audience.

Additional Forms

Any number of combination forms can be created for a given production. Some productions have employed proscenium, thrust, arena, and open actor-audience arrangements spread throughout the theatre space.

AESTHETICS AND PRACTICALITIES

Every form and every theatre exemplifying every form has its own set of aesthetic and practical characteristics. Some of the general

Figure 4.11 Extended stage.

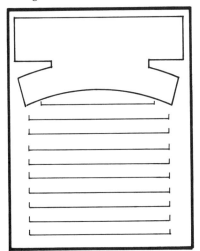

claims made in favor of or against specific forms need to be taken with a grain of salt or applied only to specific theatres. For example, the claim that the arena form is the most intimate of the forms simply does not hold true when the form is manifest in a theatre that seats two thousand spectators and is compared to a proscenium form theatre that seats three hundred. Likewise, the claim that a proscenium theatre offers greater scenic potential than other forms is totally invalidated if the proscenium stage has no wing or fly space, when compared to arena and thrust stage theatres that are fully equipped with fly potential or hydraulic floor traps. It probably does no good whatsoever to try to make wide-ranging claims or lists of potentials and limitations for the various forms. The only factor that is important to the designer regarding theatre forms is the specific nature of the form in which the design must be executed. Considerations such as the general limitations concerning vertical scenic units in arena and thrust forms seem too obvious to need explaining. The problem-solving ability and aesthetic sense requisite to being a set designer will lead one quickly to understand these things.

Nevertheless, some considerations regarding the various forms are not so obvious and have driven even experienced designers into awkward traps. The single most important of such considerations is the establishment of viable and helpful traffic patterns. In the proscenium form, the general tendency is to design movement flow that follows the natural horizontal configuration of the form. Very often proscenium stages, especially those with problematic sightlines from the side seats, force the designer into a shallow setting that leaves almost no possibility for upstage and downstage movement. If that situation applies to your setting, then you must take whatever steps you can to alleviate the problem and try to create the sense, if not the actuality, of nonhorizontal move-ment potential for the director (Fig. 4.12). In thrust stages, which tend to be significantly longer than they are wide, a similar ten-dency for monolinear movement exists (Fig. 4.13). One way to cause movement patterns other than monolinear ones is to design ob-structions to the traffic flow, thereby forcing the actors to detour. However, such devices can be counterproductive if, in breaking one traffic pattern, you eliminate it entirely as an option. Careful discussion with the director regarding the problem or potential problem is an essential part of the planning process.

In the arena form, a major traffic problem is the tendency to keep actors circling so they can remain open to all parts of the au-dience as the play progresses (Fig. 4.14). Here, again, recognition of the potential for problems will lead you and the director to confront the situation and to adopt solu-tions appropriate to the play and your par-ticular production goals.

In the proscenium form, the size of the proscenium opening itself can create poten-tial aesthetic problems. The designer who tries to upscale what is supposed to be an intimate and small room to fill a fifty-foot proscenium opening will wind up with a nightmare. When faced with a proscenium opening that is larger than the production needs, cut the space down with a false pro-scenium. If faced with too small an opening, try moving to an open stage arrangement that uses the proscenium arch as part of the setting. In the setting shown in Figure 4.15, the acting area was moved outside the pro-scenium arch (an opening of approximately twenty-four feet immediately upstage of the ramps in the foreground). The result created a stage area stretching from one wall of the auditorium to the other, kept the prosce-nium backstage area intact, and gave the pro-duction the scale that the play and style de-manded. However, changing the size of the proscenium opening in an existing theatre also changes the characteristics of sightline angles and the potentials for audience visual discomfort as discussed earlier in the chap-ter. In general, the guidelines on the next page for production type and proscenium size can guide you in your decision making.

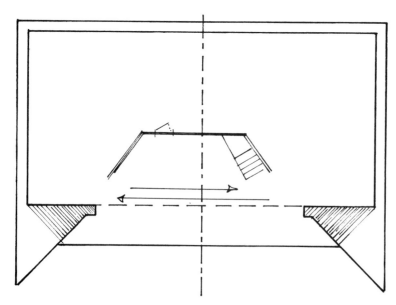

Figure 4.12 Movement patterns in a shallow proscenium setting.

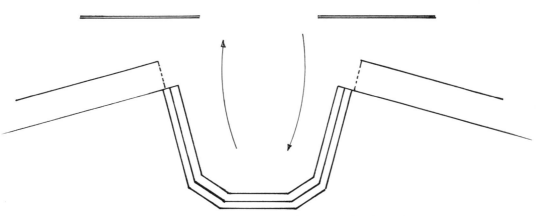

Figure 4.13 Movement pattern tendencies in the thrust form.

Type	General Proscenium Widths Maximums and Minimums (in Feet) for Various Production Types*	
	Minimum	*Maximum*
Drama	26	40
Revue	30	45
Musical Comedy	30	50
Opera	40	80

*Burris-Meyer and Cole, p. 71.

OPTIONS WITHIN THE FORMS: UNIT, SIMULTANEOUS, AND MULTIPLE SETTINGS

The specific characteristics of the individual theatre, whatever its form, will ultimately force itself on the designer, especially when plays of more than one scenic locale are produced. From the Shakespearean repertoire to modern plays such as *Dylan*, with its

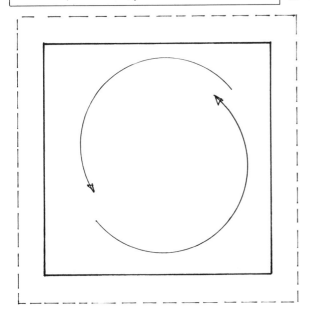

Figure 4.14 Circular movement tendencies in arena form.

Figure 4.15 Euripides, *The Bacchae,* University of Illinois at Chicago. Dennis J. Sporre, designer.

twenty-two separate scenes, the designer must face the challenge of solving aesthetic and practical problems inherent in such productions. As we have seen, history presents us with many options from which to choose; or we may invent or combine to meet our needs. Production goals will shape our decisions. For example, the multiple setting with its visual elaborateness was the favorite of nineteenth-century audiences, who watched Shakespearean revivals with a different expectation than did the Elizabethan audiences, who saw the same plays produced in simple, unit sets. The simultaneous setting stimulated the Roman and medieval audience. We are free to choose one or all of these to solve our design needs.

Multiple Settings

In some circumstances, the needs of production will be met well by the multiple set-

ting, in which a separate and complete set is designed for each required location. Such a design calls into play a designer's creative understanding of scene shifting and its intricacies. Even if the theatre plant is well endowed with wing space and fly systems, the organization of designs that facilitate rapid scenic changes is required. Often the play is written in such a way as to suggest solutions. For example, many Broadway musicals work out their dramatic structures so that the concept of the "in one" technique is built into the play itself. In this case, scenes are arranged in progression from small to large. The production, then, begins with several sets in place, each inside a larger one. Shifting is executed by removing a smaller set which then reveals a larger one. The shift is economical because the need to put a second set in place has been accomplished ahead of time.

Of course, there are numerous means of

shifting multiple settings using standard running, rolling, or flying techniques. Shifts at scene breaks are much more critical than at act breaks, inasmuch as scene break shifts do not have an intermission and its time and noise to cover them.

In addition to whatever shifting solution is chosen, the multiple setting should meet two criteria. First, all of the settings should achieve some sort of stylistic unity with the production as a whole. Second, the means of shifting must be efficient and quiet so as not to detract from the rhythmic flow of the production.

Unit Settings

The unit set has come to be a very practical solution for the multiscene play. It provides a means for staging the play without the need for settings for each different scene and the need to shift from one setting to another (see Figure 2.26). Unit sets range from a single design that sustains itself and the play for the entire production to units that form a basic environment to which various elements are added to suggest the various scenes. A unit set may be conventional—that is, nonrepresentational—or it may be illusionistic, suggesting heavily the time and place. A unit set may represent any style. It can be stationary or it may move. At its simplest, and perhaps best, the unit set can provide the perfect ambiance for a play whose language is so strong as to require nothing in the way of representational suggestion for the audience. A look back to chapter 1 reinforces the conclusion that the great classical plays of history, those whose language is high and poetic, were produced in the simplest of unit settings, settings that were architectural and formal in essence.

Above all, the unit setting must be seen in its aesthetic role. Platforms, stairways, and ramps that provide appropriate acting space must also have design integrity. A setting, whether standing alone or with actors and accoutrements on it, must meet the criteria for sound visual design. It must be like an independent work of sculpture. It must have interest, variety, and unity; and, of course, it must be appropriate to the mood, message, and style of the play. In a very selfish sense, the unit set must contain enough visual stimuli to sustain itself from the audience's point of view throughout the running time of the production. The danger of approaching the unit set as a practical expediency first and a design second is a very real one and should be avoided at all costs.

Simultaneous Settings

Simultaneous settings are not new in the theatre, but they have gained in popularity in the last several years. Lee Simonson and Jo Mielziner made use of simultaneous settings in several memorable productions, such as *Desire under the Elms* and *Death of a Salesman.* The device itself dates back to the Roman comedy and the medieval mystery, miracle, and morality plays. In the simultaneous setting, the designer creates two or more settings which remain totally within view of the audience and are united within an overall design picture. Many plays actually call for a simultaneous setting; an example is *Look Homeward, Angel,* in which two rooms in two separate houses plus a statue in a park occupy the stage throughout the play. Plays such as *Brighton Beach Memoirs* and *Broadway Bound* solve the need to move from one room in the house to another by placing the entire house on stage, and sectioning through the middle to reveal living room, dining room, hallway, and upstairs bedrooms. Audience focus is controlled by action and lighting. The same considerations adhere to the simultaneous setting as adhere to any design: It must be a design first, and technical practicality second.

Two major limitations for use of the simultaneous setting are the size of the stage space and sightlines of the theatre. A simultaneous setting that is not skillfully organized and carefully designed can end up with too little space for the necessary action. As a result, the actors move in fear of bumping against walls and furniture, and the director may not be able to utilize the kind of actor movement that may be best for the scene. In addition, especially where a second level is used, it may be impossible for major portions of the audience to see anything but the downstage action or the upper bodies of the actors if great care is not taken in plan-ning or if the theatre is not suited to elevated sightlines. In some theatres, a second level may drive the lighting designer to distraction because of limitations in possible placement of lighting instruments or problems in lighting the areas independently.

Whatever the solutions, the options for multiscened shows are many. In every case, however, the scenic options are closely tied to the facility, if not dictated by it. If you design for the same theatre, production after production, you will be able to learn from your mistakes, and the facility may become your ally rather than your adversary. If you have no control over the physical facility and must take it as it stands, you will often need as much creativity in dealing with the theatre as you will expend in composing the design.

Figure 4.16 Edward Albee, *A Delicate Balance,* Old Globe Theatre, San Diego, CA. Mark Donnelly, designer.

Figure 4.17 *Billy Bishop Goes to War,* Old Globe Theatre, San Diego, CA. Mark Donnelly, designer.

EXAMINING SOME POSSIBILITIES

The designs in Figures 4.16 and 4.17, as well as those in chapter 11 and throughout the text, provide a survey of approaches to various theatre forms. Your study of these approaches will provide you with many suggestions for solving the demands of other plays to be produced in the proscenium, arena, open, thrust, and extended stage forms.

CHAPTER FIVE

WORKING
IN THE
THEATRE

As Howard Bay said in his book on stage design, "actors are the primary element, the given quantity, but designers are the craftsmen embedded in the workings of stage creation." He spoke of design as a "visual progression of a dramatic event" and of style as a "concept." It is advisable to keep these thoughts in mind when the designer begins to face the realities of the professional world of theatre in our current cultural climate, in which motion pictures are classified as "entertainment" and television is ruled by commercial advertising companies.

In spite of the lure of money and security, the creative artist needs to retain his or her grasp of the true goals of the art, which will allow the designer to develop fresh imagination in the execution of the design work. However, too many students of design are ill prepared to face the demanding realities of the commercial marketplace as well as the competition of contemporary professionals.

Designing is basically a developed skill or craft, and the neophyte artist needs a combination of formal study and practical experience. Most colleges and universities offer courses in design and technical theatre, and many offer undergraduate and graduate degrees in theatre. In selecting a school, one should carefully examine the courses of study offered in the catalogues, the number and expertise of the instructors, the type of buildings available for producing plays, the location of the institution, and its relationship to possible community involvement.

Professional drama schools can be found in several large cities and are staffed by instructors recruited from local professional theatres. Any formal study of theatre design should include scenery construction, scene painting, drafting, sketching, perspective, and related areas.

Practical experience may be obtained in several ways: through laboratory courses in schools; by working as an apprentice with a professional designer, usually at a minimum wage; or by designing plays for community efforts, for little or no recompence. The novice designer must stay actively aware of current trends in all types of contemporary productions, including operas, ballets, television productions, and motion pictures, as well as legitimate theatre.

Although many theatre critics have a tendency to ignore or treat the theatre's visual effects lightly, a few give honest, worthwhile evaluations of design elements. The beginner should note such reviews in order to gain a reasonable view of the critical reaction a design might evoke in audience members.

Finally, regarding preparation for working in the field, we need to observe that educational theatre puts a great emphasis on academic degrees, whereas the commercial theatre believes this is not a requirement. However, of the ten most active designers on Broadway, only one does not possess a university or college advanced degree. Such a fact gives reasonable credit to the training presently obtainable in institutions of higher learning.

BROADWAY THEATRE

Most theatre artists consider the Broadway theatre to be the ultimate goal to be achieved in the profession. Actors, directors, and playwrights, as well as designers, relate success with the commercial New York area. Much of this regard is reinforced by the theatre unions, which are most active in New York.

The designers' union is the United Scenic Artists of America (USA) Local No. 829, which is affiliated with the Brotherhood of Painters, Decorators, and Paperhangers of the United States and Canada, AFL-CIO. Its members are scenic, lighting, and costume designers; diorama and display designers; television and motion picture art directors; mural artists; costume stylists; and theatre, motion picture, and television artists. Membership is restricted because of complicated and costly examinations and limited employment opportunities. The union sets minimum wage scales and fees, worker responsibilities, and working conditions for its members. Besides its offices in New York City, the USA maintains offices in Chicago and Los Angeles, and members frequently transfer their membership from one local to another, depending on their residence location. Local No. 829 works with the League of New York Theatres and Producers, Inc., to set minimum pay scales, including the fee rates for additional settings for single productions, for single unit settings for multi-scene plays, and bare-stage productions. As with any contract, there can be additional benefits such as weekly royalties, incidental expenses incurred in designing, and other, related expenditures (Fig. 5.1).

The specific services required of the scene designer are carefully described by the union and include (1) a complete working model of the settings or complete color sketches and working drawings for construction; (2) color schemes and color sketches for painting contractors; (3) the design or selection and approval of properties, draperies, and furniture; (4) the design or supervision of special scenic effects (including projections); (5) supplying of specifications for construction; (6) supervision of the building and painting of settings and properties; (7) providing of estimates available for discussion sessions; and (8) attendance at the be-

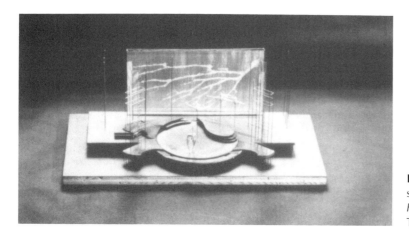

Figure 5.1 Peter Wexler, scene design for *The Happy Time.* Broadway Theatre, New York City.

ginning pre-Broadway setup, the Broadway setup and all dress rehearsals, the first public performance, out-of-town openings, the first New York public performance, and any scenic rehearsals as needed.

The International Alliance of Theatrical Stage Employees (IATSE) is the union that represents stage carpenters, stage hands, electricians, property personnel, audiovisual personnel, light board operators, follow spot operators, sound technicians, pin rail personnel, rigging personnel, loaders, and unloaders. IATSE, like the USA, is affiliated with the AFL-CIO.

The number of workers for each job assignment depends on the type and size of the production and the landlord's agreement with the local union office. The union is responsible for setting a minimum wage scale and the fees for each of the specific categories as well as for determining the workers' responsibilities in each category. The union also will specify safety measures and conditions involved in the work areas. For example, the minimum call for a show is three or four hours at a set minimum fee— that is, the minimum the worker is to be paid hourly. The union requires lunch and dinner breaks to be observed; any work after

midnight, no matter what the starting time, requires time-and-one-half payment.

Applications for membership require a unanimous vote of the active members. An examination in each of the areas of expertise must be accomplished before an applicant can be accepted as an apprentice member. After an established length of time, the full membership can be awarded.

The responsibilities of the apprentice membership differ from those of the more skilled journeyman. For each production job, the union appoints a steward to carefully monitor the working conditions and safety programs established by the local.

Work outside the member's local can be handled by trading one's membership for a temporary card in the geographic area of the job. When the assignment is completed, the temporary card is exchanged for the local membership card.

Other theatrical groups and unions involving production organizations are Legitimate Theatre Employees (LTE), United States Institute for Theatre Technology (USITT), Technical Assistance Group (TAG), and National Association of Broadcasting Engineers and Technicians (NABET).

The New York designer must be prepared

to accept the fact that he or she is a temporary employee hired for one job at a time, and who will need to supplement his or her income from designing with additional income that might even be outside the profession. Faced with the costs of setting up a single business office-studio, a number of professional artists have recently begun partnership arrangements similar to those made by lawyers and architects. This helps to offset the costs of equipment, secretarial and drafting services, and high rent costs.

New designers with little or no professional background can begin or reinforce their careers by working as an assistant to an established designer. Most Broadway designers supplemented their early training in this fashion. It is always good for the neophyte to view firsthand how professional designers handle the actual business of designing, and, specifically, how a particular artist approaches his or her works creatively. These positions are usually secured by recommendations from other designers or by individual interviews reinforced by a strong portfolio and references.

Assistants to a designer may be required to draft, work on models, and do research for the particular project. Other assignments could include securing samples of materials, searching for set props, and checking progress at scene shops. An assistant's weekly payments and length of service on a New York theatrical production can be negotiated by the designer with the management of his design contract; all details must meet USA union approval before any work begins.

WORK OUTSIDE THE THEATRE

Other work in metropolitan areas may be available to individuals with a strong background in the art of scenic design. Architec-

tural firms employ drafting technicians, as well as office workers, who can understand the requirements of architectural design. Diorama or model construction positions can be found with museums and display firms. Television stations frequently need individuals with design backgrounds (Fig. 5.2). Advertising companies require settings for filmed commercials (Fig. 5.3). Video production organizations require elaborate staging techniques and effects. Industrial shows sponsored by corporations for professional purposes use visual effects to emphasize sales. Display companies and department stores specialize in presentations of their merchandise.

UNION EXAMS

Although the United Scenic Artists membership exams vary with regard to individual projects, the form of the test is consistent. Traditionally, the exam was held once a year in the spring, but in 1987 midwinter and fall exams were added to accompany the spring examination period. There are two tracks, A and B. Track A is for professional designers who wish to join the union. Track B is for designers who have not attained professional status—for example, recently graduated students of design or individuals who may have mastered the required skills but have not yet worked in the profession.

The first exam, called Track A, is tailored to test artists who are presently working in art and scenic design and who have a minimum of at least two years of constant employment in one of the following areas: lighting design, scenic artist, costume design, or scenic design. The actual exam involves an evaluation of the applicant's résumé and references. Each area is assigned to a single weekend day.

The Track B exam is for the nonprofes-

Figure 5.2 John Wright Stevens, scene design for *The Lathe of Heaven* television film for Public Broadcast Service. New York City. Photograph by John Wright Stevens.

sional applicant and consists of an interview, a portfolio review, and an involved project to be completed at home. For scene designers, the project will be a multiset production set design for a specific theatre. The ground plans and sectional theatre plans will be provided. In addition, an eight-hour exam can be scheduled covering the rendering for a scene from a selected play, including a 1/4-in. ground plan of the same play. Four historic periods can be selected, and the applicant is asked to draw an article of furniture, such as a chair, from each of the periods. Several quick sketches of specific architectural features can be requested. A Georgian fireplace, a Greek column, a gothic doorway, or a rococo panel might be reasonable examples. A final assignment might be to draft from a postcard picture a ground and longitudinal plan that would indicate the best way to achieve a dimensional effect of the painted scene. The exam areas are lighting design, scenic artist, costume design, and scenic design. The first two areas involve two days of interviews and two days of practical examinations. The remaining one-third of the examination involves a practical scene painting and lighting project set up in an actual location and supervised by a panel of judges.

The exam may seem difficult, but it establishes a union membership of theatre artists with the highest-calibre credentials available to the professional theatre scene.

PRODUCTION ORGANIZATION

The Broadway theatre is essentially a single-production business company headed by a producer who is responsible for estimating the costs of production and for raising the

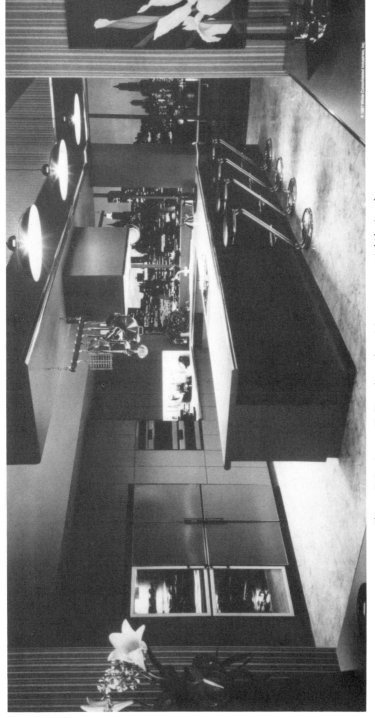

Figure 5.3 James T. Singelis, advertising commercial design for Frigidaire. New York City.

money to achieve the presentation of the production. After opening, the box office sales must cover the weekly operating expenses and begin to repay the investors. The producer is responsible for selecting the show's designer, sometimes with recommendations from the playwright and the director (if the designer has not been selected earlier). It is not unusual for a producer, before establishing a cast and even a director, to use the services of the designer to help raise capital on the basis of his or her attractive sketches and models. Most professional theatre design assignments are made through personal contacts rather than by application. Occasionally, off-Broadway shows are moved to Broadway, out-of-town productions are moved to New York theatres, and contracts made with directors in regional theatres are continued on Broadway. Association with a successful hit will nearly always ensure the designer's next assignment. Sometimes a strong positive review of scenic effects by an established critic, even though the play was poorly received, may be an advantage to the designer, although nothing can take the place of a solid and successful hit.

The United Scenic Artists Local No. 829, together with the League of New York Theatres and Producers, Inc., have established the minimum rates for scene designers. Since all contracts have fringe benefits, additional monetary terms can be negotiated. Some designers can get royalties, specific weekly fees, weekly percentages of the gross, or a combination of these payments. These are worked out with the producer as are additional reimbursement for expenses incurred in the design process. Theatrical lawyers are sometimes hired by busy designers to handle their business matters.

The designer is not allowed to work on any design until the contract between the producer and the designer has been approved and filed by the union and returned to the designer. Included in the contract are billing specifications for the theatre program and advertising.

THE OFF-BROADWAY THEATRE

The off-Broadway theatre was a reaction to the commercialism of the Broadway theatre in the 1950s and 1960s. Its purpose was to foster new plays and experimental productions and to produce the works of new playwrights. The area of the off-Broadway theatres is described as anywhere in Manhattan outside the defined Broadway area, which is bounded by 5th and 9th avenues from 34th to 56th streets or from 5th avenue to the Hudson River between 56th and 72nd streets. The seating capacity of an off-Broadway theatre must be under 499 seats. Originally established as a low-budget showcase theatre organization, off-Broadway theatres were eventually unionized, which increased production costs and encouraged commercialization. Today, the number of seats is not as important as the possible weekly gross of the theatre's box office ticket sales.

The design services for the off-Broadway theatre are similar to those of Broadway, but the union contracts require royalty payments to the designer based on the seating capacity. Although most off-Broadway productions have limited runs, a production such as *The Fantasticks* is a notable exception. The show may, because of its success, move to a Broadway theatre and the original designer may be included in the move, a factor that would mean additional income for a new setting designed for the Broadway theatre. Production budgets may be small, but the designer may be challenged by the limitations of the theatres, a restricted budget, or minimal stage crews. In addition, designing off-Broadway usually involves situations less stressful than those exerted on Broadway.

Assignments in the off-Broadway theatre are secured by much the same means as the more lucrative Broadway ones—that is, by interviews, good résumés, attention-getting portfolios, and, more importantly, personal recommendations and contacts. Since theatre is essentially a cooperative art, friends in the business can be extremely important to career advancement (Fig. 5.4).

THE EQUITY WAIVER AND SHOWCASE THEATRES

An Equity Waiver theatre has ninety-nine or fewer seats, and it must never be able to seat more than that number. At present, Equity Waiver theatres exist only in Los Angeles. Showcase Theatres operate in a house of less than 100 seats and could originally operate without union employees. However, now Showcase theatres are subject to jurisdiction by Equity under the Showcase Code, which allows for audience contributions, limited ticket prices, or both. A Waiver theatre can run a production for six to eight weeks, with a possible open-ended run for additional performances. A Showcase theatre can opt for runs of four weeks, eight weeks, twelve weeks, or twenty-four weeks, depending on box office sales.

Securing a design assignment in a Waiver or Showcase theatre would be similar to that in off-Broadway organizations, but with less renumeration. The prospective designer should obtain as much information as possible concerning the organizational procedure and facilities for this type of production. One item affecting the work of the designer that could be a major factor in decisions is the budget for the production. A Showcase theatre budget can range from nothing to $2,000.00. The designer's salary or fee could be included in the show budget or could be handled separately and could range from $150.00 to $2,000.00. Whatever the show budget, the designer should always make certain that enough is held back to handle the overage that is bound to occur.

Another factor to consider is whether or not the theatre has a shop with work space and, if so, where it is located. Find out how

Figure 5.4 Peter Wexler, scene design for *Jockeys*. Promenade Theatre, New York City.

crews are obtained and if they are paid personnel or volunteer workers. The existence of a permanent staff such as a technical director, an electrician, or a janitor should be ascertained before agreeing to a contract. Additional information such as supply sources, electrical facilities, lighting and sound equipment, and scheduled production meetings will help the prospective designer get the job completed efficiently and with few problems. Inasmuch as efficient shop tools may not be readily available in many theatre shops, it would be helpful for the designer to have a personal collection of suitable tools and brushes that would allow him or her to accomplish goals in a productive fashion.

Most theatres have a floor plan of the stage and off-stage areas. If one is not available, it will be necessary to draft plans before attempting to design. Ceiling height, complete with lighting instrument hanging positions, and wing space, should be included. Limited stages will dictate much of the possibilities for shifting scenery for set changes. Although shift crew training is not necessarily the designer's problem, the choice of a shifting device is. Many of the small Waiver and Showcase theatres lack reasonable wing or fly space, and so the designer's ingenuity will have to solve the problems (Fig. 5.5).

THE REGIONAL THEATRE

Beginning in the 1960s, regional theatres had developed sufficiently to exert an important influence over the American theatre scene. Although the decentralization of the professional theatre was encouraged by such organizations as the American National Theatre and Academy as far back as the mid-thirties, they lacked the financial clout to effect a change. Although they possessed a congressional charter, they had no public funding.

The early 1960s produced the National Endowment for the Arts, as well as a number of theatre arts councils, which contributed financial support with direct funding, grants, and contributions for struggling, nonprofit resident theatres. As these theatres grew, they created and developed audiences in numbers and areas never before imagined by the Broadway theatre. Regional theatre productions, being essentially nonprofit, were based on creativity, imagination, and originality, as opposed to the commercial efforts of Broadway. Today, a majority of the most stimulating productions in the art can be found in such urban cultural locations as Minneapolis, Dallas, San Francisco, San Diego, Louisville, Milwaukee, Tucson, Los Angeles, Denver, Chicago, and Seattle, as well as in central Manhattan (Fig. 5.6).

Because of the decrease in Broadway productions, many designers began to seek assignments in theatre organizations outside the New York area. Since most regional theatres produce a season of plays, it is economically beneficial to establish a position of resident designer, which enables the artist to enjoy a more secure income for a longer period of time than does the Broadway system of single show productions. Less affluent regional theatres could hire beginning designers or nonunion designers, thereby providing an additional step between academic training and the commercial theatre scene.

Today practically all established professional scene designers divide their time among assignments in regional theatres, Broadway theatres, off-Broadway theatres, opera companies, ballet companies, television, and motion pictures. The hiring of personnel in regional theatres is the responsibility of the artistic and managing directors, and it is necessary to deal with either or both of these individuals in contract negotiations

Figure 5.5 Richard Rorke, scene design for *Babe's All-Nite Cafe*. By permission of Megaw Theatre (an Equity Waiver Theatre), Northridge, California.

Figure 5.6 Vickie Smith, scene design for *The Marriage of Bette and Boo.* Arizona Theatre Company, Tucson, Arizona. Photograph by Tim Fuller.

as well as initial application activity. Housing, travel expenses, and assistants will frequently be involved in these agreements.

THE EDUCATIONAL THEATRE

The past twenty-five years have seen the educational theatre replace the private professional schools of the 1920s as training grounds for serious students of theatre arts. Before 1950, most scene design students studied at private art schools, with occasional apprentice positions in summer stock or professional design studios. Productions in colleges and universities were considered extracurricular activities sponsored by honorary clubs and similar to athletic events. Slowly the educational process was expanded, not only to degrees in music and graphic arts but also to drama and even

dance. The affluent sixties also brought about expansion of physical facilities until many campuses could boast of theatre structures that far surpassed any commercial Broadway centers for presentation. Not only were theatre auditoriums built, but shops, storage areas, and rehearsal rooms were judged equally important. The new structures allowed for more intense training, more flexibility in presentation, and more inspiration in execution. The security of the teaching profession attracted many talented and outstanding theatre artists, and many professional artists accepted short-term positions on university faculties between professional engagements.

Whereas secondary schools require a teaching certificate as well as a degree, colleges and universities require an advanced degree for their instructors. The growth of departments of drama, both in enrollment and teaching staff, doubled during the sixties and seventies. However, today's economy has slowed development and further expansion to a minimum, and most positions on faculties are replacements rather than new teaching posts.

Competition requires strong preparation, both in practice and academic areas of design and technical theatre. For some, the responsibility of presenting basic course information year after year may prove tedious in its repetition, but this can be offset by the numerous vacation periods and allowance for outside employment in varied theatre situations. Applications for faculty positions are generally channeled through a departmental faculty committee that recommends a select number of candidates to the department head for consideration.

Many universities have strong connections with professional Equity companies that give students an added contact with the profession through association. Some professional designers work as guest lecturers or professors in schools with professional programs, a combination that provides additional financial security as well as satisfaction in contributing to the development of young artists (Fig. 5.7).

THE COMMUNITY THEATRE

The community theatre is essentially a nonprofit, urban project that involves enthusiastic but amateur artists. Beginning in the twenties and thirties, it has become a means of artistic expression for individuals who do not consider it their profession but more a responsible hobby. Reinforced by municipal funding, many organizations are contributing vitality and enthusiasm to a cooperative community activity (Fig. 5.8).

Most of the involved citizenry are nonsalaried amateurs dedicated to producing plays that are performed for local neighbors. The organization is generally headed by a board of directors that will hire at least two

Figure 5.7 Robert C. Burroughs, scene design for *The Guardsman*. University of Arizona Mainstage, Tucson, Arizona.

Figure 5.8 Thom Gilseth, scene design for *The Miser.* Phoenix Little Theatre, Phoenix, Arizona.

paid theatre artists, generally a managing director and a designer-technician. Community theatres usually operate under a seasonal plan of productions, and the paid staff is hired by the season. Some communities have their own theatre buildings, but they are in the minority. More often than not, community theatres are found in temporary quarters such as stores, field houses, ballrooms, and school or civic auditoriums.

The theatre's scene shop can be located at a different place than the theatre itself, which presents a number of obvious problems. The prospective designer-technician should seek information on working conditions in similar fashion and with similar goals to those suggested for possible employment with off-Broadway organizations. Salaries or fees for the designer may be ar-

ranged by individual projects or for an established length of time, such as a season, a summer, or even a year, all subject to renewal. Community theatres do not require college degrees or professional experience for employment, although leadership abilities are definitely needed to handle the problems that frequently arise with production.

THE DESIGN PORTFOLIO

The necessity of assembling a design portfolio should be apparent to every serious student of scene design. As with any graphic artist, it is the only means of presenting a visual overview of the individual's talent, artistic abilities, and accomplishments. It is essential, in transferring from one educational institution to another, as well as in job applications, to present tangible evidence of past work.

The portfolio content will depend on the particular level of the individual artist and his or her major interest in the area of design. It is essential that each piece of work be properly identified with the name of the play, the playwright, the name of the designer, the date of completion, and the scale that was used. If the work was actually produced, additional information concerning the theatre, the producer, and the director should be included to allow for a more objective evaluation.

The following items would be considered minimum content for the portfolio of a graduate of a four-year college:

1. Colored renderings (six) no larger than 20 in. by 30 in.
2. Scaled models or photographs of same (one or two).
3. Scaled floor plans of above models (one or two).
4. Shifting plans if necessary (indication of hanging or suspended elements included).
5. Construction drawings of at least two of the designs in 1/2-in. scale.
6. Property sketches of one of the renderings, in scale with suggested construction techniques.

The portfolio of a recent graduate with a master's degree in theatre would be more involved and should contain at least the following items.

1. Colored renderings (twelve) matted, and of a variety of types of plays in various historical periods. Operas and ballet as well as drama should be included. Also, at least two different styles of presentation should be indicated, such as arena or proscenium. One Shakespeare play should be included, as well as a multiset show.

2. Colored photographs of scaled painted models for at least three to six of the colored renderings.
3. Scaled floor plans for each of the three to six renderings.
4. Front elevations, construction drawings, isometric drawings in scale (1/2 in.) for at least one of the renderings.
5. Painter's elevations, to scale with color formulas or mixing instructions, for a drop or an involved hanging. Additional painter's elevation samples indicating foliage, wood paneling, or marble.
6. Property sketches.
7. Any color photographs or slides of actually produced work. These need to be carefully indentified.

Because the portfolio may be too bulky to mail for job applications in distant locations, it is essential to consider additional presentation methods. These could include a slide collection carefully numbered in sequence. If possible, it is wise to have production information printed on the bottom of the slide, furnishing easy identification when projected. If the design was actually produced, follow the design rendering with an actual photograph so that the design execution can be carefully observed.

Another means of presentation comprises photographic records of actual productions, including the initial rendering, floor plans, and working drawings. Because some items may not photograph well, it is possible to fold and include actual drawings in a book.

Slides, prints, or both also can be used for recording student work in school files. In so doing, the school helps to maintain a reasonable background for evaluation of past work. Such evaluation forms the basis for letters of recommendation, which can help in establishing a worthwhile reputation for a career in the design field.

COMPOSING A RÉSUMÉ

A designer's résumé needs to be short, neat, and to the point. Preferably, it should be a single-spaced page and should never be more than two pages long. It should include only essential information on the individual and only recent accomplishments. It must be well organized and easily read and understood.

Head the résumé with the title or position for which you are applying, such as designer, teacher, scenic artist, set and costume designer, and so on. Next come your full name, your business address, or home address, or both, and your telephone numbers, including area code.

The next section should be devoted to one's education and training with degrees from institutions of higher learning. Include separate special courses of study that did not apply toward a certificate or a degree. Listing a recognized, important instructor might be a significant addition. Do not include secondary school information or courses of study that have no relevance to the area of design.

Any union affiliation needs to be cited before beginning to list productions designed. The list should be in chronological order beginning with the most recent production and including the name of the show, the year, the name of the theatre or the organization, and exactly what was designed. If more than one design was for a particular theatre or organization, that should be set up as a separate heading followed by each show, year, and design area.

Identify any original script productions, because they are not previously designed shows and provide greater challenges to the designer. Any assistant designer position could now be listed, if applicable, naming the show and the year. Other work in related fields might be the next item of documentation, followed by honors and awards, if applicable.

The last item would be a list of three or four names of individuals for reference. Any letters of recommendation can be included separately. Try to use individuals who are recognizable and well known (Fig. 5.9).

Separate from the actual résumé, include a personal letter requesting consideration for a specific assignment and stating your availability for the position. Never use a form letter for this enclosure. Keep the letter on a personal level, and comment on recent company productions you might have seen. If you have not seen any because of distance, express your wish to observe their work in the very near future. The letter should also state why you want to design for that particular theatre organization. Show that you know of the organization and its purpose. If you know that the theatre already has a resident designer, you may wish to be considered for an assistant design position. This may be a way of getting your foot in the door.

After mailing your résumé, begin an interview log in which you record the mailing addresses, names of company administrators or directors, postage and printing expenses incurred that could be helpful for income tax records, and information on organizations for future employment possibilities. In addition, a follow-up phone call or letter of inquiry would be in order if you have not received a reply within a reasonable length of time. The letter could reiterate your interest in the organization and your desire for a meeting at some future date when you would be in the vicinity of the theatre. Enclosing a self-addressed, stamped postcard, with a questionnaire concerning the receipt of the letter and whether the person is interested in future communication with you, is a further possibility.

Résumés can be sent to professional resi-

JOHN DOE   SCENIC DESIGNER

    BUSINESS—123 Circle Square
                Suite D
                New York City, New York 10023

RESIDENCE—425 W. Huntington Drive
                Apt. 1068
                New York City, New York 10008
                (212) 111-4876

Education

2 years Crawford Community College, Patterson, Ohio
B.A. Catholic University of America, Washington, D.C.
M.F.A. University of Wisconsin, Madison, Wisconsin—
   Graduate Assistantship in Technical Theatre

Additional studies at UCLA and San Francisco Academy of Design

Memberships

United Scenic Artists Lu350; USITT

Productions

      Oblong Repertory Company—SCENIC DESIGNER:
      Nicholas Nickelby 1989

      Soho Cellar Theatre Company—SCENIC DESIGNER:
      Miss Firecracker 1988

      Sandusky Ballet Company—SCENIC DESIGNER:
      The Nutcracker 1987

      T.V. Crisco Commercial, New York 1987

      T.V. Pilot Film—ASSISTANT DESIGNER:
      Burbank Blues Bull's Eye Productions, Los Angeles 1986

Honors and Awards

      Phi Beta Kappa; Honorable Mention for Design, American
      College Theatre Festival, 1984

      Outstanding Theatre Arts Senior, Catholic University
      Theatre Arts Department, 1982

References

      Dr. O.T. McCullough   Ms. Phyllis Smith
      Dean of Creative Arts   Artistic Director
      University of Wisconsin   Oblong Repertory Company
      Madison, Wisconsin 92013   Oblong, Idaho 62311

      Mr. Daniel Foster
      Designs Limited—Suite B
      34 West 82nd Street
      New York City, New York 10022

Figure 5.9   Sample résumé.

dent theatres, repertory theatres, summer stock theatres, package houses, musical tent theatres, showcase theatres, community theatres, and university theatres with resident companies.

THE CONTRACT

Someone once remarked, "Paper remembers, people forget," and that is undoubtedly the reasoning behind a written contract, which is a legally enforceable agreement between two or more people. The agreement consists of an offer that is accepted and for which something is given in return. There are essentially three types of contracts: oral, implied, and written. Written is the most easily enforceable. The details of the other two are much more difficult to prove.

The United Scenic Artists' basic contract is a good pattern for composing a reasonable agreement between a designer and a producer. A dependable contract needs to contain elements such as the following:

1. A concise description of the job, distinguishing between a production that is assembled from stock items or designed originally. It could be a combination of the two and, if so, should be carefully indicated.
2. Dates of performance, production meetings, technical rehearsals, and dress rehearsals should be stated, and the required attendance indicated.
3. Fee payments and amounts should be listed specifically. Any arrangements and fees for design assistance need to be handled here.
4. Any royalty fees should be established.
5. Ownership rights of the designs agreed upon.
6. The possibility of a sale of the production, which could call for overseeing remounting of the production, should be mentioned. This would include any film, television, and taping arrangements. Designers should be allowed to negotiate their individual fees for this.

7. Availability of per diem and travel expenses incurred in execution of shopping trips for production materials.
8. Complimentary tickets or house seats available for the designer.

Agents are more adept at, or at least they are more familiar with, negotiating contracts than is the average scene designer. They look upon the job as a business deal. Individual designers have problems in deciding on their own worth. Consequently, present-day professional designers are resorting more and more to agents and lawyers to handle the business side of the job.

At times, some producers in off-off-Broadway situations are reluctant to sign letters of agreement or completed contracts, but they might be agreeable to a simple, written statement involving the fee payment, the production budget, and a production schedule. If the producer still avoids such a general commitment, the wise designer will seek work with other theatre producers.

THE COPYRIGHT

The designer may wish to copyright his or her designs. Copyright can be accomplished by signing and dating the front or back of the piece and adding a circled *C* next to the signature. A series of drawings can be registered for a small fee of $10.00 per application for Copyright Registration for the Visual Arts from:

Information and Publication Section
Copyright Office
Library of Congress
Washington, D.C. 20559

A copyright is the exclusive right to use the precise product of an individual's own creation for a definite period of time. If the design was created on or after January 1,

1978, the copyright will last for one's life-time plus an additional fifty years. The owner of the copyright has the exclusive right to reproduce the work, display the work, and distribute copies of the work. The work is essentially the owner's domain and must be original. Ideas cannot be copyrighted; only the treatment of an idea can be copyrighted.

Scene designing today is in a period of rapid development as we move into the electronic age. Computers, projections, lasers, and complicated electronic sound are being used for startling effects. Videotapes of rock music are excellent examples of the ingenuity in lighting and sound displays currently being used. Examples such as *Cats, Starlight Express,* and *The Phantom of the Opera* are not in the same category as drawing-room drama. It is important for today's designers to familiarize themselves with current technology by investigating trade journals, attending trade fairs, and learning computer techniques.

CHAPTER SIX

THE DESIGN CONCEPT
AND
PROCESS

To create a proper environment for a play, the designer must be able to analyze the writing, the author's intent and purpose, discover suggestions and descriptions in the writing, understand the director's philosophy, and coordinate all of this with the various other technical departments. We must have a knowledge of mechanical drawing, freehand and mechanical perspective, and painting. The arts are means by which artists transmit some vision—in our case, a vision manifested in the medium of theatre—to an audience. As designers, we use the playwright's eyes and insights as the basis for our vision. Ultimately, however, our design must have something of its own to say to the audience. If our hopes are realized, our understanding of the play, coupled with our creativity, will give us something important to say. Beyond that, our "message" depends on our ability to put our thoughts into a form

that adequately reflects them. As designers, we must first be able to make visual images from our creative insights. Simply, we must be able to draw and to paint, because our medium begins with the pencil sketch and the color rendering. The pencil sketch, the color rendering, and the model are what the designer "sells" to the director or producer. They must represent our talent and ingenuity and be executed to the best of our ability. All working drawings must be neat, clear, concise, and, above all, complete. In the professional theatre, the designer will be held at fault if a costly mistake appears in the construction because of inadequate drawings.

The procedures of design can be learned if one is willing to expend some effort and use some discipline. Execution of the design idea is, among other things, a matter of learning techniques and then applying them. In the following section, we will trace design procedures from the preliminaries through the final product.

THUMBNAIL SKETCHES

The thumbnail sketch represents a short-hand method by which we commit our first visual ideas to paper. Thumbnail sketches are rough, rapidly drawn, basic conceptions. They are concerned more with feelings than with details. They also are progressive; that is, they provide us with a means to work quickly through an emerging set of ideas toward a finished product. One technique of developing thumbnail sketches is to divide a page of sketchbook paper into a series of small rectangles whose proportions represent, roughly, the proscenium opening or the frame of visual reference for the audience if production format entails some other form or environment (Fig. 6.1). After dividing up the page, begin in the upper left rectangle with some simple concepts of line and form. Move to the next box and refine these. Add more detail or redo the concepts. You may wish to develop alternative or parallel ideas so that you can compare them side by side. You will discover that your original sheet of paper will be filled quickly, and you will be surprised at how many pages and sketches you can exhaust as your ideas become clearer and more refined. Ultimately you will reach a point at which you feel comfortable that your last sketch fairly well represents the ideas you have about the dynamics, mood, basic forms, unity, and production needs of the design (Fig. 6.2).

Figure 6.1 Format for the thumbnail sketch.

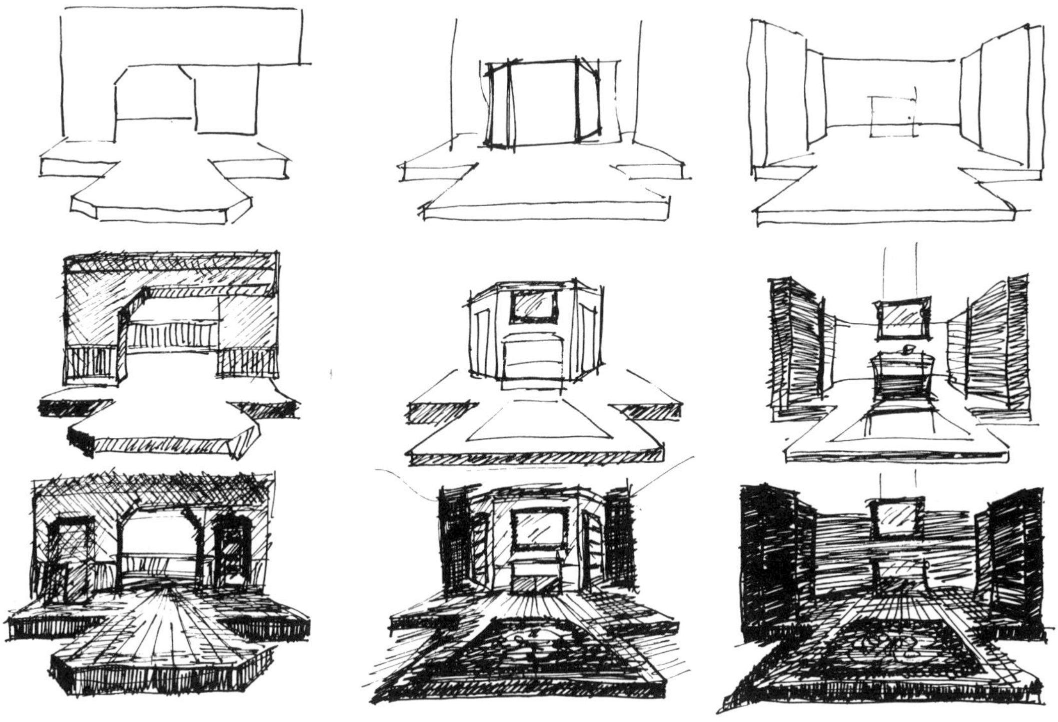

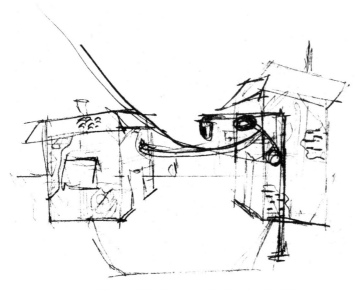

Figure 6.2 Thumbnail sketch, *The Liar,* by Carlo Goldoni, Hilberry Repertory Theatre. Tom Macie, designer.

When you have reached that point, the thumbnail sketches will have served their purpose, and you will be ready to move on to a more finished sketch that will be acceptable to show to the director and other designers.

PRESENTATION SKETCHES

Remember always that what you show in public is a reflection of your professionalism, skill, and overall competence as a designer. Everything you present to the director should be as complete, clear, and professionally done as possible. Sloppy work, even in the early stages of production, casts a bad light on you and may taint your ability to sell your work to those for and with whom you work. You are an artist, but you are also a salesperson of your own ideas and work. As a beginning designer, you must earn the respect of your production col-

leagues. Your presentation sketches are your initial opportunity to make your way in the production, and, ultimately, in the profession. Well-executed sketches can help to sell your ideas to the production team. Even the best design ideas can be crippled by poor sketches.

The presentation sketch (Fig. 6.3) is a black-and-white sketch large enough in scale to show clearly all of the necessary details of the design. It is not necessary to execute the presentation sketch in the 1/2-in. scale customary for the color rendering, but anything smaller than 3/8-in. scale may not carry the necessary clarity of detail for the director and other designers to understand what you intend, and, thereby, to make accurate decisions about its acceptability. Since, at this meeting discussions about color and texture will occur, you may wish to append to the presentation sketches some color chips, fabric swatches, and texture details. Verbal discussions about color are highly imprecise.

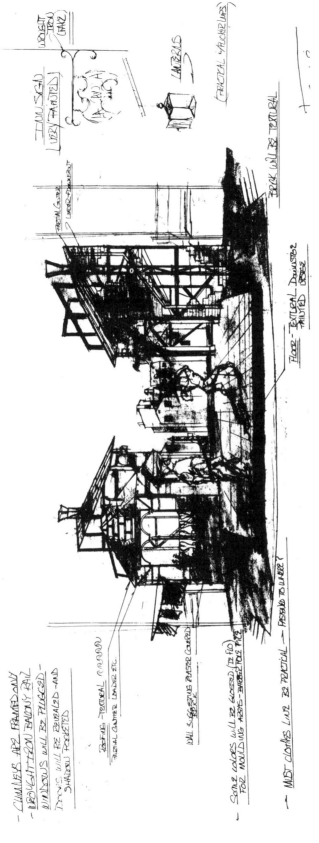

Figure 6.3 Presentation sketch, *The Liar*, by Carlo Goldoni, Hilberry Repertory Theatre. Tom Macie, designer.

127

Your clear impression of "institutional green" may not be anywhere near the *director's* impression of the same term. Discovery of that fact after you have spent a dozen or so hours on your color rendering will be a shattering and frustrating experience.

Your presentation sketches need not take a great deal of time to prepare, but they must be complete enough so that you can come away from the production meeting confident that your color rendering will meet the director's expectations.

COLOR RENDERINGS

The color rendering is the part of the process of scene designing that is, perhaps, the most familiar. However, as we have seen, it is only one step in the entire process of design. It is important in showing what the finished setting will look like under production conditions (Figs. 6.4 and 6.5). The color rendering is usually the device by which the director can assume what the completed set will convey in the way of mood, color, and atmosphere. The sketch is not only used by the director; it is also needed by the costume and lighting designers to give them visual information that will aid them in their work. If the sketch is badly executed or too vague to give definite information, it will not achieve its purpose. The scenic artist must remember that the rendering is our "sales talk," and like a salesperson, we must be able to represent the product fairly and accu-

Figure 6.4   Color rendering, *The Liar,* by Carlo Goldoni, Hilberry Repertory Theatre. Tom Macie, designer.

Figure 6.5 Production photograph, *The Liar,* by Carlo Goldoni. Hilberry Repertory Theatre. Tom Macie, designer.

rately. Also, no amount of striking rendering techniques will excuse the designer's inability to "deliver the goods." The designer must be certain that the design can be executed in the third dimension. Failure to be able to execute a set that looks like the rendering will result in unemployment in the near future.

As we have noted, the designer usually draws a very simple thumbnail sketch followed by a presentation sketch early in the design process. These sketches are useful in consolidating ideas and in preliminary discussions. However, in certain stock companies, in some educational theatres, and in television designing, it is possible to use a simple pencil sketch in lieu of an elaborate color rendering. Such practices are allowable only when time will not permit the exe-

cution of a color rendering. This is understandable when we realize the time it sometimes takes to render an acceptable design. Some designers can execute a workable design in as little as two hours, whereas others will require as long as thirty hours, depending on the particular style of rendering. The length of time devoted to the execution of a drawing has very little bearing on its degree of excellence as a stage design, and so the student of design should learn to work as rapidly as possible, using as many acceptable shortcuts as possible, but keeping in mind that the completed rendering must have a professional quality.

Although the designer can use many different media for the rendering (for example, pastels, pencil, crayon, ink, wash, gouache, or temperas), the most universal medium is watercolor. The reason for this is that transparent watercolors will most closely approximate the appearance of the finished setting under stage lights. Watercolors also are inexpensive, take less time to work (once the technique of using them is mastered), and can most easily express the artist's feelings.

Materials

Watercolor painting, like drafting, requires special tools and equipment. It is important to be acquainted with the many different commercial items available at local art stores so as to select those which will best suit our particular needs. The beginning artist will need the following:

1. Drafting equipment for laying out in pencil the details of the color rendering.

2. Illustration board. This is available in several grades and thicknesses. The heavier the board, the better. Thin board will warp when wet and result in unsatisfactory results. Illustration board comes in 30 in. by 40 in. sheets. The painting surface may be either flat or pebbled. Your own taste and style will dictate which you wish to use. Most art stores will cut the board to any size: 30 in. by 20 in. and 15 in. by 20 in. are preferred.

3. A color slant (Fig. 6.6). This device is used for your palette and is a plastic or ceramic tray containing depressions or sinks for mixing colors and water. Plastic egg crates and metal muffin tins are acceptable substitutes. However, the white surface of the commercial slant makes it easier to ascertain whether your mixture is the color you desire. Inasmuch as watercolor is transparent, testing your colors on a spare piece of board before applying them to your rendering will ensure accuracy.

4. Drawing pencils. For most purposes, 2B or 3H pencils will suffice.

5. Brushes. The selection of brushes is extremely important. Red sable is the best because of its resilience and long life. However, camel's hair is a good substitute. Most beginners make the mistake of selecting brushes that are too small for their work. Although a small brush may be useful for detail work, large brushes are superior for all other work, especially large areas of wash. The following list indicates brush sizes and potential uses (Fig. 6.7).

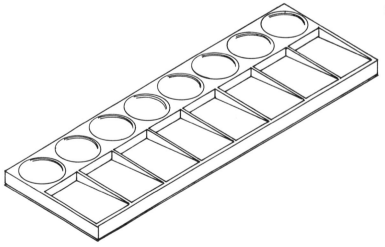

Figure 6.6 Watercolor slant.

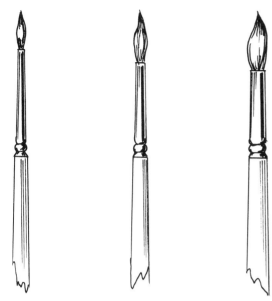

Figure 6.7 Watercolor brushes.

a. No. 2, 3, 4. To be used for intricate detail or highlights.

b. No. 5, 6, 7. To be used for small detail such as furniture. May also be used for some lay-in work.

c. No. 8, 9, 10. To be used for lay-in washes of moderate sized areas.

d. No. 11, 12. To be used for large areas of lay-in wash.

e. 1/2-in. flat, straight-edge brush. Used for medium-size lay-in areas.

f. 3/4-in. flat, straight-edge brush. Used for medium-size lay-in areas.

g. 1 1/4-in. flat, straight-edge brush. For large-area lay-in washes such as skies and backgrounds.

6. Sponge. Small fibered sponge for blotting up superfluous moisture from the sketch.

7. Eraser. An art gum eraser for removing unnecessary pencil lines and for removing smudges on the illustration board.

8. Tube or pan water colors. Although tube colors are generally preferred, many students use inexpensive pan colors with excellent results. The better pan sets will have at least twelve to sixteen colors: yellow, yellow-orange, orange, red-orange, red, fuchsia, purple, Prussian blue, blue, blue-green, green, yellow-green, brown, black, and white. Tube colors, on the other hand, are available in a wide range of colors, but the following colors will be adequate for the beginning designer: gamboge yellow, yellow ochre, burnt sienna, sepia, light red, alizarin crimson, cerulean blue, new blue or phthalo blue, emerald green, charcoal gray, lamp-black, hooker's green, and Chinese white.

Techniques

There are several methods of painting with watercolor. The beginner needs to experiment with the materials to realize his or her potential. However, the following basic steps and suggestions can be helpful to the beginner learning to render the setting.

Step 1. Draw the setting in pencil on a sheet of tracing paper in the desired scale or size. This can be done using freehand or mechanical perspective. Do not use any shading on the drawing. The pencil sketch can be as complete as the artist wishes, even including furniture and props. When the pencil sketch is finished, it should be attached to the top edge of the illustration board; but first the sketch must be centered on the board. Trace the pencil sketch by using a light graphite paper or by penciling the back of the tracing paper. Draw in only the lines defining the large areas. Leave all details until later. When the large areas have been traced, turn back the tracing paper, check the drawing on the illustration board, and fill in any uncompleted lines.

Step 2. Before beginning the brush work, mask the edges of the sketch with masking tape that is at least 1/2-in. wide. Some artists prefer to wet the entire picture with clear water, while others will moisten only the specific area immediately before filling in with color. Regardless of the method used, be sure to cover the area evenly with water, picking up any surplus moisture with a clean, dry brush or sponge. Be careful not to get fingerprints and eraser marks on the drawing before using the water; water will not cover these grease marks. The board should be *damp* when the color is applied—not wet or dry. Select the color of the side and back walls of the set first, filling them in with swift, broad strokes, and working from left to right (if you are right-handed). Do not make the wall color too dark, or it will be difficult to cover with detail. Pick up any excess paint with a dry brush or with a sponge. Next, fill in the ceiling and the floor areas, keeping in mind the source of light and its effect on these areas. Flat surfaces are always lighter in color the closer they are to the light source, and darker when farther away. In general, stage lighting will leave the tops of wall areas darker than the bases. So you will need to learn how to control your pigments to create a graduated effect from light to dark. It is necessary to complete one full surface before pausing. If the paint is allowed to dry before the area is covered, an ugly water line will result. Also, be sure that an area is nearly dry before filling in its neighbor. If this is not done, the colors will run together leaving unsightly blotches of light and dark color. Remember that watercolor is transparent. You must be careful, even when the pigment is dry, not to spill over from one area to another. If you do, the result will be a third color where the two areas have overlapped. When all large areas have been filled in, allow the paint to dry fully.

Step 3. Place the tracing paper sketch over the watercolor rendering, and trace in the significant details such as doors, windows, woodwork, and large pieces of furniture. Turn back the tracing paper and paint these items. For visibility and contrast, these items should be darker in value than the background areas. It is possible to cover one color with another only if the second color is to some extent darker than the first. Good judgment and trial and error, in addition to your design sense, need to be your guides. Expect to make some mistakes on your first few renderings. In painting the larger detail objects, remember the light sources. Highlight and shadow (chiaroscuro) give the effect of depth to your rendering. Remember also that furniture pieces cast shadows on the floor and walls. Do not forget to put shadows where necessary. In painting details, occasionally you will need to use Chinese white mixed with a color to cover the underpainting completely. This makes the paint opaque and should not be used too frequently. Allow all detail time to dry.

Step 4. Trace in, or lay in freehand, any small details such as highlights or lowlights on objects, patterns, decor, small properties, and so on. Generally these will be the darkest or at least the most opaque objects of all. When you have finished these, allow the painting to dry thoroughly, and then remove the masking tape, carefully, from around the edge of the painting. Clean up the illustration board with an eraser. The sketch is now completed. A 1/8 in. to 3/16 in.-wide black border can help to frame the design if time or expense does not permit matting.

Learning to use watercolors requires trial and error, experience, great patience, and application. However, we must remember that anyone who is determined can learn to draw and paint. You may never be able to produce work of great artistic finish (neither could several of history's most notable designers), but diligence will result in renderings of sufficient quality to convey your ideas to another person, which is the entire purpose of the scene design rendering. It is, after all, the quality of the *design,* and not slick rendering technique, that is important. Slick effects such as those which can be achieved with devices such as an airbrush can make a rendering look terrific. They do not, however, change the inherent quality of the design behind the rendering that will appear on stage quite naked and apart from the artist's rendering techniques.

While working with watercolors, keep a few simple additional rules in mind.

1. Keep the brush well filled with color.
2. Keep your paints clean.
3. Use large amounts of water, with frequent changes.
4. Brushes should be kept clean and not be allowed to soak in the water jar.
5. Do not use greasy or kneaded erasers on watercolor board or paper.
6. Store brushes to protect the points.
7. Keep tube colors capped at all times.
8. If the tube cap sticks, loosen it by heating with a match. Do not try to force it open.
9. Protect the finished watercolor by covering it with cellophane, tracing paper, or a fixative.
10. Mix plenty of color. It may be difficult to match and will leave a mark if you run out before an area is completed.

MODELS

Some directors prefer models to sketches, believing that they can visualize the finished setting more easily from a scaled, three-dimensional replica. Unfortunately, there is always the danger that the tiny model will give an appearance of quaintness or cuteness which will be impossible to achieve in the real setting. Accurately detailed models will involve three or four times the amount of time to execute compared to a watercolor rendering. Therefore, if time is essential, do not waste it by constructing a model.

However, models are very useful for settings requiring many platforms and levels (Fig. 6.8), because a model will give both the designer and the director a definite picture of the areas. Models also are invaluable for exhibition and display purposes; most people are enchanted with scale miniatures. Historical models can be most helpful in teaching certain dramatic arts courses, and many schools have fascinating collections. Sometimes the design student will believe that he or she can express the design better in a model than in a two-dimensional rendering. Inasmuch as either format is generally acceptable to a producer or director, this medium should be experimented with. The young designer needs to remember, however, that his or her portfolio, which must be shipped or carried to prospective employers, is much more manageable if it consists of renderings rather than models. Your prospective employer will want to see your actual work, not a photograph of it.

Models can be made in almost any scale, but 1/2 in. = 1 ft. is preferred. Whichever scale is chosen, be sure that the scale dimensions are within reason. A historical model of Covent Garden, built to a 1 in. = 1 ft. scale would need a crane to lift it. An intricate model of the Teatro Olimpico in the scale of 1/8 in. would prove almost impossible to execute.

Materials

The model builder must have proper materials before attempting any model work. The following items are useful:

Cardboard. Should be Bristol board of medium weight. Shirt board can be used as a substitute.

Figure 6.8   Scenic model. *Edmond,* by David Mamet, University of North Carolina at Wilmington. Tom Macie, designer.

Illustration board is too heavy and does not bend easily.

Drawing board and drafting equipment (triangles, T square, pencils)

Masking tape

Rubber cement

Airplane glue

Razor blades (single edged)

Exacto cutting knife set

Straight pins for holding parts while glue is drying

Scissors

Balsa wood

Watercolors and brushes

Procedure

Select the board to be used for the floor of the model. The floor should be made of Upson board, thin plywood, or very heavy cardboard that will not warp. A temporary model can be mounted on an old drawing board. The floor of the model should approximate the entire area of the theatre's stage floor, including wing space and backstage area. Of course, if the area is enormous, some reduction will be necessary. Trace the outline of the ground plan on the board.

Draw the side walls and the back wall on the Bristol board. Use the front elevation drawings for this task. Add at least three tabs at the bottom of the walls so they can be glued to the floor. Putting tabs on the sides of the walls allows these to be glued together also. Thicknesses should be attached to the inside of wall openings, such as for windows, arches, and doors. Cut out the walls carefully. Attach the thicknesses of doors or windows and so on with glue or masking tape. The walls now can be painted and trimmed. When this is finished, attach the back wall to the side walls with glue or masking tape, and then fasten the assembled walls to the floor, according to the ground plan. Backings then can be painted and glued in place. The floor should be painted carefully and allowed to dry before adding furniture or properties.

Many designers find it easier to use small cubes and rectangles rather than elaborately constructed model furniture.

After the model itself is completed, a piece of cardboard cut to scale in the shape of the proscenium arch should be attached at the front of the model. This can be painted to look like a particular proscenium opening or remain merely a neutral, colored frame for the model of your setting.

Outdoor scenes frequently make use of drops or sky cycloramas that can be constructed of cardboard, painted, and, if necessary, curved to conform to the shape of the theatre's cyclorama. Borders, whether sky or foliage, are cut out of cardboard, mounted on sticks, and placed across the top of the cyclorama parallel to the proscenium arch.

Steps, ramps, and levels are often carved from balsa wood, rather than being made of cardboard. A platform made of balsa is easier to make and join together, and it has the necessary weight to stay glued to the floor. However, balsa wood must be coated with a sealer before it will take paint.

The ingenious model builder will find uses for many little items available in variety stores and toy shops. If it is necessary to build models frequently, you should keep a box for storing these materials so they will be easily available. Parts of old models can be stored and reused from time to time.

Remember that the model is only a point of departure and not the finished set. It is entirely too easy to spend more time on making a scale model than on constructing the actual set, and many a beginning designer has discovered this trap too late.

GROUND PLANS

The ground plan or floor plan shows the dimensions and placement of the setting as seen from above. It is a scale, mechanical drawing (Fig. 6.9). It must be executed carefully to show the position of all walls or units, all backings, dimensional thickness, hangings, ground rows, platforms, steps, ramps, and furniture. The plan must also show the relationship of the set to certain physical aspects of the stage, such as the proscenium opening, the apron, and the back wall. This, of course, cannot be done if the setting is designed with no particular stage in mind or if the production intends to tour.

After framing the paper with a margin (see chapter 7), the designer puts in the centerline halfway between the two side margins. The width of the proscenium opening is measured and drawn in. Some designers like to begin at the tormentor line and work toward the back, filling in the side walls. Others prefer to work from the back to the front, planning the back wall first. Either way is correct; it is a matter of preference only.

SIGHTLINE DRAWINGS

The plan also must take into consideration any problems of sightlines that may be involved. Horizontal sightlines can be checked easily by using a horizontal plan of the theatre and projecting imaginary lines from the seats farthest right or left to the back of the setting (Fig. 6.10). Vertical sightlines are similarly checked by using a vertical section drawing of the theatre and stage (Fig. 6.11).

FRONT ELEVATIONS

The front elevation of a setting is designed to show the actual details of the audience side of the scenic units (Fig. 6.12). It is executed in scale, usually 1/2 in. = 1 ft., and shows the position and design of such units as doors, windows, fireplaces, moldings, or

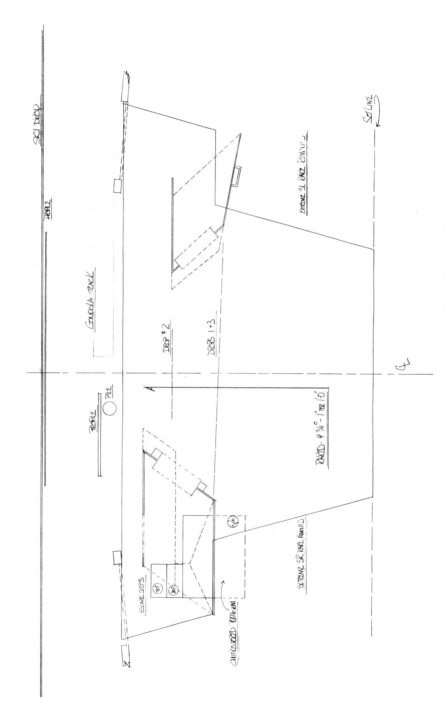

Figure 6.9 Ground plan. *The Liar*, by Carlo Goldoni. Hilberry Repertory Theatre. Tom Macie, designer.

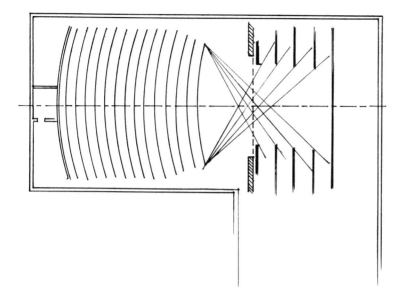

Figure 6.10 Sightline drawing from horizontal plan.

other details, depending on whether the setting is a realistic interior or something else.

As in executing the ground plan, we frame the paper with a margin and place a legend box in the lower right-hand corner (see chapter 7). Usually it is possible to divide the paper in half horizontally if the scenic units are less than fourteen feet high. Beginning with the stage right side of the stage,

the flats or units are drawn in scale along the top half of the paper, starting at the left. For a simple box set, this would include the tormentor, the stage right wall, then the back wall, and the stage left wall and the stage left tormentor. Next the backings are drawn, as are any additional units. Corners or changes in plane along these walls are indicated by a vertical line. Walls are separated by narrow

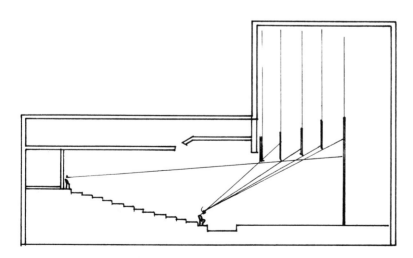

Figure 6.11 Sightline drawing from vertical plan

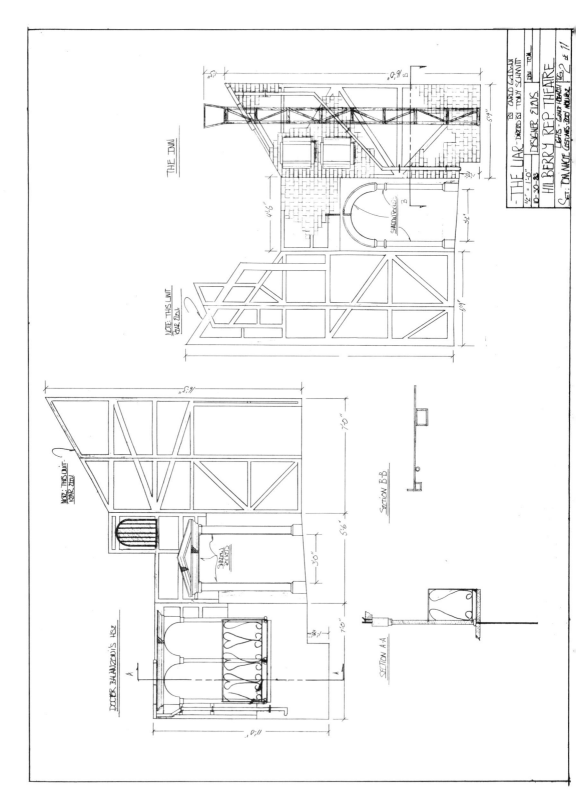

Figure 6.13 Paint elevation at ½" scale. Robert C. Burroughs, scene design, *Girl Crazy.* Patio scene. University of Arizona, Tucson.

spaces. When the top section of the paper is filled, the flats or units are continued along the bottom half, beginning at the left and working to the right. Usually it is necessary to use at least two papers to include all the units. The bottoms of all the units must be lined up as though they are resting on the stage floor. The various walls and units should be labeled. It is wise to keep the front elevation free from all but the most essential measurements, so as to keep the drawing simple and easy to read.

PAINT DETAILS

The paint detail is used specifically for the scene painters or the paint crews. Differing from the watercolor sketch, the paint detail presents the flats or units as they will be painted, without the benefit of stage lighting or the illusion of distance (Fig. 6.13). The paint detail is like the front elevation except that it is colored, and it frequently includes the color formulas for the mixing of paint. The paint detail can be placed on a 30 in. by 20 in. piece of illustration board. The front elevation can be traced onto the board to save time. Some designers prefer to use tempera paints on their paint details because temperas more closely approximate opaque, flat, scene paint; however, watercolors will serve just as well. When the paint detail is finished, the entire board should be covered with cellophane to protect it from being soiled in the paint shop.

The design process is straightforward. It is likewise fundamental. Although, as we have

Figure 6.12 Front elevation drawings. *The Liar,* by Carlo Goldoni. Hilberry Repertory Theatre. Tom Macie, designer.

indicated, circumstances may dictate short-cuts in the design procedure, the young designer is well advised to resist the temptation to omit one component or another. Each part of the process serves an important purpose; an omission of any part leaves one vulnerable to oversights that may well cause problems far more time-consuming than the omitted step.

CHAPTER SEVEN

DRAFTING

Regardless of the style or graphic clarity of a designer's renderings or models, every scene design eventually must be translated into exact symbols and measurements so that the set can be constructed properly and accurately. Drafting, then, becomes the means of communication whereby pictures in the form of drafting conventions translate a visual idea into a specific reality. As any experienced designer can testify, the need to master the conventions and techniques of drafting and to use proper equipment can represent the difference between satisfactory completion of a setting and disaster. In this chapter, we will examine mechanical drawing or drafting to learn about those instruments which can improve our efficiency, accuracy, and clarity, those drawing surfaces which can reduce hand and eye strain, plus the symbols and techniques which will make our drawings readable and understandable.

DRAFTING EQUIPMENT

Drawing Boards

Mechanical drawings require for their preparation a special surface called a drawing board (Fig. 7.1). A drawing board is a large flat surface constructed of a variety of materials. Above all, it must be sturdy, flat, smooth on both the edges and the surface, and large enough to exceed the size of the drafting paper or other medium.

However, with the exception of beginning student projects, normal scenic design will require a more elaborate drawing board, or support for the drawing board, called a *drafting table* (Figure 7.2). This is a drafting board mounted on a stand. Drafting tables range in size, complexity, and price, but to be of most value, the drafting table should have an adjustable top (from 0° to 20°) and should

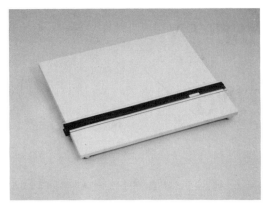

Figure 7.1 Drafting board with parallel blade. Courtesy Teledyne Post.

cover the surface of the drafting board with a *drafting board cover.* Specifically designed vinyl and paper covers that have tinted and grid surfaces can be purchased. If this is not available, the designer needs to cover the drawing board with heavy paper so that the drawing process itself does not score the surface of the board, eventually making smooth work impossible.

T Square

The T square is the basic tool of the draftsperson (Fig. 7.3). Whether it is in the form of a separate tool, as in Figure 7.3, a part of the drafting board assembly, as in Figure 7.1, or part of a drafting machine (Fig. 7.4), the T square or its substitute enables the draftsperson to draw consistent and accurate horizontal lines. The blade of the T square should reach completely across the drafting board. T squares are constructed of wood,

have a minimum surface size of 24 in. by 30 in. The table must be sufficiently well constructed that it is absolutely free of wiggle or vibration when one is drawing or erasing.

Most experienced draftspersons prefer to

Figure 7.2   Drafting table. Courtesy Teledyne Post.

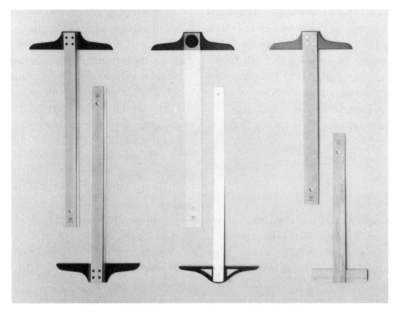

Figure 7.3 T squares. Courtesy Teledyne Post.

plastic, stainless steel, and composites. Some thought needs to be given to the purchase of the T square by those for whom cost is a consideration. The most expensive T squares are probably not essential. However, a cheap, wooden T square whose blade edge is susceptible to denting and whose head is not securely attached to the blade with glue and screws will soon lose its square and its smooth edge and become useless. A T square

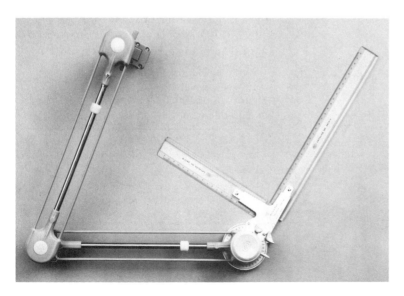

Figure 7.4 Arm drafter or band and pulley drafter. Courtesy Teledyne Post.

with clear plastic edges for the blade allows the draftsperson to see his or her work, keeps the blade off the drawing surface, thereby preventing smudges from ink from creeping under the blade, and resists most traumas that could nick a wooden blade. The beginning designer must constantly remember that the quality of work in theatre design often depends upon the quality of the equipment used.

Triangles

Basic to any set of drafting equipment are a 30°–60° (*minimum* size: 10 in.) triangle and a 45° triangle (*minimum* size: 8 in.) (Fig. 7.5). These two triangles can be used for a variety of different work. Vertical lines are drawn by using these triangles in conjunction with the T square. Usage of the triangles requires proper technique for maximum ease, accuracy, and efficiency. The triangle should be faced so that the light source comes from the side on which the line is to be drawn. This eliminates the confusing shadow that occurs when the light source is behind the working edge. The recommended size of the triangles is important because smaller triangles will require moving the T square, an inefficiency and potential for inaccuracy, when long vertical lines must be drawn. Vertical lines should be drawn from the bottom to the top of the triangle. The two triangles can be combined as in Figure 7.6 to produce 75° and 15° angles.

A useful addition to the basic set of drafting instruments is the adjustable triangle (Fig. 7.7). Without the adjustable triangle, the draftsperson must use a protractor to draw all other angles in addition to those possible with the fixed triangles.

Dividers

Transferring measurements and dividing lines can be done efficiently by using dividers (Fig. 7.8). Dividers are particularly helpful in transferring measurements from

Figure 7.5 10″ 30–60-degree triangle; 8″ 45-degree triangle. Courtesy Teledyne Post.

Figure 7.6 Combining triangles to produce 75 and 15-degree angles.

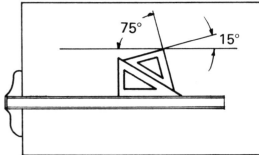

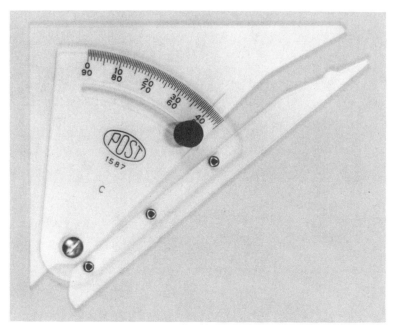

Figure 7.7 Adjustable triangle. Courtesy Teledyne Post.

models to drawings and vice versa. They also can be used to make trial measurements without marking the drawing. The friction joint of the divider allows fingertip adjustment, and the pinpoints on the legs allow for absolutely precise measuring.

Figure 7.8 Dividers. Courtesy Koh-I-Noor Rapidograph, Inc.

Bow Compass

The bow compass (Fig. 7.9) looks like the divider, but it has a pencil point on one leg which allows the draftsperson to draw circles and arcs. The standard bow compass can draw circles up to one foot in diameter. Extremely small circles can be drawn with a special instrument called a drop bow compass (Fig. 7.10). Both the bow compass and the drop bow compass have threaded crosspieces between the legs to allow precise adjustment. Large circles and arcs require either a beam compass (Fig. 7.11) or a large bow compass with an extension bar (Fig. 7.12). Compasses may be equipped for pencil or ink drawings.

French Curves

Irregular or asymmetrical curves occur often in scenic design drafting, and the temptation to draw them freehand often

Figure 7.9   Bow compass. Courtesy Koh-I-Noor Rapidograph, Inc.

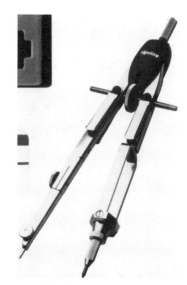

Figure 7.11   Quick set compass. Courtesy Koh-I-Noor Rapidograph, Inc.

overtakes the designer. However, a freehand curve probably will not be accurate and definitely will ruin the professional look of your plate. To accomplish irregular curves, use a French, railroad, or ship curve (Fig. 7.13). Using the French or other curves is different from other drafting aids in that probably

you will need to adjust the device one or more times to complete the desired curve. The best procedure involves, first, laying out the rough shape of the curve with a series of moderately spaced dots. Then, to effect the drawing, connect the dots using whatever part of the curve duplicates the desired arc of that particular portion of the curve.

Figure 7.10   Drop bow compass. Courtesy Koh-I-Noor Rapidograph, Inc.

Figure 7.12   Large bow compass with extension bar. Courtesy Koh-I-Noor Rapidograph, Inc.

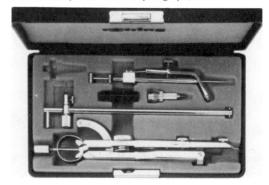

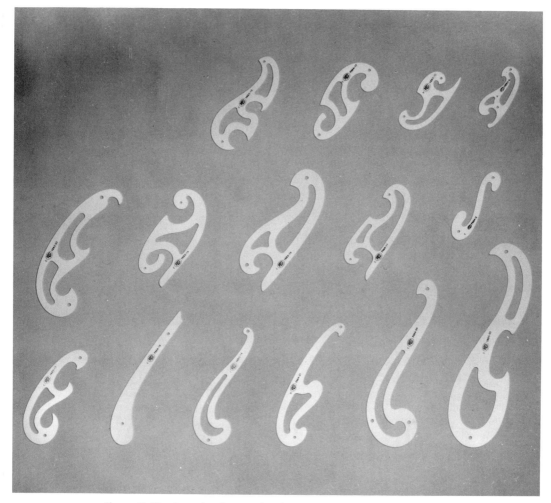

Figure 7.13 French, ship, and railroad curves. Courtesy Koh-I-Noor Rapidograph, Inc.

Templates

Other curves, arcs, circles, geometric shapes, and symbols can be drawn easily and accurately by using a template. Hundreds of shapes, from lighting instruments to directional signs, are available on templates, and a perusal of various drafting and theatrical supply catalogues will give you every choice you can afford (Fig. 7.14). Lettering and furniture templates benefit the stage designer significantly.

Scale Rules

The scale rule converts measurements so that drawings can represent feet and inches accurately and conveniently in a size that will fit the drawing paper. Scales are avail-

Architectural

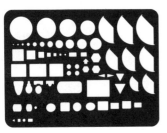

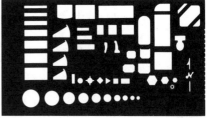

1151/House Plan Fixtures
1151I/House Plan Fixtures - Inking Template
Template contains basic symbols for professional use.
Scale: ¼":1'. Size: 5" x 9" x .030".

1150/House Plan & Plumbing
1150I/House Plan & Plumbing - Inking Template
Template contains symbols used in every house plan.
Scale: ¼":1'. Size: 5" x 7" x .030".

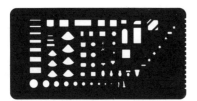

1152/House Plan Fixtures
1152I/House Plan Fixtures - Inking Template
Template contains an improved selection of symbols for
the professional. Same as 1151 except scale is ⅛":1'.
Size: 4" x 8" x .030".

1153I/House Plan Fixtures - Inking Template
Template contains an improved selection of symbols for
the professional. Scale: ¼":1'.
Size: 8" x 10" x .030".

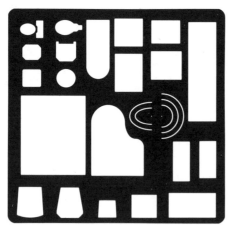

1157I/Interior Design & Home Modeling - Inking Template
A useful template for designing interiors of new homes
or remodeling the interiors of existing homes. A one-half
inch scale permits easy visualization of desired results.
Scale: ½":1'. Size: 9½" x 10" x .030".

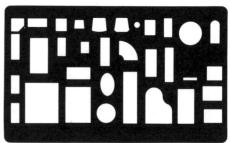

1155/Home Furnishings
1155I/Home Furnishings - Inking Template
A handy working tool for interior designers and room
planners. Enables one to plan and rearrange a room
without having to touch the furniture. Scale: ¼":1'.
Size: 6" x 10" x .030".

Figure 7.14 Templates. Courtesy Chartpak-Pickett.

able in shapes and patterns designed to meet the needs of architects and engineers. For the scenic designer, the triangular architect's rule (Fig. 7.15) provides the most convenient scales. On this rule, ten different scales are indicated: 1 ft. = 3/32 in.; 1 ft. = 1/8 in.; 1 ft. = 3/16 in.; 1 ft. = 1/4 in.; 1 ft. = 3/8 in.; 1 ft. = 1/2 in.; 1 ft. = 3/4 in.; 1 ft. = 1 in.; 1 ft. = 1 1/2 in.; 1 ft. = 3 in. Learning to read the inch equivalents on each scale takes some effort and attention. The drawing in Figure 7.16 can assist us. Observe that the scale labeled 1 1/2 on one end and 3 on the other represents the conversion of the regular linear foot to scales in which 1 1/2 in. = 1 ft. (reading right to left on the top) and 3 in. = 1 ft. (reading right to left on the top). Above the scale, we have drawn the way the indicators are read for the 3 in. scale. When the distance between two points is to be measured, the scale is placed so that the point on the left corresponds to a foot indicator. The point on the right then will correspond to some portion of the part of the scale representing inches. In Figure 7.16, the distance represented by points at the left and right dimension lines would be 2 ft. 6 in. Observe also that as the scales diminish in size, so does the possibility for representing fractions of inches. The smallest indicator on the 3-in. scale is 1/8 in.; on the 3/8-in. scale, it is 1 in. Test yourself by determining whether you can read the dimension 2 ft. 7 in. on each of the four scales shown in Figure 7.16.

Drafting Pencils

Most drafting for the theatre is not intended for permanent display and usually

Figure 7.15 Architect's rule. Courtesy Koh-I-Noor Rapidograph, Inc.

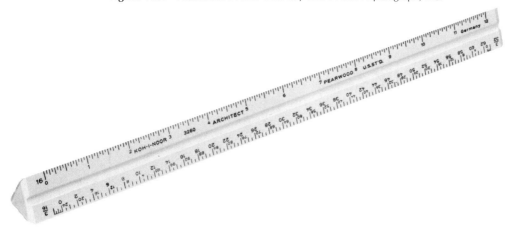

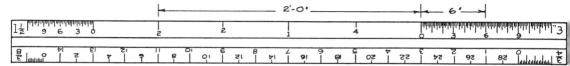

Figure 7.16 Architect's rule. Courtesy Koh-I-Noor Rapidograph, Inc.

must be done as rapidly as possible. As a result, pencils remain the drawing instrument most popular and practical for scenic designers. However, only high-quality, graphite drawing pencils are suitable for this type of work. Leads range in hardness from 9H, the hardest, downward: 8H, 7H, 6H, 5H, 4H, 3H, 2H, H. Medium leads are labeled F, and softer leads, B: HB, B, 2B, 3B, 4B, and 5B, the softest. Soft leads should be used only for sketching or rendering, and not for drafting. Softer leads rub off onto triangles and T squares and give the drawing a smudged and dirty appearance that is wholly unacceptable. On the other hand, the hardest leads tend to mark too lightly to trace and duplicate, and also can tear the drawing when lighter-weight vellums are being used. Therefore, the theatre technician should stick to 2H, 3H, and 4H for best overall results.

Pencils themselves come in three varieties: wooden, mechanical, and automatic (Fig. 7.17). Wooden drafting pencils, similar in appearance to an everyday pencil, but without an eraser, have the advantage of being inexpensive. However, they must be sharpened continuously, and thereby become shorter and less balanced in the hand. *Mechanical pencils* are metal sheaths that hold individual leads. As the leads are sharpened, more lead is fed out of the holder, and then replaced when it is used up. The holder, then, stays constant and balanced. Leads can be retracted into the holder for protection when not in use. *Automatic pencils* offer the advantage of holding lead of a specific size which creates a line of that same specific

width. Mechanical pencils do not need to be sharpened, which constitutes a considerable advantage. However, a separate pencil is required for each line weight. As we will see, more than one line weight is required for theatre drafting, and so more than one automatic pencil will need to be purchased. A *mechanical lead pointer* (Fig. 7.18) is a helpful instrument for pointing leads in mechanical pencils. Sandpaper pointing devices also are available at lesser cost, but these are not as convenient or as precise.

Drafting Pens

At one time or another, every designer will need a drawing pen (Fig. 7.19). These seldom are used in day-to-day drafting, but occasionally permanence is desired, and ink must be used. We have found drafting pens to be extremely useful in making color renderings when black bordering lines or background around small details are required. So, purchase of a drafting pen becomes worthwhile, if not necessary. It may be tempting to use some of the finer, fiber-tipped pens available on the general market. Avoid such temptation. In the first place, even the best fiber tip will not work well with your drafting triangles and straightedges. You will also discover that the ink used in these pens is not permanent. In a year or less, especially on renderings, the ink will bleach out, leaving open spaces of light beige that formerly were black. These inks also are not waterproof and can be smudged even by the perspiration on your fingers. Probably the best choice, for convenience alone, is the techni-

Figure 7.17 Drafting pencils. Courtesy Koh-I-Noor Rapidograph, Inc.

cal pen, which is available in up to seventeen different point sizes, each of which carries its own ink cartridge and fits into a single housing. Care must be taken to keep these tips, especially the fine tips, clean. A clogged pen wastes valuable time and increases your frustration level exponentially.

DRAFTING ACCESSORIES

Drafting Tape

You must not confuse drafting tape with masking tape, which looks similar. Drafting tape is much less adhesive than masking tape; it is designed to hold your drawing medium to the board and to be removed without roughening or tearing the medium. Masking tape is designed to adhere securely to any surface, and its use in drafting will prove unacceptable. Drafting tape is applied across the corners of your medium, and if you follow a few suggestions, it will give you the results you wish. First, hold the drafting medium securely with one hand while applying a piece of tape to one corner with the other hand. Be sure that the medium is aligned carefully with the blade of the T square, and be careful to keep the tape as far up on the corner as possible. Nothing is quite so frustrating as the discovery that your tape covers the area where your margin lines are to be drawn. So, the tape must not intrude more than 1/2 in. into the drawing.

Figure 7.18 Lead pointer. Courtesy Koh-I-Noor Rapidograph, Inc.

Be sure to smooth the medium carefully before taping down the subsequent corners. You will discover that not all drafting media are cut perfectly square, and you must take note of any discrepancies before taping, so that your medium is as parallel as possible to your margin lines, whose purpose is to square your paper.

Erasers

For best results, you will need several erasers, each of which has a specific purpose. Erasers are designed to remove lead lines and ink lines and to do general cleaning. The single criterion for any eraser is the capability to remove ink or pencil without damaging the drawing surface or leaving

shadows or smudges. One should purchase this accessory as selectively as any specialized piece of equipment. The local art store or professional drafting supply store, not the local dime store, should be your source. Also available are electric and cordless erasing machines (Fig. 7.20).

Erasing Shield

An erasing shield is a thin metal template-like device (Fig. 7.21) designed to mask the drawing while exposing only those areas to be erased. This is a very helpful tool, as is a *dusting brush* to whisk away eraser residue. *Eraser dust,* a commercially manufactured fine, eraser residue, often is used by draftspersons to keep the drawing free from the inevitable smudges caused when triangles and T squares pick up minute amounts of lead residue and spread it onto other parts of the surface. Eraser dust is sprinkled on the surface and helps keep it clean, picking up lead residue as the T square and triangles pass over.

DRAWING MEDIA

Several kinds of drawing media are used by draftspersons. Not all are paper, and so the term *medium* is used. The following media come in various sizes; 18 in. by 24 in. is standard for most theatre drafting.

Drawing Paper

Drawing paper is a heavyweight paper colored white, buff, or green. This medium is seldom used by professional draftspersons, although it was a staple for many years.

Figure 7.19 Technical pen. Courtesy Koh-I-Noor Rapidograph, Inc.

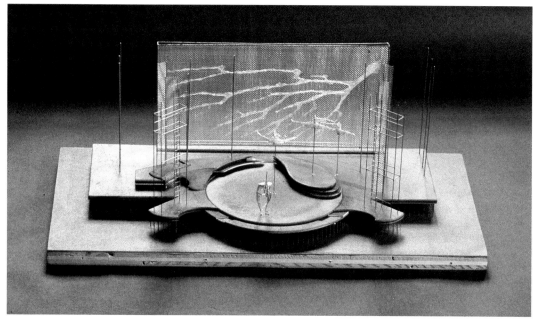

Figure 5.1 Peter Wexler, scene design for *The Happy Time.* Broadway Theatre, New York City.

Figure 11.35 Ming Cho Lee, scene design for *Roberto Devereaux,* New York State Opera. Courtesy of University of Arizona Theatre Collection, Tucson.

Figure 11.36 Robert C. Burroughs, scene design for *Peer Gynt.*
University of Arizona, Tucson.

Figure 11.42 Douglas W. Schmidt, scene design for *Over Here!*
Shubert Theatre, New York City. Courtesy of University of Arizona Theatre
Collection, Tucson.

Figure 11.70 John Wright Stevens, scene design for *La Bohème,* act 2. Cincinnati Opera Company, Cincinnati, Ohio. Photograph by John Wright Stevens.

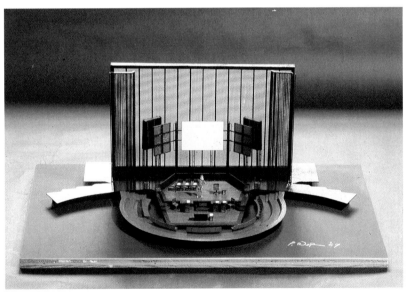

Figure 11.74 Peter Wexler, *The Matter of J. Robert Oppenheimer.* Repertory Theatre of Lincoln Center, New York City.

Figure 11.75 Hal Tiné, scene design for *Jerry's Girls.* National Tour, U.S.A.

Figure 11.77 Tom Benson, scene design for *Cabaret,* Mainstage, University of Arizona, Tucson.

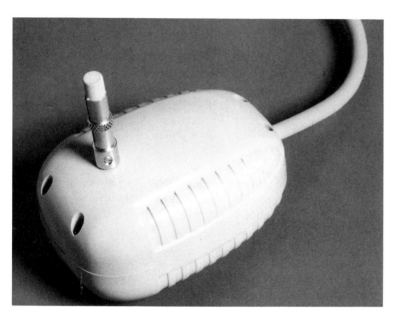

Figure 7.20   Electric erasing machine. Courtesy Teledyne Post.

Tracing Paper

Tracing paper is a translucent medium that is inexpensive and can be used for overlays or for tracing. Because of its physical weakness, it is not a medium for making permanent drawings, which must stand up to frequent handling.

Figure 7.21   Erasing shield. Courtesy Teledyne Post.

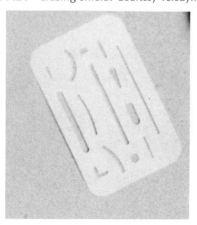

Vellum

Vellum is a specially treated 100 percent rag paper. It is designed to accept ink or pencil on one or both sides and is the staple in contemporary drafting.

Drafting Film

Drafting film is a polyester sheeting of various thicknesses manufactured so that one or both sides will accept special leads or inks. This material is strong, stable, and transparent. It is, however, expensive, and despite its widespread use in industry, it may be impractical for use in many theatre programs.

All media come in a variety of weights and costs. You will need to consider, in addition to your budget, whether the particular variety of the medium you choose to use is strong enough to draw upon and sustain the kind of handling you intend, stable enough to withstand temperature and humidity over time without warping, capable of being erased without damage, and capable of accepting either ink or pencil. Some media are one-sided—that is, designed to be used only on one side; others are two-sided. You need to know which kind to buy and which kind you are buying.

ADDITIONAL MATERIALS

If you have the budget and the storage space, you will find a myriad of special tools, accessories, materials, cleaners, and so on available at every professional drafting supply store. If you live in a small community that does not have a store of this type, you may be able to find what you need in the many mail-order catalogues that are available.

REPRODUCTION

In even the smallest of production programs, it is essential to have copies available for various members of the production staff. Only the most foolhardy designer would allow his or her original drawing plates to go into the shop or paint room, or to be given to a director or stage manager. Our advice to the working designer, especially in the educational theatre, is to purchase a blueprint maker (Fig. 7.22). Otherwise, you will need to spend valuable extra time running to the university print shop (if one is available), or to a commercial reproduction service, which may be miles away. Your time and effort, and cost itself, will pay for your investment in short order. Blueprint makers come in two types, ammonia and non-ammonia. Personal preference more than anything else will dictate which to buy. Obviously, the need to deal with a strong chemical, ammonia, is seen as a significant liability, by some, for that type of machine.

DRAFTING TECHNIQUES

Any skilled task such as drafting rests not only on the choice of good equipment and knowledge of the terminology and conventions of the craft, but also on good work habits and disciplined technique. The following paragraphs contain our advice to

Figure 7.22   Blueprint maker. Courtesy Teledyne Post.

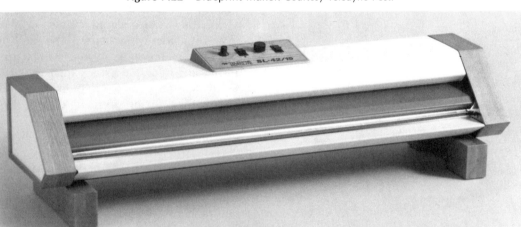

help you develop the procedures and habits that will allow you to use your knowledge of drafting practices and your tools to best advantage.

The Work Environment

Before you begin, make sure the immediate area in which you will be working is orderly and clean. Your equipment should be located so that you can reach everything you need conveniently. All extraneous materials should be removed, and this includes food, drinks, cigarettes, and any other nondrafting objects of personal habit which you may normally want at hand when you are doing a time-consuming task. Coffee stains, cigarette burns, bread crumbs, and so on are unacceptable additions to your drawings. You must think of yourself as a professional, and professionals do not produce sloppy work.

As you prepare your equipment, laying it out for convenient usage, take the time to clean everything. In the interval since its last use or cleaning, your equipment will have accumulated graphite dust and general house dust, each of which can cause smudges on the drafting surface. It is essential that your work environment have enough surface area within reach of the drawing board so that you can keep all materials off the drafting surface, away from the path of your T square. If you are right-handed, you probably will find it most convenient to keep your equipment to the right of your board and to operate your T square against the left edge of the drawing board. If you are left-handed, the opposite conditions should prevail.

Your Equipment and Layout

Earlier we noted the use and placement of drafting tape to secure your medium to the drafting board. Do not make the mistake of using masking tape or transparent tape to secure your medium, and never use thumbtacks. Place your medium approximately three inches from whichever edge of the board will accommodate the head of your T square. Position the medium far enough above the bottom of your board so that you are able to draw comfortably across the bottom of the plate with the top edge of your T square. With your plate securely and properly in place, you should be able to move the T square freely from top to bottom so that with a single stroke you can draw a horizontal line completely across any part of your drawing. The *top* edge of your T square is your drawing guide for horizontal lines; it also will support your triangles, which you will use for drawing all vertical and angled lines. *Never use your scale rule as a drawing guide.* If you are using a detachable T square, you must learn immediately how to go about your tasks of drawing while using one hand to hold the head of the T square firmly against the edge of the drawing board.

Pencil and compass leads must be kept well sharpened. If your leads become rounded, you will not be able to draw consistent lines of the proper width. As we will note momentarily, drafting conventions require specific widths for various kinds of lines. You will quickly learn the proper pressure needed to execute the proper line width; however, you will never master this technique if your pencil point is allowed to deteriorate. You also will discover through experience that, without proper technique and a properly pointed pencil, you cannot draw a line that has a consistent width along its full length. Inconsistently drawn line widths are easy to do, but they are never acceptable. Whether you use sandpaper or a pencil-pointing device, you must learn how to create a perfectly symmetrical point on your lead. A properly pointed lead will be approximately 3/8 in. long and will taper evenly to a conical point. After pointing your lead, wipe it free of all residue before continuing to draw. The lead of your compass is sharpened on a sanding block to a chiseled point. The needle point and lead point should be approximately equal in length (Fig. 7.23).

Using the Pencil

Although the drawing pencil is held in the same manner as an ordinary pencil, it is not used in the same way. It will take some practice for you to become proficient in making your pencil do what you want it to do. In the beginning, you may expect some frustration in trying to keep your pencil evenly pointed, trying to manipulate the pencil, trying to avoid breaking the point of your lead, and making your lines dark enough to read and copy easily and consistent in width and darkness. Rule Number One is *Keep your pencil perpendicular to the edge of your guide at all times* (Fig. 7.24). Some separation must be kept between the lead and the bottom of your guide, or graphite will get under the guide and smudge the drawing. If the pencil is allowed to tilt back and forth, your line will not be straight. Rule Number Two is *Tilt the pencil at approximately 60° in the direction in which it will move* (Fig.

Figure 7.23 Pointing the compass.

7.25). Always pull the pencil; never push it. Pushing the pencil is the surest way to rip your paper and break the lead. Twirl the pencil slowly as you pull it, moving away from the head of the T square for horizontals, from bottom to top for verticals and right-handed diagonals, and from top to bottom for left-handed diagonals. Your lines must be clean, crisp, and consistent in width, and must be dark enough to read and copy but must not dent the paper. The same principles apply to using your compass: Pull, do not push. Keep the tapered edge of the lead toward the outside, as in Figure 7.23, and mark the center of the circle to be drawn with a "+" sign so that the center of the arc can be placed precisely. Lines drawn with the compass also must be crisp, clean, and consistent, and they must be of the same weight or darkness and width as are the other lines.

MECHANICAL DRAFTING CONVENTIONS

Every discipline, whether theatre, painting, biology, or psychology, has its technical vocabulary, which must be learned in order to communicate effectively in and to understand the concepts and messages of that discipline. Mechanical drafting, likewise, has its vocabulary, and this section will introduce it to you in two parts. The first is a brief set of definitions and explanations that relate to and are illustrated by the second, which comprises the United States Institute for Theatre Technology Graphic Standards Board Recommendations for Standard Graphic Language in Scenic Design and Technical Production.

Definitions: Line Types

1. **Visible Outline or Object Line.** A thick, solid line that is drafted to the precise

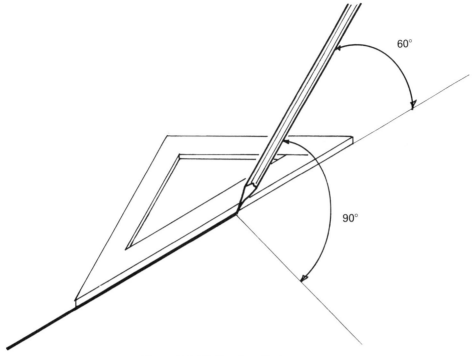

Figure 7.24/7.25   Pencil placement.

shape of an object, showing all edges and planes visible in the view drawn.

2. **Hidden Outline or Hidden Construction.** A thick, dashed line, with each dash 1/4 in. long and separated by 1/8-in. spaces. This line is drawn to the precise shape of an edge or plane that is not visible in the view from which the drawing is made, but whose presence is important to understand the drawing. A typical application of this line would be to show the structure of a platform frame that was hidden underneath its top.

3. **Section Line.** A thin, solid line outlining the actual shape of a surface that has been cut through to expose the interior structure.

4. **Section Line or Section Interior.** A series of thin, solid lines drawn between section outlines at an angle less than 90° to the edge of the paper. These lines indicate the presence of mass that has been cut through in the sectional view. A variety of angles and patterns may be used to distinguish different materials shown in the view.

5. **Informational Lines.** A thin line composed of long dashes separated by short spaces; the usual rhythm of this line is 1/2-in. line, 1/8-in. space. This line has a variety of applications, each requiring a label.

   a. *Plaster line.* Drawn at the upstage side of the proscenium from the stage right to the stage left edge of the opening. The line is labeled "Plaster Line."

b. *Set line.* Drawn at the extreme downstage edge of a proscenium setting or at the perimeter of a thrust, arena, or nontraditional set to indicate the edge of the acting area. The line is labeled "Set Line."

c. *Curtain Line.* Drawn at the extreme upstage edge of the plane that the act curtain travels or falls upon. The line is labeled "Curtain Line."

d. *Ceiling Line.* Drawn at the perimeter of the ceiling over a set. The line is labeled "Ceiling" or "Ceiling Line."

6. **Phantom Line or Alternate Position Line.** A thin, dashed line composed of a long dash and two short dashes; the usual rhythm of this line is 1-in. line, 1/8-in space, 1/4-in. line, 1/8-in. space, 1/4-in. line, 1/8-in. space. This line is used to show that an object or elements of an object repeat between two points, but the repeating portions are not drawn—for instance, the spindles in a railing. The line may also be used to indicate that an object will move or will be used in more than one position. The primary position of the object is drawn as a visible outline, and the alternate position of the object is drawn as a phantom line. The phantom line may also be used as a secondary centerline, and for locating a transverse axis for use as a centerline on an arena stage.

7. **Cutting Plane.** A thick line that may be drawn in one of three styles. The traditional cutting-plane line is composed of a long dash and two short dashes separated by shorter spaces. The usual rhythm for this line is 1/2-in. line, 1/8-in. space, 1/4-in.

line, 1/8-in. space, 1/4-in. line, 1/8-in. space. The line terminates with a 90° angle and a solid arrowhead. The arrowhead is three times as long as its width. The arrow points toward the portion shown in the sectional view. The name of the section (for instance, A-A) is placed at the point of the arrowheads, with the letter oriented toward the bottom of the page. An alternative to this style of line uses thick dashes of equal length; the line terminates as described above. A third style of cutting-plane line uses only a pair of thick 90° angles, arrowheads, and labels placed at either end of the cutting plane with no connecting lines between the arrowheads. This approach identifies the cutting plane without interrupting the content of the drawing. There are some limitations to the use of this style of line, especially for showing offset sections.

8. **Centerline.** A thin line composed of a long and short dash separated by shorter spaces. The usual rhythm for this line is 1-in. line, 1/8-in. space, 1/4-in. line, 1/8-in. space. The line is labeled near its lowest end on the page. The centerline is used to indicate the primary center of an object or a space.

9. **Breaklines.** A thin, serpentine line that indicates a portion of an object is removed from the drawing. Note the difference between long and short breaklines.

10. **Leaderline.** A thin, serpentine or angled line terminating in a half-arrowhead or a dot. The half-arrowhead is six times as long as its width. This line leads the eye of the reader from printed information located outside the drawing to the object or location described. The arrowhead or dot is placed at the object or space de-

scribed—not at the note. A half-arrow-head is normally used; however, a dot is occasionally used to refer to an entire surface. Drafting for television and film requires the use of only straight leader-lines.

11. **Extension and Dimension Lines.** These thin, solid, straight lines are used in combination to identify the size of an object or space.

   a. *Extension lines* are drawn perpendicular to the point or plane at which a measurement is taken. The line never touches the surface measured; 1/16-in. clearance is maintained between the line and the point it identifies. Each extension line is of sufficient length to extend at least 1/8-in. beyond the dimension lines it encloses.

   b. *Dimension lines* are drawn parallel to the surface they measure. They terminate in a whole arrowhead at the extension lines or the surface from which a measurement is taken. The arrowhead is drawn three times as long as its width. Dimensions are placed in a break near the center of the line.

   c. *Dimension lines used in television and film drafting* are solid, unbroken lines that terminate in an arrowhead, a dot, or a diagonal slash. Dimensions are placed above the line in horizontal planes and outside the line in vertical planes.

12. **Borderlines.** A thick, solid line or a pair of thick, solid lines spaced 1/8-in. apart and located 1/2-in. in from the edge of the paper. These lines enclose all the information on the drawing with a squared frame.

Graphic Standards Board Recommendations for Standard Graphic Language in Scenic Design and Technical Production

GENERAL DESCRIPTION. The concept of a standard must evolve from a logical basis. In this case, that basis is rooted in the only inflexible rule of technical drawing: that any graphic communication must be clear, consistent, and efficient. While these recommendations will not include specific guidelines for the spacing of objects on each plate, any graphic presentation should adhere to the general recommendation of clarity: Do not crowd nor unevenly space individual items on a plate. Equally important, all line weight, line types, symbols, conventions, and lettering should be consistent from plate to plate and in a given set of drawings. This does not mean that everyone will be expected to letter in the same manner, nor draw arrowheads in precisely the same way. It means that each draftsperson should be able to establish a style within the guidelines of the recommended standards and conform to that style throughout the drawings for a particular project or production. Finally, the standards and symbols used in any recommended guide should be efficient, both in ease of drawing and in ease of comprehension by the reader.

GROUND PLAN. A great deal of drawing in technical theatre, both in presentation and symbology, is directly related to the drawing of the floor plan or ground plan. The specific definition of the ground plan is as follows: A floor or ground plan is a horizontal offset section with the cutting plane passing at whatever level is required to produce the most descriptive view of the set, normally a height of 4 ft. above the stage floor (see Fig. 6.9).

LINE WEIGHTS. The United States Institute for Theatre Technology recommends a modified American National Standards Institute (ANSI) standard two-thickness line system. The approved line weights are as follows:

Pen	Thin:	.010″–.0125″ width.
		(ANSI standard .016″)
	Thick:	.020″–.025″ width
		(ANSI standard .032″)
Pencil	Thin:	.3 mm
	Thick:	.5 mm

In either pen or pencil, an extra-thick line of .035 in.–.040 in. (.9 mms) may be infrequently used, as necessary, for emphasis (plate border, suitable section cutting plane line, and so on).

CONVENTIONS. There are a number of standard theatrical units, such as chandeliers, shelves, and fireplaces that, because of their varying styles and sizes, should not be represented by standard symbols but need to be easily and repetitively drawn.

The drawing of these items should subscribe to the general guideline offered under the definition of the ground plan. Shelves, fireplaces, and similar items should be drawn using a sectional cutting plane of 4 ft., unless another view would be more descriptive. Chandeliers should be indicated by a circle using a hidden line, as they are not at the 4 ft. cutting plane. The circle should be drawn, in scale, the diameter of the chandelier at its widest point. The graphic should be placed in its proper position on the floor plan. Other suspended objects such as beams, drops not in contact with the stage floor (such as an Act 2 drop on an Act 1 floor plan) would be drawn in their appropriate outline using the hidden line type.

When flats are drawn in section view, as in a ground plan, they should be in scale thickness and should have the space darkened between the two visible lines that are outlining the thickness of the flat.

LETTERING. Lettering should be legible, and the style should allow for easy and rapid execution. Characters that generally conform to the single-stroke Gothic style meet these requirements. Only uppercase letters should be used on drawings unless lowercase letters are needed to conform with other established standards or nomenclature (see Fig. 7.26).

TITLE BLOCK. The title block should be in the same location on all drawings of a single project. The title block should be located in either the lower right-hand corner of the drawing or in a strip along the bottom of the drawing (see Fig. 7.27). In either case, the block should include the following information:

1. Name of the producing organization or theatre
2. Name of production, act, and scene, if appropriate
3. Drawing title

Figure 7.26 a, Single-stroke vertical Gothic. b, Single-stroke slant Gothic.

ABCDEFGHIJKLMN
OPQRSTUVWXYZ
1234567890

ABCDEFGHIJKLMN
OPQRSTUVWXYZ
1234567890

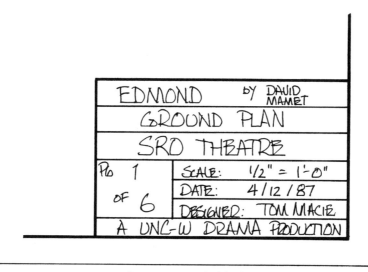

Figure 7.27 Title block.

4. Drawing number
5. Predominant scale of the drawing
6. Date the drawing was drafted
7. Designer of the production
8. Draftsperson, if different from the designer
9. Approval of drawing, if applicable

DIMENSIONS

1. Dimensions must be clear, consistent, and easily understood.
2. Dimensions should be oriented to read from the bottom or the right-hand side of the plate.
3. Metric dimensions less than one meter are to be noted as zero, decimal point, and portion of meter in numerals. All measurements one meter and greater shall be given as a whole meter number, decimal point, and portion of meter, for example, 0.1 m, 0.52 m, 1.5 m, 2.35 m.
4. Dimensions less than 1 ft. are given in inches without a foot notation, such as 6″ or 9 1/2″.
5. Dimensions 1′-0″ and greater include the whole feet with a single apostrophe followed by a dash, and then inches followed by a double apostrophe: 7′-1/2″, 18′-9 1/4″, 1′-3″.

6. Dimensions that require more space than between extension lines are placed in proximity to the area measured, parallel with the bottom edge of the sheet, and directed to the point of reference by means of a leader line.

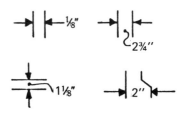

7. Platform and tread heights are given in inches above the stage floor. Such heights are placed in circles at or near the centers of the platform or tread.

8. Direction of arrows (when used to indicate elevation change on stairs, ramps, and so on) points away from the primary level of the drawing.

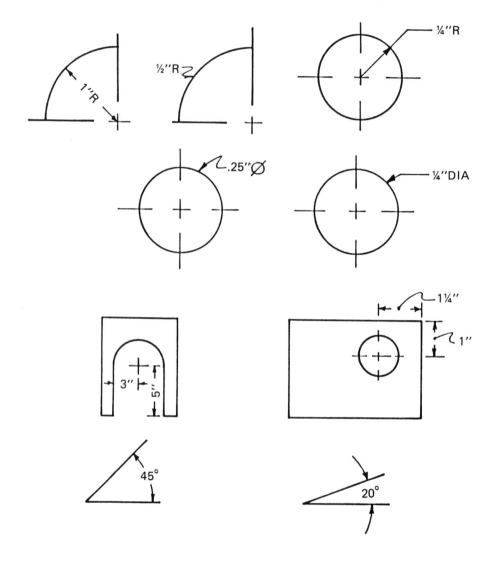

LINE TYPES

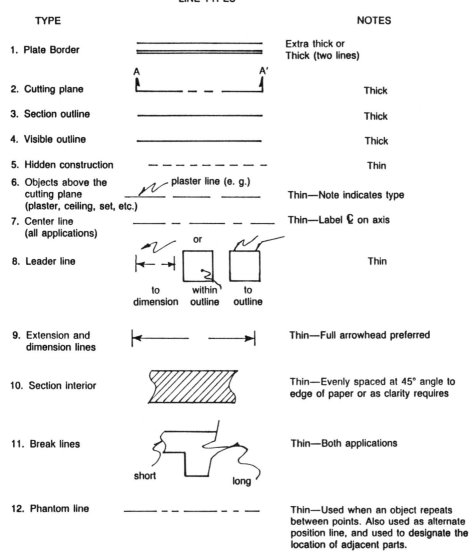

TYPE		NOTES
1. Plate Border		Extra thick or Thick (two lines)
2. Cutting plane	A — A'	Thick
3. Section outline		Thick
4. Visible outline		Thick
5. Hidden construction		Thin
6. Objects above the cutting plane (plaster, ceiling, set, etc.)	plaster line (e. g.)	Thin—Note indicates type
7. Center line (all applications)		Thin—Label ℄ on axis
8. Leader line	or	Thin
	to dimension / within outline / to outline	
9. Extension and dimension lines		Thin—Full arrowhead preferred
10. Section interior		Thin—Evenly spaced at 45° angle to edge of paper or as clarity requires
11. Break lines	short / long	Thin—Both applications
12. Phantom line		Thin—Used when an object repeats between points. Also used as alternate position line, and used to designate the location of adjacent parts.

13. Any "special" lines not listed above should be noted in the legend of each sheet.

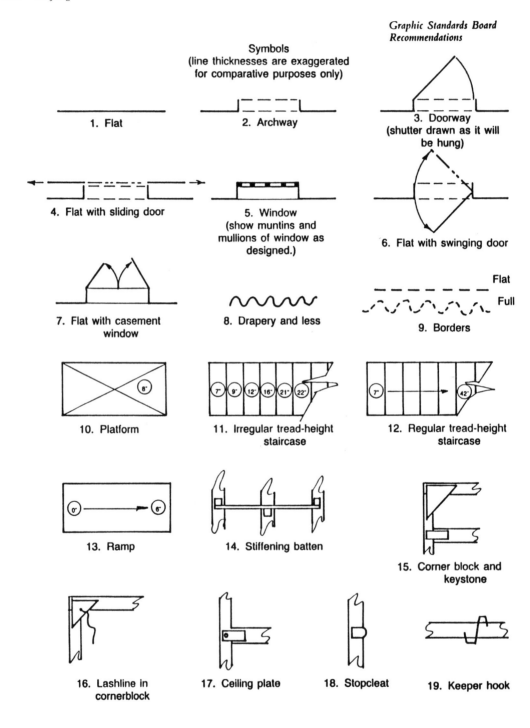

Symbols
(line thicknesses are exaggerated
for comparative purposes only)

*Graphic Standards Board
Recommendations*

1. Flat

2. Archway

3. Doorway
(shutter drawn as it will
be hung)

4. Flat with sliding door

5. Window
(show muntins and
mullions of window as
designed.)

6. Flat with swinging door

7. Flat with casement
window

8. Drapery and less

9. Borders

Flat

Full

10. Platform

11. Irregular tread-height
staircase

12. Regular tread-height
staircase

13. Ramp

14. Stiffening batten

15. Corner block and
keystone

16. Lashline in
cornerblock

17. Ceiling plate

18. Stopcleat

19. Keeper hook

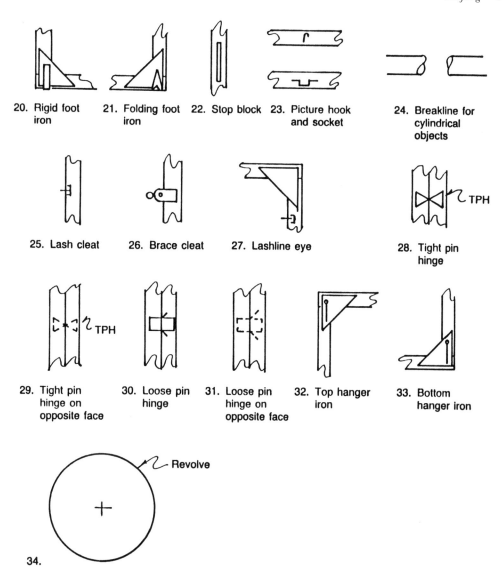

20. Rigid foot iron
21. Folding foot iron
22. Stop block
23. Picture hook and socket
24. Breakline for cylindrical objects

25. Lash cleat
26. Brace cleat
27. Lashline eye
28. Tight pin hinge

29. Tight pin hinge on opposite face
30. Loose pin hinge
31. Loose pin hinge on opposite face
32. Top hanger iron
33. Bottom hanger iron

34.

SCALE

Logic tells us that drawings must be smaller than the objects they are meant to represent. To reduce depictions to a manageable size, the designer needs to choose an appropriate *scale*. When working in the scale, great care must be taken to ensure accuracy, because often a measurement in the shop must be taken directly from the drawing and from a section in which no dimensions are noted. If the drawing is not precise, the unit cannot be built correctly or interpreted, regardless of the scale indicated.

Different scales may be used within the same set of drawings in order to show a detail of a unit with greater clarity. However, with the exception of detail drawings, normally only one scale is used on a single plate of drawings. What follows is a list of scales and some of their more common uses:

Scale	Use
1/8″ = 1′-0″	Designer's thumbnail sketches and preliminary plans. Plans for extremely large settings.
1/4″ = 1′-0″	Some design drawings, renderings, design elevations, plans, and lighting plots for large sets or large theatres. Plans and elevations for film.
1/2″ = 1′-0″	Most plans, design drawings, elevations, and working drawings for scenery and props.
3/4″ = 1′-0″	Detail construction drawings for film.
1′ = 1′-0″	Detail construction drawings and painter's elevations.
1 1/2″ = 1′-0″	Construction and design details.

(Source: Harvey Sweet, *Graphics for the Performing Arts*, pp. 48–49).

TYPES OF DRAWINGS

Orthographic Projection

One of the simplest and yet most effective means for accurately describing an object in a two-dimensional drawing is the orthographic projection (Fig. 7.28). In this type of drawing, the object is drawn as if it were encased in a glass cube, with each side projected onto different sides of the cube, and the cube, in turn, unfolded to a single plane.

There is a specific relationship to all sides and views of the object in orthographic projection, as indicated in Figure 7.28. As you can see, this is a simple and effective means for quickly drawing the required object. Of course, occasions will present themselves in which a surface of an object will be at an angle to the plane of the orthographic cube. If a true scale of that side is essential, then a separate, auxiliary projection parallel to the angled side of the object needs to be drawn. Such auxiliary views are not always necessary, even though an object may have an angled side. Your experience and common sense as a designer will tell you when such views are needed.

Isometric Drawing

Often the complexity of a unit requires a view that conforms to our normal, three-dimensional way of seeing. In such cases, one option is the isometric drawing (Fig. 7.29), in which the object is tilted and rotated into such a position that the viewer can see three sides simultaneously. However, although this viewpoint appears three-dimensional, it is not in perspective—that is, with foreshortened sides. The lines of the object are placed on 30° angles to parallel and are called isometric planes. Lines parallel to the isometric planes are true in scale; these are called isometric lines. Nonparallel lines are called nonisometric and are not true in measurement.

CIRCLES. Circles or circular forms can be drawn in isometric projection by noting the relationship between a square and its inscribed circle (Figure 7.30). Notice that the circumference of the circle contacts the sides of the square at the midpoint of each side. To draw an isometric circle, first locate a square on the desired isometric plane, and then establish the points of contact. Using

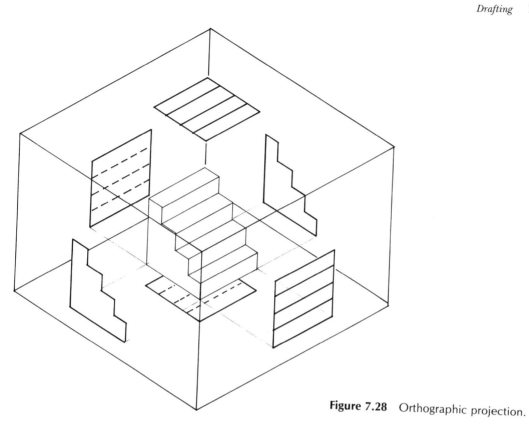

Figure 7.28 Orthographic projection.

Figure 7.29 Isometric drawing.

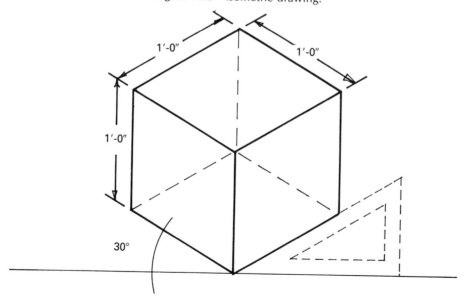

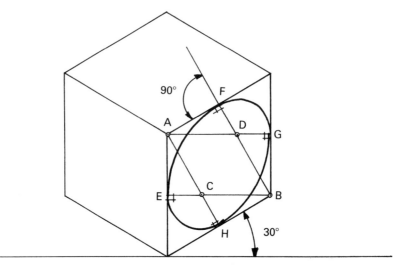

Figure 7.30   Isometric circle.

the contact points as a reference, draw the circle using a French curve. Notice that the isometric circle is not, in appearance, a true circle. An accurate isometric circle also can be drawn using a compass and establishing arcs by placing the point of the compass at C and the lead at G. Draw an arc from G to H. Using the same setting, draw an arc, with the pivot at D, from E to F. Now, with the compass point at A, set the distance to H. Draw an arc from H to E. Repeat the process with the pivot at B and the arc from F to G.

We need to be aware that not all objects lend themselves to isometric projection drawing. Because this form of drawing does not allow for perspective foreshortening, some large objects will appear so distorted that the communicative value of the drawing is lost entirely.

Oblique Drawing

Oblique drawings combine characteristics of both isometric and orthographic projections and are useful especially for objects with curvilinear features (Fig. 7.31). This

Figure 7.31   Oblique drawing.

type of drawing has one face of the object parallel to the drawing surface, and adjacent sides drawn at a receding angle. Three types of oblique drawings may be used, as seen in Figure 7.32. In using the oblique drawing, you should strive to keep the most complex plane of the object toward the viewer and the least complex plane away from the viewer (Fig.7.33).

Sectional Views

The discussion thus far has focused on external views of objects. Occasionally, however, an internal view is necessary. Sectional drawings answer this need. Earlier we presented the conventions for indicating sectional views. When sectional drawings are used, they should be kept as close to the primary drawing as possible. Several kinds of sectional views are shown in Figure 7.34.

COMPUTER DRAFTING

Computer Aided Drafting and Design (CADD) promises to be a significant time-saver in the design process. Should you be able to afford the hardware and software, many options are available. Digital computers, such as those shown in Figure 7.35 and 7.36, can be used by computer-aided draftspersons. When the entire system is assembled, full and complex drawings can be executed (Fig. 7.37).

This text is designed to teach principles and techniques and to advise on the purchase of various kinds of materials which are fundamental to scenic design and execution. CADD systems do not yet fall into the realm of the necessary. So, we face a multi-faceted dilemma in choosing details for this subject. First, the present generation of students stands an excellent chance of some exposure to CADD. Giving the subject only a passing reference makes the text less useful than it might be otherwise. On the other hand, the majority of theatre education programs in this country still cannot afford CADD systems, and the beginning design student without an operational CADD system for reference will not find much help even in the most detailed textbook treatment. Practically speaking, effective instruction in the use of CADD systems requires a *specific* system at hand. In addition, both hardware, that is, the equipment, and software, the programs which drive the equipment, are changing so rapidly that virtually any specific reference we might include here is

Figure 7.32 a, Cavalier. b, Cabinet. c, General oblique.

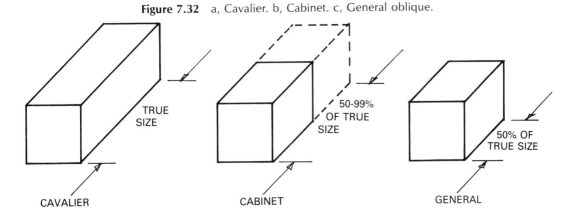

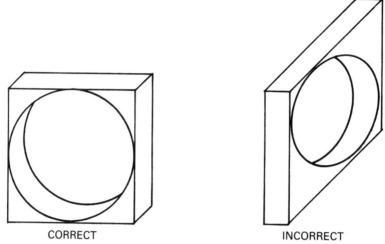

CORRECT   INCORRECT

Figure 7.33 Proper positioning of the oblique drawing.

guaranteed to be out of date by the time the book is published. Furthermore, each of the systems currently available has loyal supporters and strident detractors, and so, making applicational recommendations in this space would prove highly counterproductive.

Nonetheless, we can draw a quick and simple overview that may be helpful to the beginner. First, you must have the basic hardware. This includes a CPU (Central Processing Unit) or processor, which is the main processing mechanism of a computer system. Macintosh, Apple II and IIGs, IBM

Figure 7.34 Sectional views: a, Full section. b, Half section. c, Revolved section. d, Removed sections. e, Sectional plane.

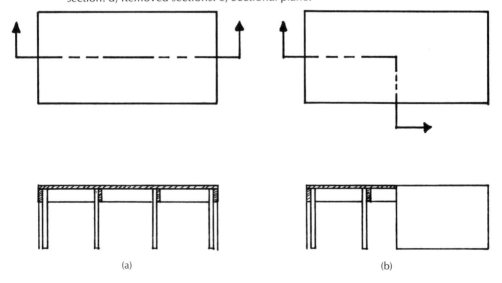

(a)   (b)

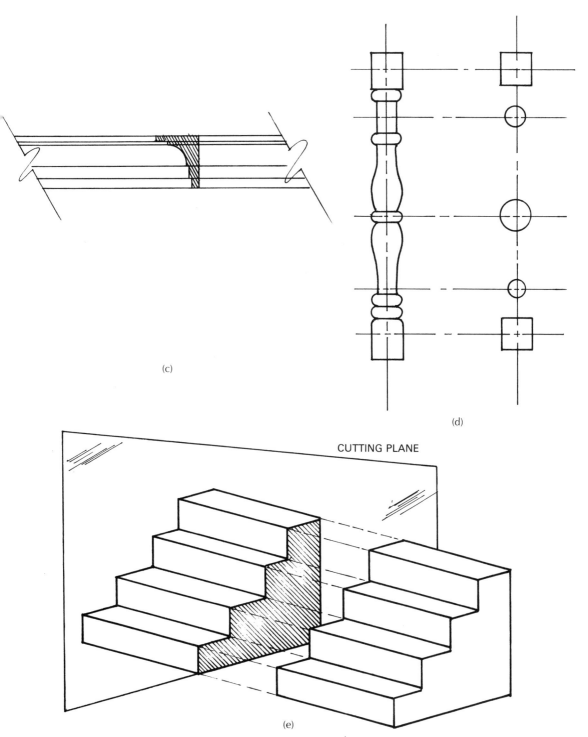

(c)

(d)

CUTTING PLANE

(e)

Figure 7.34   *(continued)*

Figure 7.35 PS/2 Model 80 with a 8514 high resolution monitor; a PS/2 model 50; and a 3118 image scanner. Courtesy IBM. PS/2® is a trademark of the IBM Corporation.

Figure 7.36 ALDUS PAGEMAKER running on an IBM PS/2 Model 80 and printed on an IBM 4216 Personal Page printer. 300 DPI Laser printer, Courtesy IBM. PS/2® is a trademark of the IBM Corporation.

PCs and IBM clones fall into this category. Next, you must have a visual display. For graphics, a color monitor is mandatory. The third piece of essential hardware is a printer. Printers include daisywheel, dot-matrix, and laser printers. However, for effective CADD you will need a specialized printer rather than the normal office printers associated with microcomputers. The size of design drawings necessitates this. Finally, some kind of networking hardware may be helpful in order to tie microcomputers together (especially with laser printers) for efficient usage.

Commercially-available programs, such as

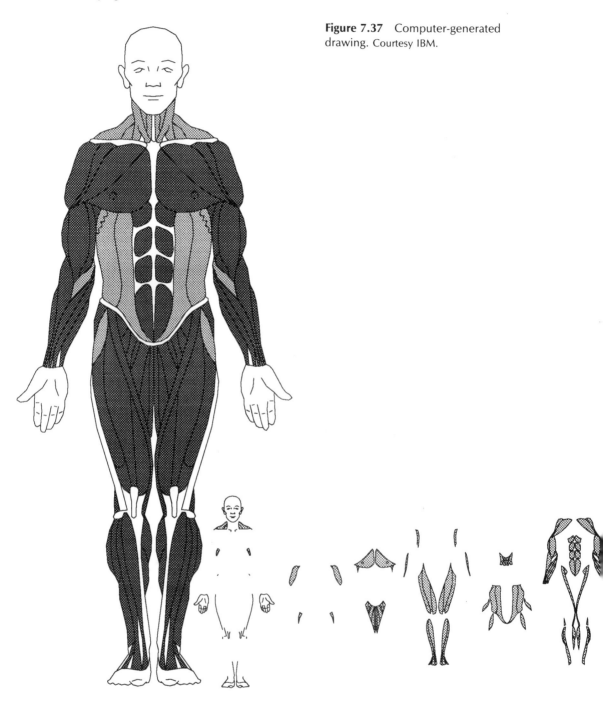

Figure 7.37 Computer-generated drawing. Courtesy IBM.

MacPaint, are available for instructing the computer hardware to do what you wish. Numerous programs exist for each available system. However, anyone interested in CADD must invest the time in hands-on exposure to several systems. Do not rely on salespersons; talk to individuals who have CADD systems and whose programs and needs are similar to yours. You must know what your specific needs are going to be, and you must know that, while CADD systems can be tremendously helpful, they may not save time or be cost effective for *your* type of theatre operation. You also must be prepared to budget for repair and maintenance when the initial manufacturer's warranty expires and for upgrading in the future. Many individuals working with CADD systems for the first time are shocked by the tremendous amount of time required to both learn the system and enter into it the numerous figures and symbols which will allow the computer and its software to draft and design for you. Do not assume that the computer will speed up your work schedule initially: It probably will slow you down for several months, until everything you need is in the system, and you have mastered its operation. Finally, do not assume that the computer will make you a better or more creative designer. It will not. CADD systems are tools which, when used properly and over time, may assist you in translating your design from conception to paper. They are especially helpful in making changes which, in hand-drawn circumstances, would require redrafting an entire plate. Cost, set up, and learning time may make the CADD system nothing more than a fancy toy of questionable use for some programs. In short order your new system may become an antique of questionable value even as a teaching tool. We can guarantee that a CADD system cannot supplant your need to learn how to draft, draw, and paint "the old-fashioned way." The first time

your system goes down at an inopportune moment, you will learn that lesson with excruciating clarity. Those who are interested in learning more about the subject should read David L. Goetsch's *Introduction to Computer-aided Drafting* (Prentice-Hall, 1983). In it are detailed explanations sufficient for using this tool.

PERSPECTIVE DRAWING

The kinds of drawing we discussed earlier relate primarily to the parts of the design process that occur after the designer has presented his or her ideas in the form of a sketch or rendering. The sketch and rendering are discussed fully in chapter 6. However, in order to present an effective sketch or rendering, the designer first must master the means by which a three-dimensional entity, the setting, is translated into a two-dimensional medium—that is, the sketch or rendering. The means by which such translation occurs is called perspective drawing. It is partially a mechanical formula, discovered in the Italian Renaissance, which allows us to make a rational presentation of the *foreshortening* that occurs in nature when we perceive three-dimensional space. We recognize the effect of perspective when we stand in the middle of a highway or railroad track and see it seemingly disappear on the horizon (Fig. 7.38). The governing factors in this phenomenon, called *linear perspective,* are the height of the horizon line and the placement of a vanishing point on that horizon line. The height of the horizon line corresponds to the height of the viewer's eye above the ground, and the vanishing point corresponds to the angle of the side of the object in view, relative to the viewer's direct line of vision. In the theatre, we can apply these factors to make a perspective drawing of the setting if we have the following information:

Figure 7.38 Linear perspective.

(1) a ground plan of the setting; (2) the distance from the stage to any specified seat in the auditorium; and (3) the height of the viewer's eye (in that specified seat) above the stage floor (Fig. 7.39). With that information we can, through a repetitive process, translate the ground plan of setting into a pictorially accurate rendering.

In our experience of teaching scenic design, nothing has posed so great an array of

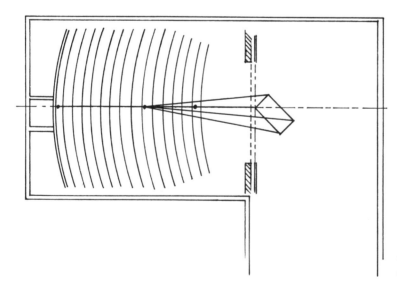

Figure 7.39 Viewer observation point, center of vision.

frustrations for both teacher and students than has the teaching and mastering of mechanical perspective. Nonetheless, for all but the very few who have outstanding abilities in spatial thinking and drawing, mechanical perspective is the only sure-fire means of presenting an accurate picture of the setting. However, following the tedious repetitions of the mechanical, or drop-point, procedure, tends to require such rigor and discipline that it becomes an absolute turnoff for beginning students. A few options exist, and what follows is a brief synopsis of some of the approaches that can be used in mastering mechanical perspective.

Drop-Point, Multiple Vanishing Point Perspective

Figure 7.40 illustrates the basic procedures needed to use the drop-point method. The *tormentor plane* corresponds to an arbitrary plane such as the edge of the stage (whether proscenium, arena, thrust, and so forth), a curtain line, or some other identifiable part of the performance area. In our example, a simple rectangle ABCD represents a portion of the stage floor to be translated into perspective. A *picture plane* is established parallel to the tormentor plane at a distance from TP equal to the distance from the observer to TP in the actual theatre. The *observation point* (OP) represents the position of the observer. The OP can be in the center, as it is in Figure 7.40, or at any point along the PP, just as an observer may sit in any seat in the auditorium. The position of the OP changes the view one gets of the setting. The *center of vision* (CV) represents a point on the TP directly above CV. The horizon is established by drawing a line parallel to PP at a height equal to the actual height of the observer's eye above the stage floor. Vanishing points for all sides of objects not parallel to the TP are found by measuring the angle of

each side as it or its extension meets the tormentor plane. This angle is duplicated at OP and extended to the TP. At the point of intersection, a perpendicular line is dropped to the horizon line. The point of intersection with the horizon line is the vanishing point for that side and for *all other sides of all other objects that are parallel to that side.* There will be as many vanishing points as there are nonparallel sides of all walls, objects, and so forth in the setting. *Every* vanishing point is determined by the procedure just outlined.

A careful study of Figure 7.40 will lead you to understand how transference from ground plan to perspective depiction is determined. Note that every point on the TP is the spatial equivalent of a point directly below it on the PP. Therefore, corner A, which happens to be at CV, is the equivalent of point A′ at OP. Were A somewhere else on the TP, its equivalent (A′) on the PP would be directly below it, and diminution lines to the vanishing points would be drawn from that point on the PP. Objects that do not rest on the TP need to be extended so that an intersection with TP occurs, as in Figure 7.41. Finding corners B and D consists of drawing a line from OP to B and D and, where that line crosses the TP, dropping a perpendicular to line A′—VPL or VPR. All objects, walls, and so on in the set are transferred by repetition of this simple process.

Heights of objects are established by measuring at PP (only at PP are measurements true) and carrying back toward the vanishing point, as in Figure 7.42. If the rectangle ABCD were a platform 3 ft. high, once we established A′B′C′D′ using the procedure just described, we would measure, using the scale of the ground plan, a height of 3 ft. at A′, and establish A″. Because the top sides A″B″C″D″ of the platform are parallel to the bottom, sides A″B″C″D″ are controlled by the same vanishing points as A′B′C′D′. All heights for all objects, walls, steps, doorways,

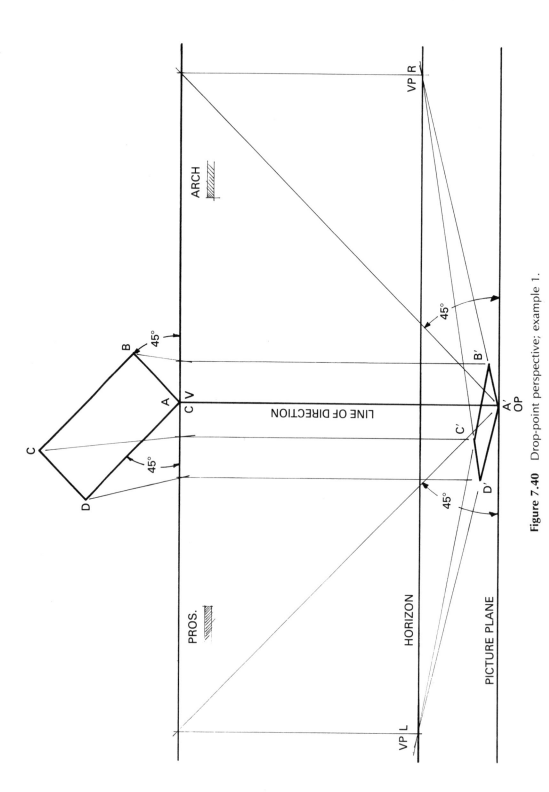

Figure 7.40 Drop-point perspective; example 1.

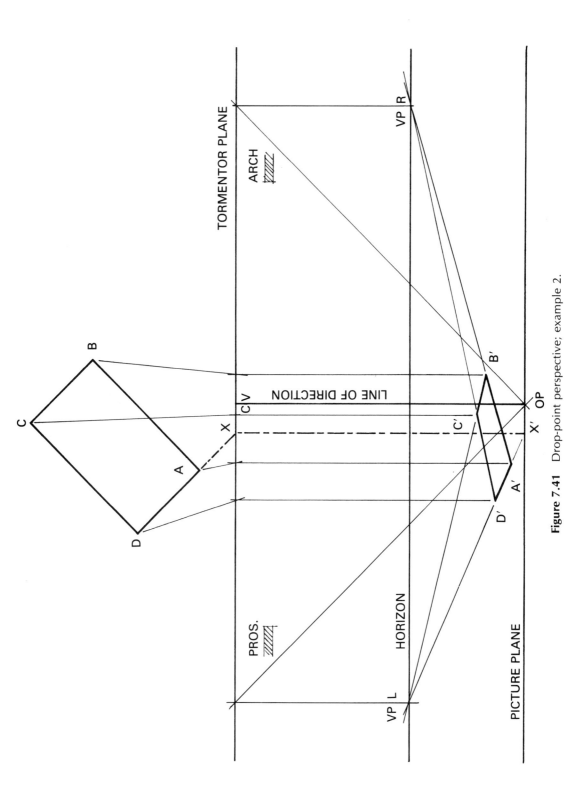

Figure 7.41 Drop-point perspective; example 2.

179

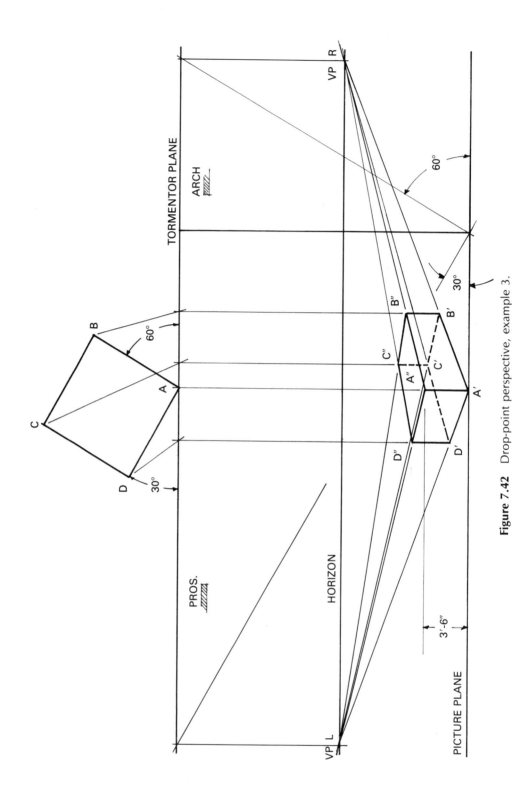

Figure 7.42 Drop-point perspective, example 3.

180

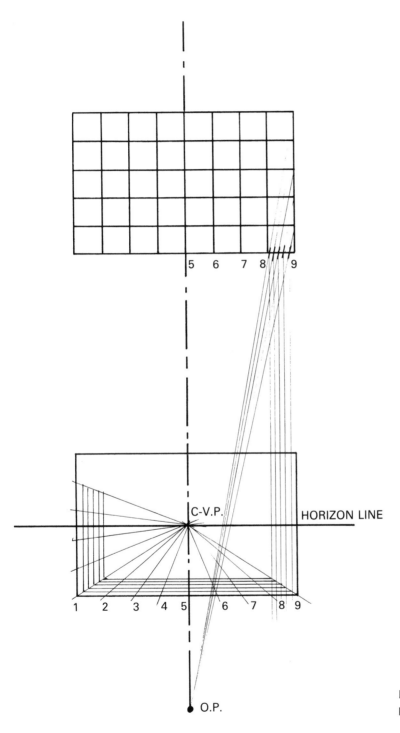

Figure 7.43 Grid method perspective.

and so on, are established by repetition of this single procedure.

Obviously, a setting is much more complicated than a rectangle, but it is, nonetheless, nothing more than numerous multiplications of the procedure used for a rectangle. Even decorous, curvilinear furniture can be drawn by this method, by encasing it in a rectangular form. This process, then, carried through on every wall, alcove, door, window, sofa, table, and so on, represents hundreds of repetitions, and *can* become tedious. Nonetheless, when completed, this process will result in a pictorially perfect perspective representation of the setting.

Grid-Method Perspective

A less tedious method of creating the perspective rendering or sketch is illustrated in Figure 7.43. Using the drop-point procedure, create a grid in perspective to correspond to the grid in the ground plan. When that is established, wall lines can be set in easily, and heights established by measuring at the PP, determining vanishing points, and carrying back. This method is less precise, but it will give an accurate picture of the setting. Perspective floor grids also are available commercially.

Our experience has taught us that different systems will work differently for different individuals. Some people, who can think and visualize spatially, seem to need no system at all. They are able to render perspectively accurate renderings at will. Others, even with the aid of the mechanical systems, seem totally unable to translate rational perspective into their renderings. Therefore, we propose only that you decide for yourself which system works best for you, and then carry on to polish your skills. For those who wish further reading on this subject we suggest Henry Morgan's *Perspective Drawing For The Theatre* (Drama Book Specialists).

CHAPTER EIGHT

BUILDING THE SET

Fundamental to every scenic designer's approach is a thorough working knowledge of the practicalities involved in executing the design. It does little good to design a stage setting that cannot be built or to victimize the actors because the wrong materials were chosen. A good scenic design requires a working knowledge of basic technology, because, to reiterate, if you cannot translate into space, time, budget, personnel, tools, and details the design you have envisioned and sold to the director, then you will not survive as a scenic designer. The reality of the situation in which you work may dictate that you act as your own technical director, in which case a detailed knowledge of scenic execution is absolutely essential. You may work in a situation in which someone else is hired to build your design. Without suggesting that you need to look over the shoulder of another professional, let us simply state

that occasionally you will need to second-guess or at least advise on what materials will be best to execute what you have in mind. In either case, you need to know this material. What follows in this chapter is a layout of the basic information required for executing the design: the choices, uses, and standard techniques for translating the scenic design from rendering to actual stage setting.

SCENERY UNITS

Stage scenery can be divided into two categories: two-dimensional units and three-dimensional units.

Two-Dimensional Units

These units are vertical and horizontal and are not considered to have any important thickness. They can be framed for support or they can be suspended in a hanging position on the stage.

Framed Scenery. Framed scenery consists of several variations of a standard piece of construction called the plain flat. All of these can be constructed in a well-organized scene shop with proper materials and advance planning. There are many ways of achieving the final product, and today's technological advances have relaxed a number of methods previously used as rigid guidelines for construction. The methods related here are suggested rather than dictated. A number of solutions always exist for any problem advanced by the design.

The flat is, essentially, a lightweight screen constructed of lumber and covered with cloth. A variation of the flat can be taken apart and rolled up for easy storage. Flats should be light enough to be lifted by a single stagehand and no wider than the usual width of scenic muslin or canvas, adjusted for shrinkage—that is, approximately 5 ft. 9 in. The height or length of a flat is usually governed by the length that can be accommodated by available transportation or access doorways. In general terms, 18 ft. is the maximum height for a single flat. If a unit is constructed in place—that is, on stage—and there are no plans for storage after the production, then, obviously these limitations do not apply.

Lumber used to construct the flat frame must be selected with care, because the resulting finished product must be straight and without knots and defects that would interfere in the alignment of the unit with other scenic units. A select grade of white pine is the most suitable for scene construction, and the ideal size is the standard 1 by 3. The bottom and top boards of the frame are called the rails, and the vertical boards on the right and left sides of the frame are called the stiles. The toggle bars are the horizontal boards that keep the stiles the same distance from each other across the length of the flat. Diagonal braces are on the same side of the frame and prevent the frame from warping (Fig. 8.1).

Corner blocks cut from 1/4-in. plywood into right triangles with 10-in. sides are attached 3/4-in. from the outside edge of the flat frame to reinforce the butt joints. To give maximum strength, the grain of two of the layers of the plywood should run across the butt joint. Keystones are pieces of three-ply cut in 3 in. by 8 in. rectangles and used to attach the toggles to the stiles. They must also be placed 3/4 in. from the outside edge of the stile. Keystones are used also to secure the two diagonal braces for the flat.

The hardware attaching the plywood to the flat frame will vary depending on shop procedures. Accepted fasteners are 1 1/4-in. clout nails, 3/4-in. wood screws, or 1-in. pneumatic staples. If clout nails are used, a clinch plate must be employed to clinch the nails as they are nailed through the frame.

After the flat frame is assembled, the covering of canvas (lightweight) or unbleached muslin is measured for attachment to the frame. The material should extend over the outside edges of the frame by at least 1 in. The material is then attached to the frame on the inner edge of the stiles and rails by staples or tacks placed approximately 18 in. apart. The material is then folded back, and an adhesive of either watered-down polyvinyl glue or animal glue is applied to the wood frame. The material is pressed against the adhesive on the frame and smoothed with a small wooden block. After a reasonable drying time (approximately eight hours) the material is trimmed to the edge of the flat frame with a sharp knife.

Before the finished flat can be painted, it must be sized to tighten the fabric, which enables it to accept the scene paint more

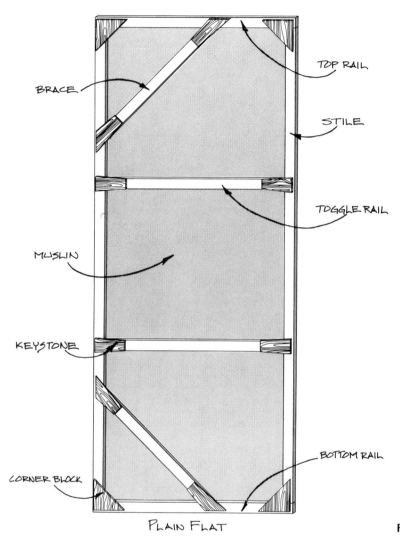

BRACE

TOP RAIL

STILE

TOGGLE RAIL

MUSLIN

KEYSTONE

BOTTOM RAIL

CORNER BLOCK

PLAIN FLAT

Figure 8.1 Plain flat.

evenly. After sizing the front of the flat, and before applying the scene paint base coat, attach the required stage hardware to the flat, including, for example, lash line cleats, stage brace cleats, lash line eyes, and hinges.

Variations of the plain flat include flats with openings such as windows, doors, bookcases, and fireplaces (Figs. 8.2 and 8.3). Construction of such units uses rails, stiles, toggles, and diagonal braces in essentially the same manner as in a plain flat, with allowances for modifications to accommodate the openings. Scenery designed for motion pictures and television usually requires flats constructed of materials more rigid than canvas or muslin. The ever-discerning camera eye readily exposes the instability of a canvas unit. Area stages and outdoor productions also make use of strong and durable scenery. The flat frame in these circum-

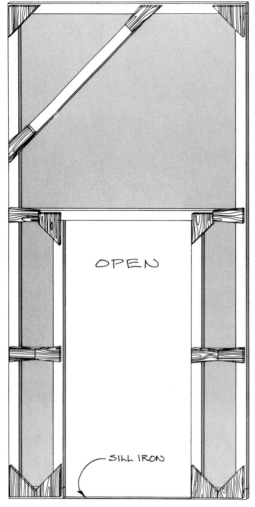

Figure 8.2 Door flat.

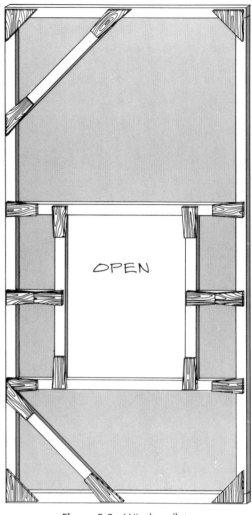

Figure 8.3 Window flat.

stances is nailed together as a box with a cover of 1/4-in. plywood or Masonite. These flats employ construction to fit 4 ft. by 8 ft. plywood sheets and are held together with clamps and bolts rather than stage hardware. This type of flat works best when assembled with wood screws rather than nails; the hard plywood facing eliminates the need for plywood corner blocks.

Another variation of the plain flat is the profile flat, which is a plain flat with irregular edges added. Used primarily as wings, unusual borders, and ground rows, these flats employ the same construction techniques as the standard plain flat to which additional framing of 1 by 2 or 1 by 3 lumber is appended.

Ceiling units, which find less usage today than in the past because of the trend away from realistic settings, are very large, framed units that are not unlike the standard flat. The ceiling unit utilizes 1 by 4 framing for strength because it must be suspended above the stage. Muslin or canvas is attached only to the stiles of the ceiling unit so that it can be dismantled and rolled up for storage. The unit hangs from ceiling plates attached to an overhead batten. Sometimes the unit is divided into two pieces hinged together to allow the ceiling to fold in half for storage in the files when not in use. This is called a book ceiling (Fig. 8.4).

Unframed Scenery. Unframed scenery comprises drops and curtains. However, a drop can be framed, in which case it belongs in the category just mentioned. Drops usually employ a weight at the bottom, either a pipe or a heavy chain. Loose edges are rein-forced with webbing and are pierced by metal grommets so that the drop can be laced to a frame or batten with cotton rope. Canvas or muslin drops are seamed horizontally for smooth hanging. Drops should be constructed of the widest material available. Supply houses carry 9-ft. widths that will give the drop only one visible seam. Gauze and scrim drops normally do not have seams; some gauzes are available in 30-ft. widths. Because of the size of an average drop—that is, 38 ft. by 22 ft. high, the construction of a drop requires a large and clean area of a scene shop for assembling.

Drop size depends on the design and size of the theatre's stage. After the drop is sewn together, a strip of webbing is sewn along the top edge, and No. 2 grommets are placed on one-foot centers. Cotton rope of 1/8-in. di-

Figure 8.4 Book ceiling.

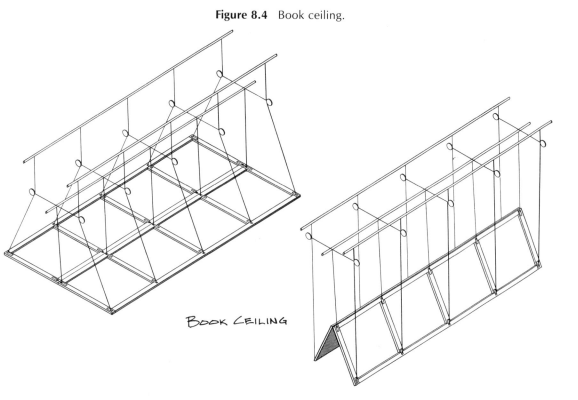

BOOK CEILING

ameter and 3-ft. lengths is then threaded through the grommets with half-hitch knots. These will serve to tie off the drop for flying. The bottom of the drop requires a double hem to allow for the insertion of a pipe, wooden batten, or metal chain to serve as a weight to make the drop hang as taut as possible.

A variety of soft drops can be used for the stage, including cut drops, transparencies, translucent drops, borders, leg drops, cycloramas, ribbon drops, rope drops, and others, depending upon the designer's creativity.

Draperies function primarily to control what the audience sees. They can also define the performance space as well as conceal the offstage space. While performing such functions, draperies also can provide an attractive stage decoration. Stage draperies can be made of many different fabrics or materials, depending on the principle purpose for their use. Durability, decoration, masking, and expense all must be considered in selecting the weave, texture, and color of drapery fabric. Drapery construction usually allows for 50 to 100 percent fullness. Fullness can be sewn into the top of the drapery panel by box or plain pleating; or fullness can be included in the overall width of the panel, which is then gathered by tying the tie lines at the top closer together. A 6-in. hem should be included in draperies that hang to the floor. All seams connecting the panels of draperies need to be vertical to assure fewer wrinkles. Before hemming, the drapery should be hung for a short period of time to allow the material to stretch. Finally, the finished draperies must be fireproofed to meet local fire codes.

Three-Dimensional Units

Weight-bearing Structures. The most important and most often used structure for the stage is the platform, which is utilized to elevate stage areas for more interesting visual effects. The folding platform represents one type of platform, called a parallel. It consists of a platform top with cleats and sits on a base that can fold for storage. The base has four sides held together by hinges, and its construction is similar to that of a flat. When the top is set in place, the cleats prevent the unit from folding. The hinges on the platform base need to be specifically placed to allow the base top to fold for storage (Fig. 8.5).

Rigid platforms (Fig. 8.6) can be constructed of a 3/4 in. plywood top supported by 2 by 4 legs and frame. Rigid platforms are heavy as well as strong and can present problems in moving and shifting. The platform legs can be secured by nails, screws, or bolts. The use of bolts and wing nuts allows the legs to be removed easily without damage to the structural members. Remember that wood can splinter and that bolt holes do enlarge with use. Consequently the length of service of the rigid platform is limited. Perhaps a more efficient method is the use of pipe or preformed steel for supporting legs. Welded frames are the best for weight, strength, and durability. Although the expense is greater, the practicality is superior. Construction of this type of platform requires proper welding equipment and an experienced welder. One-and-one-half-inch black steel pipe with flanges and pipe clamps also can be used to support platform tops. Most platforms are rectangular, but pipe construction can be easily adapted to irregular or even curved shapes. These units can be disassembled and stored when not in use.

Some other flexible systems of metal platform construction can be used. The first employs a slotted angle iron with perforated slots and holes. The pieces of angle iron can be easily cut with special angle iron cutting tools and can then be joined together with

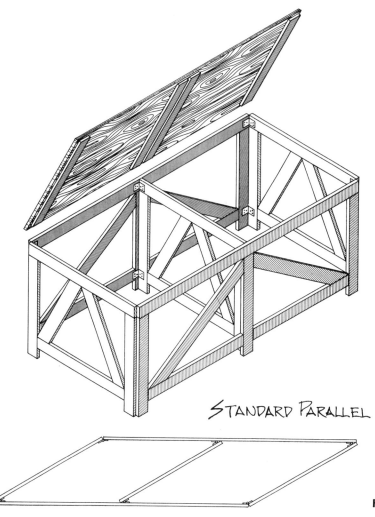

STANDARD PARALLEL

Figure 8.5 Standard parallel.

bolts. A second type employs Unistrut channel—steel pieces made with special channels and grooves that hold spring-held nuts bolted to special fittings. A third type, another product of the Unistrut Company, is made of lengths of steel tubing logs formed in squares that can fit into each other, allowing the tubes to telescope (Fig. 8.7). This system allows for flexibility in platform height. The legs can be attached to a plywood top whose support frame consists of slotted angle metal.

Wagons are simply platforms on casters. They can be of standard platform sizes, such as 4 ft. by 8 ft., or they can be as large as a full-stage acting area, thereby moving an entire setting. Rubber-tired casters from 3–6 in. in diameter provide the best support for wagons. Casters come in three types: rigid, which move back and forth in one direction only; swivel, which can move in any direction; and brake, which allow the caster to lock into position.

Platform and wagon tops should be cov-

Figure 8.6   Rigid platform.

ered with padded material to reduce noise caused by footsteps. Carpet padding covered with heavy canvas or muslin can be painted as desired.

Steps and stairs, another type of three-dimension unit, consist of three sections: (1) the carriage, which provides the fundamental support; (2) the tread, which is the horizontal surface of the step; and (3) the riser, which is the vertical facing separating the treads. The height and depth of the tread depend on the type and size of the unit, but one should remember that any steps with a riser height of over 7 in. will present problems for short actors. In addition, the tread must be deep enough to accommodate the actor's foot comfortably. Offstage or escape steps need not be so accommodating (Fig. 8.8).

Non-weight-bearing Structures. Non-weight-bearing, three-dimensional scenery such as rocks, trees, ceiling beams, fireplaces, and pillars are usually built on frames of wood covered with muslin or with wire and muslin to provide contours. These units must be as lightweight as possible. Additional material can be used to establish a proper surface effect, for example, different-sized mesh wire, corrugated cardboard, wooden strips, papier-mâché, impregnated fabrics such as Celastic or Sculpt-o-fab and fiberglass.

Three-dimensional scenery units attached to or inserted in flats—for example, for doors, windows, and archways—give the appearance of reality and architectural style. Door units are composed of three parts: the casing, the shutter, and the thickness. The casing consists of a frame with decorative

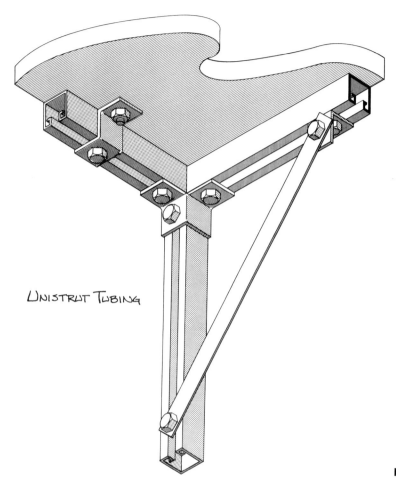

UNISTRUT TUBING

Figure 8.7 Unistrut tubing.

trim for the opening. The shutter is the two-dimensional panel that opens and closes in the door opening. The thicknesses are the pieces of the opening that suggest the wall depth. The entire door unit fits into a flat opening and can be attached as permanently as desired. In some cases, the door needs to be removable for shifting. In others, it needs to be braced for maximum solidity. Windows are similar in construction, with the exception of the panel, which can be changed into a glass frame called a sash. Glass, of course, is not generally used for stage windows because of its fragility and safety hazards. Sashes, like door panels, come in several types, among them casement, sliding, and double-hung. Archways usually consist only of thickness frames, and they conform to various shapes and sizes. Bookcases, niches, and fireplace units are constructed in a fashion similar to doors and window units.

Curved Units. Curved units are built on a wooden frame, curved in the desired radius, and covered with sheets of 1/8-in. laminated

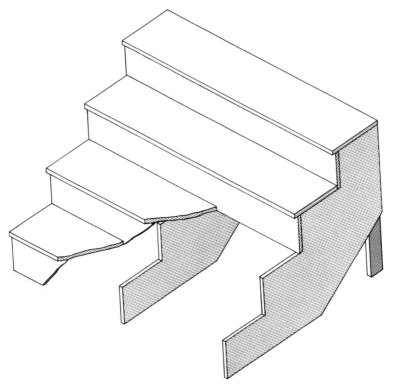

Figure 8.8 Steps.

paper product such as Upson board or fiber board attached to the rails and toggles of the frame. Any joints must be carefully covered with a dutchman to mask effectively.

SCULPTURED EFFECTS AND TEXTURES

Wooden Trims

Architectural trim on scenery gives dimension and interesting chiaroscuros to the setting. Beginning with profile frames, wooden moldings, thin and narrow strips of lumber, additional decor can be added using cardboard, wooden blocks, plastic forms and fiberboard or cardboard attachments. Cornices, moldings, rails, paneling, fireplaces, doors, doorways and other trims can be con-

structed for strong architectural effects. Precision in measurements for these pieces must be emphasized because careful fit is essential.

Applique

Sometimes dimensional effects are required to give the appearance of stone, brick, rough plaster, and other surfaces on flat areas. Burlap, pieces of styrofoam, sawdust, padding, newspaper, and the like can be glued or pasted to specific areas and covered with muslin or cheesecloth dipped in a heavy size solution and molded around the forms. After drying, the surface can be painted as desired. Sawdust, cork, or ground Styrofoam can be mixed with the size or sprinkled on the surface while wet and allowed to dry before the base coat is applied.

Papier-Mâché

A commercial preparation called Instant Papier-Mâché or Celluclay can be applied to a surface and molded by hand. Make certain that the mixture is thoroughly dry before applying a base coat of paint. Small bits of paper soaked in water for a reasonable time also can be combined with paste to mold into dimensional effects.

Plastic Foams

Styrofoam, a trade name for polystyrene, is a rigid, porous, lightweight plastic. It can be purchased from local suppliers in a variety of sizes and shapes. It can be carved into statues, trims, cornices, capitals, and bas-relief effects and is easily bonded together to frames with white glue or special Styrofoam glues available from hobby shops. It can be cut with knives, power saws, electric hot-wire cutters, soldering irons, and propane torches. It also can be sanded. Before base-coating, the plastic must be covered with cheesecloth dipped in glue. Flexible polyurethane is most useful as a molding and as a trim on curved units such as columns, pillars, and cornices.

Vacuum-Formed Plastics

Shaped plastic sheets of high-impact polystyrene are commercially available at local home decorating stores, as well as theatrical and display suppliers. It is strong, flexible, and easily cut with ordinary scissors. It is especially useful when a number of duplications of three-dimensional objects are needed. Brick or stone walls, involved lengths of intricate moldings, numerous carved panels, and other dimensional items are more easily achieved through the use of these molded sheets. Vacuum-form machines are expensive, and educational theatres may find it more economical to build their own. For reference, Nicholas Bryson's book *Thermoplastic Scenery for Theatre* is recommended. Vacuum-formed impressions are made using the following procedures.

1. The thermoplastic sheet (.02 in. thick) is heated to 750°–1,000° F.
2. The sheet is stretched over a three-dimensional, hollow replica and sealed.
3. All air is removed.
4. The plastic sheet is allowed to cool and become rigid.
5. The molded form is removed from the mold and cut or trimmed as desired.

The resulting form can be attached to the scenery unit with staples, glue, or tape.

PROPERTIES AND FURNITURE

Scenery frequently has been defined as the environment of the play, and up to now we have been discussing backgrounds and dimensional units. However, the actors frequently need portable objects and articles to move around, to use and handle while telling the story. The selection of these elements, whether useful or ornamental, is the responsibility of the designer. One expects the designer of the scenery to devote the same energies and decisive expertise to researching, organizing, designing, and sometimes locating the proper furniture and other properties as is given to the set design itself.

Properties fall into four basic types or groups, depending on their use. The first, and the type most closely associated with the actual design, is set properties. These include furniture, rugs, stoves, sinks, free-standing cabinets, rocks, plants, logs, and other large items to be found in the setting itself.

Actors use the second group, called hand properties. These are small items used by the play's characters as part of their stage business and can be placed on the set before the production begins or are sometimes carried on stage by the actors. Hand properties might include luggage, guns, trays, dishes, glassware, books, canes, swords, banners, flags, signs, papers, letters, cigarettes, watches, and so on.

Properties in the third grouping comprise those items of set decoration usually not handled by the actors, but which add to the general atmosphere of the setting. They form an essential ingredient in the total visual effect of the scene, and they serve to integrate the various areas of the setting. Usually, such items consist of draperies, window treatments, tapestries, pictures, mirrors, clocks, side tables, decorative chairs, pillows, wall brackets, flower arrangements, and plants.

The final type—essentially everything not covered in the three previous categories—includes breakaway and trick effect items that have a performance purpose. These involve breakaway objects such as bottles, dishes, and crockery, as well as furniture, windowpanes, and so on. Usually, electrical devices or exploding and burning effects, which might fall into this category, are the responsibility of the effects technicians and are not among the scene designer's responsibilities.

The successful designer understands the need for accurate research for properties and careful selection for each production. Properties must be representative of the historical period of the show. Egyptian, Elizabethan, contemporary, and Restoration periods, for example, all produced their own specific furniture, eating utensils, and wall decorations. Of course, different geographi-

cal locations also imply differences in property materials and objects. A play's location may call for a specifically identified area, exterior or interior. Properties must accurately reflect these details as well as the social status, personalities, gender, age, and preferences of the play's characters.

Research for properties generally requires searching out drawings and photographs in published materials available at local libraries. Books on decoration, design, architectural details, art masterpieces, historical manners and customs, stage and motion picture production histories, as well as magazine publications of the nineteenth and twentieth centuries contain many photographs and drawings that will provide help in identifying the proper objects needed for the production. Museums, such as London's Victoria and Albert Museum, are excellent sources for property details, as are furniture stores, catalogues, antique shops, and secondhand stores. Most professional designers develop and maintain files, called morgues, for photographs, clippings, and back issues of publications for easy reference on properties.

As is the case for the design in general, listing and assembling properties required for a particular production begins with several readings of the play to ascertain the atmosphere, period, style, and locale, keeping in mind the specific technical requirements for each scene. A list should be compiled from the author's scene description, any stage directions, any mention of properties in the dialogue, and any requirements that might be involved in the implied action.

Next comes a conference with the director to learn his or her specific interpretation and wishes for staging the production. The initial list needs a thorough discussion with the director for understanding, alteration, and suggested additions. The list must be considered to be flexible, and occasional attendance at rehearsals will allow discussions of particular problems that require solutions. When agreements are reached on the property requirements, the designer needs to plan any construction and acquisition schedules and coordinate them with the technical rehearsals.

Properties are obtained for a production in several ways. The theatre organization may possess a stockroom of properties stored from previous productions. These can include furniture items, both period and contemporary, hand props, and set decor articles. If production budgets allow, a particular property may be purchased. Renting may prove more economical for some pieces, if you can find a shop owner who is willing. Establishing a written leasing agreement with the lender is essential to avoid any legal problems that might arise from damage to the article or misunderstanding of terms.

In addition, properties simply may be borrowed from commercial businesses, antique dealers, and understanding individuals. If this is standard practice for your organization, it would be to the advantage of both the lender and borrower if insurance coverage were managed by the theatre to cover any unfortunate accident to the item.

Certain properties that cannot be secured by other means will need to be constructed. Such properties include period furniture not readily available, perishable items, and properties that might be destroyed during each performance. Some stock items may need to be altered for a particular use or changed in some way to disguise their use in previous productions. Any unusual, distorted, or extreme property pieces will need to be designed by the designer and constructed in the theatre shop.

Furniture properties are usually identified by historic or cultural periods, and the designer must have a thorough knowledge of furniture styles. While historical accuracy is important, it should not overshadow the creative artistry of the design. A museum replica of an eighteenth-century drawing room may not fulfill the visual requirements of a dramatic production that needs to accentuate the mood, plot, and characters of the particular play.

Furniture can be classified by general use, shape, and construction. Most furniture is constructed of wood, although the twentieth century has seen metals, plastics, and glass used as construction materials. Usually local availability prescribed what woods were used in the various historical periods; however, modern transportation and technology has changed that. Hardwoods are favored because of their durability, and among the most popular are oak, walnut, mahogany, fruitwoods, and maple. Exotic woods such as teakwood and rosewood were used for specialized items. Veneers have assumed dominance since the Industrial Revolution in the 1850s created techniques for manufacturing mass-produced, laminated woods. Furniture woods can be decorated in several definitive ways that will help in identifying the particular historical period.

Bending	The process of curving straight wood by the application of moisture and pressure
Shaping	A method of cutting wood into specific shapes by using various saws
Applique	Decorating wood surfaces by attaching pieces of carved wood, metal, ornaments, ceramic tile, ivory inserts, and so on
Carving	Cutting or sculpting wood with knives or chisels
Turning	Shaping pieces of wood on a lathe

In general, furniture forms can be divided into three basic categories depending on how they are used: tables, seating pieces, and containers. Tables include desks, occasionals, dining, and vanities, while seating pieces involve benches, stools, sofas, love seats, armchairs, lounges, straight chairs, settees, and so on. Containers are receptacles such as chests, bookcases, buffets, sideboards, cabinets, and dressers.

WINDOW TREATMENTS

One of the most important decorative elements of interior scene design is the window treatment. Like furniture styles, window treatments can be identified with historic periods and can be most helpful in establishing mood and locale as well. Window coverings can be composed of one or more pieces of material depending on the style of the period. Sheer fabric panels, being closest to the glass, are labeled, appropriately, *glass curtains*. The material used can be semitransparent such as lace, net, or gauzelike material. A *draw drape* is a heavy fabric panel, usually two panels for each window, that involves a curtain rod or track to allow the panels to close. The material for draw drapes is usually opaque and can be velvet, satin, damask, and so on. A *valance* is a length of curtain hung in a decorative fashion across the top of a window with an *overdrape* used to mask the sides as well as the top of the window. Heavy, decorative materials such as brocades, satins, velvets, and damasks are used to mask curtain rods and rings.

FLOOR COVERINGS

Floor coverings can be additional means of identifying periods and styles. Realistic interior settings require carpeting or rugs to aid

in establishing period and locale for the play, as well as the social status of the characters. Stage ground cloths can be painted as planking, marble, tile, stone, as well as a neutral color to unify the visual elements of the setting. If a durable scene paint is used for this covering, it should also be coated with a clear acrylic or latex to allow for easy cleaning during the play's run. Because the angle of rake in many modern theatres increases the audience's ability to see more of the stage floor, the floor takes on increasing importance in the designer's responsibility. Special effects, as well as conventional floor coverings, may be required; for example, actual dirt, sand, or imitation snow may add realism to the scene. In addition to their design possibilities, floor coverings play a purely practical role. They can control unwanted foot noise made by actors and by shifting scenery.

EXTERIORS

Living plants do not last and are expensive. Artificial plants and trees are widely available locally. Time may prevent attempting to construct "real-looking" plants in theatre shops, but sometimes budget considerations outweigh other factors. Vines, which may be needed for outdoor wall decoration, can be made of a variety of materials. Artificial hedges and bushes are very expensive when purchased, but they can be constructed easily by building a framework, covering it with chicken wire, and then attaching paper leaves. Using slightly different colors of green or shadow painting on individual leaves adds to the sense of reality and creates a necessary effect of depth.

Grass is sometimes a requirement for exterior scenes. The entire acting area usually does not need to be covered. The effect of a total covering is normally less interesting than using carefully planned areas in a pleasing design. Grass matting in 6 by 10 ft. sections is sold by wholesale florist suppliers. Outdoor carpeting with the appearance of grass also is available, but it is less reasonable in price than the matting. Light-colored pile carpet can be spray-dyed and cut for stage use if it can be secured inexpensively.

DECOR ITEMS

Most unadorned walls on stage need items of decoration such as pictures, hangings, wall sconces, bell pulls, and shelves. These must be appropriate to the period, locale, and social status of the characters in the play. Walls are not the only areas that can display decorative items. Tables, mantels, bookcases, shelves, and other units of furniture can be used to hold set dressings. Framed pictures should not contain glass, because of unwanted reflections. Reflecting surfaces of mirrors can be coated to alleviate distracting reflections. Coatings can include black netting, matte-fixative spray, or light wax. Recognizable paintings by known artists should not be used unless required in the script, because they create a visual distraction for the audience.

Other important decor items include lighting instruments such as chandeliers, candelabras, lamps, and wall sconces, all of which, again, must reflect the period and locale of the production. Open flames should be avoided whenever possible and, in fact, may be unlawful in many communities. Ornamental vases, statues, flower arrangements, clocks, plates, and other items should be included in set dressing, and all of these enhance the designer's ability to make a comprehensive statement in the set design.

Special effects may sometimes be involved with scenery and properties, and the designer must be aware of the solutions, techniques, and problems involved. Some effects, which are used repeatedly in television and motion pictures are impractical for use in the live theatre. Occasionally productions require fog, running water, rain, snow, fires, winds, and explosions. Consultation with the technical director, lighting designer, and stage managers helps to make decisions regarding the best solutions for these effects and how they can be integrated into the final design. Ideally, solutions should be simple, believable, repeatable, and, above all, safe.

THE SHOP

A scene shop should be as carefully planned as any factory assembly plant, but, unfortunately, few are. Therefore, the designer and the shop technician must constantly adjust to less-than-efficient operational procedures. Theatre building planners usually focus more attention on the auditorium and the public rooms than on the actual working areas. The stage area may be given consideration on the basis of presentation, but the scene shop areas are seldom examined. As a result, most theatre shops are inadequate for the basic production requirements of the particular organization. Because the designer often must share space in the shop for his or her responsibilities, it is essential that the designer understand how a shop should be organized, used, and equipped.

Basic Shop Requirements

The size of the shop is directly related to the size of the theatre's performance areas. Scenic units need to be constructed and assembled so they will closely approximate their position and appearance on the stage itself. If the production requires more than one setting, the shop requirements must allow for additional space to handle production demands. Frequently, one shop area must serve several performance areas, and it is not unusual for two and even three productions to be in preparation at one time. A repertory program is certain to make additional demands on shop space ordinarily committed to a conventional program. The actual construction of scenery units requires reasonable and unencumbered floor space that is in addition and unrelated to space for assembled units for trimming and painting.

The location of the shop in relation to the other theatre areas is also an important consideration. For example, a shop attached to a rehearsal or performance area is bound to create major conflicts with rehearsal, performance, and shop schedules. The noise generated by shop activity will be in direct conflict with rehearsal, lecture, or performance activity. Soundproofing in these circumstances would be an absolute necessity. The shop also must be located adjacent to, or, at least close by, the loading area to allow for deliveries of materials and equipment. Because the finished setting needs to be moved from the work area, it is advantageous to have the shop on the same level as the performance area, thereby allowing easy movement from one location to another. To permit maximum efficiency, storage spaces need to be in close proximity to the shop.

Educational theatre buildings need space for teaching students of stagecraft and design in addition to actual set building for a production, which must follow its own separate schedule. The number of workers who will use the shop facilities needs to be carefully considered, inasmuch as appropriate and adequate space must be provided. Four full-time professional technicians will require a much different organizational and spatial plan than will fifteen amateur volunteers. Finally, ascertainment must be made of the type of productions planned, whether

experimental, classic dramas, musical comedies, operas, or any or all of these. Planning should focus on the most demanding of the types planned relative to amount and size of the scenery required. That is, one should plan for the space needed to build and paint the most complicated of the possible productions.

Space Areas

The various functions of the shop need to be examined carefully in order to plan for efficiency. An area sized for reasonable construction of two-dimensional scenery as well as three-dimensional units needs to be available. Once units are built, they need to be assembled in a trial setup similar to the finished stage plan. The next step requires the painting of scenery, and those area requirements are vastly different from those of the construction space. Wall space, floor space, incandescent lighting, paint frames, plumbing, and paint storage are all special considerations for painting.

Storage areas for scenic elements, drops, properties, and electrical equipment must not be omitted; few theatrical organizations can afford to create everything new for each production. Property construction requires space for the building of small hand props and larger items such as furniture and special units. Metalworking equipment and work with plastics make special demands on safety, ventilation, and storage.

Safety and Security

The theatre scene shop is no different from any other shop involved with machinery, construction, assembly, electrical equipment, and a staff of workers. Consequently, the same safety codes and regulations apply. Advisory organizations regarding safety are the National Safety Council, the American National Standards Institute, the National Fire Protection Association, the American Society of Safety Engineers, and the National Board of Fire Underwriters. Their standards and regulations must be fundamental to any shop layout and operation.

Municipal and county governments generally adopt specific ordinances cut from various nationally established codes, such as the Basic Building Code, the National Building Code, and others, to institute minimum building standards for safety and health. Electrical safety practices set up by the National Fire Protection Association also are adopted by local and state governments. In 1970, a federal agency, the Occupational Safety and Health Administration (OSHA) was empowered by an act of Congress with broad authority. OSHA regulates

1. Building construction design
2. Building ventilation
3. Electrical equipment
4. Fire protection
5. Uses of machinery
6. Sanitary elements
7. Possible air contamination
8. Light and noise exposure
9. Protection implements on power equipment

In addition to OSHA, an organization for studies and research entitled the National Institute for Occupational Safety and Health was established at the same time.

To establish accident prevention in the well-organized shop, several safety measures need to be in constant practice. Some of the more important are

1. Sprinkler systems for fire protection
2. Numerous fire extinguishers
3. Auxiliary lighting equipment in case of power failure
4. Well-marked escape routes
5. Well-lighted areas around power tools
6. Protective guards and devices on tools and around electrical facilities
7. Adequate ventilation
8. Safety instruction for unskilled workers
9. Fireproof storage for combustible materials
10. Proper attire for workers, including proper work shoes with hard toe caps and nonslip, puncture-resistant soles. Covered hair and practical, fitted garments
11. Enforcement of no-smoking rules
12. Job assignments appropriate to and not beyond the worker's capabilities
13. Readily available first-aid equipment
14. Shop tools kept in working condition at all times
15. The shop kept as clean as possible at all times

Accidents do happen; remember: Be prepared.

Many municipal codes require fireproofing, and it may be necessary to check on what materials are to be included and which type of retardant is required. Actually, *fireproofing* is a misnomer, for it is basically a *fire-retardant* procedure. The usual items include all the standard scenery units, plus draperies and artificial foliage. The customary test made by local inspectors is to observe the effect of a match held for twelve seconds against the material in question. Most scenery materials can be purchased already fireproofed, and that is usually worth the slightly higher cost. However, a flame-proofing compound that will usually meet established standards can be prepared in the shop. The recipe for this compound is

1 lb of sal ammoniac
1 lb of borax
1/2 pint of vinegar
1 gallon of hot water

The compound can be sprayed on whatever materials and units need to be "proofed."

The application will usually be effective for a five-year period.

Tools

Every scene shop requires a set of basic equipment appropriate to construction of scenery and properties. What follows is a list of tools and their usage.

HAMMERS

Claw Hammer: Common tool and nail driver. Claw is used for pulling. Weights are 10-ounce, 13-ounce, and 16-ounce. The head is drop-forged steel with a bell face and curved claw. Handle can be steel with rubber grip or hickory. Head of wood-handled hammer is secured with a wedge. Repaired by additional wedges. Used for removing partially driven nails (Fig. 8.9).

Rip Hammer: Used for rough work (straight claw). Heavy-duty, drop-forged steel. Handle is of steel or fiberglass. Used for ripping apart.

Used for driving nails and only for woodworking. Use a block for greater leverage and for separating joined lumber. Weights are 10-ounce, 13-ounce, and 20-ounce (Fig. 8.9).

Tack Hammer: Magnetic head, weights are 4-ounce to 14-ounce. Used to tack fabric to wood. The 12- and 14-ounce hammers are used to secure webbing. Four- to 7-ounce hammers have very slender heads. Hammer has one magnetized face for tacks (Fig. 8.9).

Mallet: Made of wood or plastic for driving chisels and can be used to shape metal. Rubber mallets are also available. Tool does not leave hammer marks on work (Fig. 8.9).

Ball Peen: A 12-ounce and 16-ounce cylindrical face with a ball-shaped peen and an oval wooden handle. Used to work on metal parts and to rivet ends of bolts to prevent nut from coming off. Made of hardened steel (Fig. 8.9).

SAWS

Crosscut: A hand saw to cut across wood grain. Teeth, filed to a 65-degree angle and leaning

Figure 8.9 Hammers.

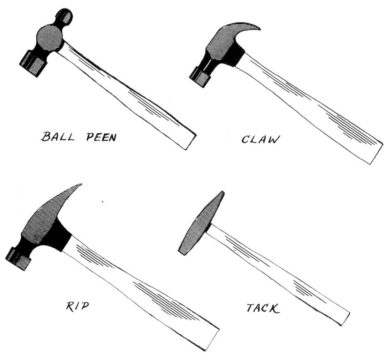

BALL PEEN

CLAW

RIP

TACK

outward in alternating directions. Low points on teeth cut faster but leave a rougher surface (Fig. 8.10).

Rip: A hand saw to cut with the grain of the wood. Six and eight points per inch is standard. Rip teeth are filed flat, like chisels, to remove wood. Has fewer teeth than crosscut saw and is slightly wider and of heavier steel. Teeth are set alternately to widen the cut. The saw cuts only on forward strokes (Fig. 8.10).

Coping: Used for delicate work, curved, or irregular shapes. Replaceable blades are 6 in. to 6 5/8 in. long. Different types of blades for plastic, metal, and wood. Blades have sixteen to eighteen teeth per inch. The blade is held in position by spring tension. These saw blades cannot be sharpened (Fig. 8.10).

Keyhole: The keyhole saw, sometimes known as a compass saw, has a narrower, tapered blade. Used for tight places that cannot be cut by other hand saws. Blades have ten to twelve teeth per inch. Used for stock lumber and plywood. Pistol-grip wood or plastic handle. Saw is crosscut-filed and must be sharp. It is suitable for making curved or straight cuts from a bored hole (Fig. 8.10).

Hack: Primarily for cutting metal. Choice of blade depends on type of metal and the thick-

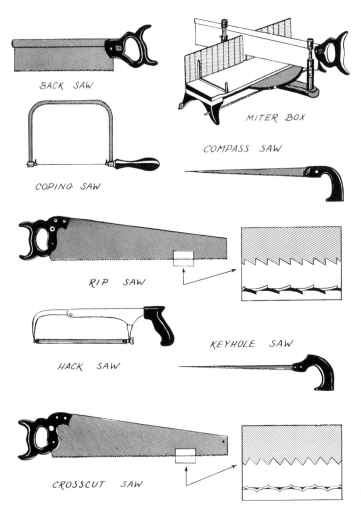

Figure 8.10 Hand saws.

ness. Steel, high-speed blades are most useful. Fourteen teeth per inch are used for aluminum, copper, brass, cast iron, or machine steel 1 in. thick or more. Eighteen teeth per inch are used for 1/4-in. to 1-in. metal. Twenty-four teeth per inch blades are used for 1/8-in. to 1/4-in. metals. Thirty-two teeth per inch used for thinner metals. Blades are 8–12 in. in length. Saws have pistol grip handles. Blades cannot be sharpened. Use oil on file and cut while operating to avoid overheating (Fig. 8.10).

Back: Used for accurate and precise angular cuts with accompanying *miter.* The blade is stif-

fened at the top by a metal spine that acts as a guide in the miter box. There are twelve or more points per inch. Miter box is adjustable for the angles which are usually 90 or 45 degrees. Saw will bend. Used for cutting accurate cabinet and furniture joints, picture frames, and cornices. Blades are 10–16 in. in length (Fig. 8.10).

TOOLS FOR MEASURING AND MARKING

Folding Wood Rule: Used for general measuring where rigidity is needed: 6 ft. by 8 ft. by 1/2 in. Very accurate but easily broken (Fig. 8.11).

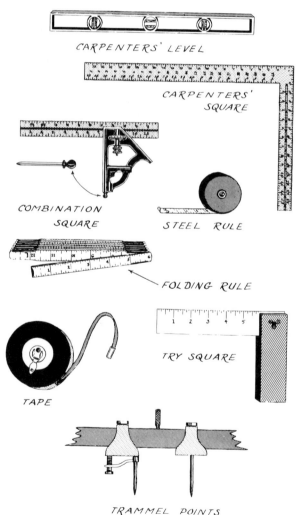

Figure 8.11 Measuring devices.

Retractable Steel Tapes: Eight, ten, twelve, sixteen, and twenty-five ft. windup tapes. Fifty and 100-ft. tapes in plastic or metal cases. Some can be locked in extended position. Tape is usually 1/2 in. wide. Reasonably accurate, flexible, and compact (Fig. 8.11).

Try Square: Used to test adjoining surfaces for squareness and to mark for angle cuts. Size is 7-in. steel blade in 5-in. wood, steel, or plastic handle. To be used on narrow stock lumber (Fig. 8.11).

Combination Square: Twelve-inch blade, 90- and 45-degree handle. A calibrated scale 1/32 in. to 1 in. Double-faced side is segmented differently. Some models have a spirit level and a steel scriber point. Used like a try square but is capable of marking a miter angle (Fig. 8.11).

Framing Square: This square measures 18 in. on the outside edge and 16 in. on the inside edge. The blade is 24 in. on the outside and 22 1/2 in. on the inside edge. Made of steel or aluminum, it has a 1/16-in. and 1/8-in. graduation on one face and 1/12-in. and 1/16-in. on the opposite face. Used for squaring, framing, and

accurate measuring. Necessary for layout of steps, flats, and platform construction. It determines true horizontal and vertical angles. Used to check right angles and right-angled joints as well as to compute any angle markings for cuts (8.11).

Bevel: Used to measure an angle cut and transfer it to another piece of wood (Fig. 8.11).

SCREWDRIVERS

Standard: Blade length ranges from 2 in. pocket size to 8 in. Blade width varies from 1/8 in. to 3/8 in. A steel shaft is flattened at the tip to fit a slot cut in the screw head; the fitted handle is of hard wood or plastic composition. Used to turn screws. It is matched to screw and size (Fig. 8.12).

Phillips: Point sizes are 0, 1, 2, and 3. Shaft length is from 2 3/4 in. to 5 3/4 in. Used for Phillips screws only. The four-flanged tip matches the slots of Phillips-head screws. This tool is also available in 6 and 8 in. sizes (Fig. 8.12).

Ratchet: Has a very handy spiral action. Shaft is

Figure 8.12 Screw drivers.

spiral ratchet with spring chuck to hold two or more sizes of bits. It has a three-position adjustment: forward, reverse, or lock position. Used for setting or removing screws quickly and needs maintenance occasionally (Fig. 8.12).

WRENCHES

Adjustable End: An end wrench with knurled adjustment set into larger jaw. Used for tightening bolts, it is an excellent general wrench. Also known as a crescent wrench. Switch jaws, 6 in., 8 in., and 10 in. are most suitable for the stage. It can be altered to fit several sizes of nuts (Fig. 8.13).

Open End: Nonadjustable with smooth jaws (Fig. 8.13).

Allen: Also called a hex-key wrench. Fits hexagonal recesses and is also a setscrew wrench.

Monkey: A heavyweight smooth-jawed, adjustable wrench for use on large units and for work too large for adjustable-end wrenches (Fig. 8.13).

Vise Grip: Seven- and ten-inch overall length. It combines advantages of common pliers with those of an adjustable wrench. The adjustable bolt in the end of one grip handle and a lock spring combines a vise action with strong pressure.

PLIERS

Slip-joint: A two-position pivot that provides normal and wide jaw openings. The 6- and 8-in. sizes are used for bending wire and for hold-

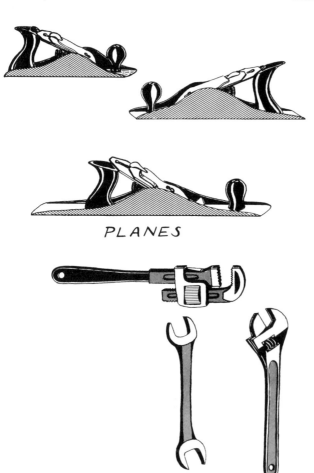

PLANES

Figure 8.13   Wrenches, planes.

ing the nut while tightening stove bolts. Used for general grasping operations. The adjustable pivot point provides two types of jaw openings. Use for clamping, gripping, bending, and cutting light wire.

Lineman's: Also known as side-cutting pliers; used for heavy-duty wire cutting and splicing.

Long-nose: Used for holding small objects in hard-to-reach locations. Used to shape wire and thin metal, often for cutting as well.

End-cutting: Used for snipping wire, small nails, and brads.

PLANES

Block: The smallest plane is 6 or 7 in. long. A 1 5/8-in. wide blade is mounted at a low angle. Used for smoothing and shaving the end grain of lumber. Depth of cut is adjustable (Fig. 8.13).

Smoothing: Eight to 14 in. long and 2 in. wide, the usual size is 9 in. It planes in the direction of the wood grain and has an adjustable cutting depth and a pistol grip (Fig. 8.13).

Draw Knife: Used for rough shaping. Also used for curved and straight-edge cuts. The cutting width is from 10–12 in. (Fig. 8.15).

Spokeshave: Used to smooth curved edges, neither convex nor concave. Must be cut with grain. This plane has removable blades (Fig. 8.15).

DRILLS

Hand: A crank-operated tool consisting of a large wheel gear working with a smaller gear which then turns a drill chuck. The drills can range from 1/32 in. to 1/4 in. The hand drill is used to drill straight holes in wood or metal (Fig. 8.14).

Breast: A heavy-duty hand drill that has a curved extension instead of a main handle to allow the operator to apply more force to the drilling. Can use bits up to 3/8 in. (Fig. 8.14).

Brace and Bit: A hand drill that can accomplish the same jobs as a power drill, only taking a longer time. It can be used where electrical power would be inaccessible. The brace works as a turning crank with a chuck to hold the bit. For use in honing holes in wood. Bits are 1/4 in. to 1 in. Countersink bits and screwdriver bits also are used with this tool (Fig. 8.14).

Push: Used for drilling small holes in wood. The bits can be stored in the handle. It has a spring-loaded shaft that works the drill points. Used for starting holes for screws. Drill size 1/64 in. to 11/64 in. (Fig. 8.14).

CHISELS

Butt: This tool is 7–9 in. long and is used for tight spaces. It is a sharp woodcutting tool and has a plastic handle. The blade is cut to a 30-degree angle. Used by tapping with a mallet (Fig. 8.15).

Pocket: This chisel is 9–10 1/2 in. long and has the same uses as the Butt chisel. It ranges from 1/4 in. to 1 1/2 in. in width and is used for cutting grooves, slats, mortises in lumber, and for general work (Fig. 8.15).

Paring: This chisel is 16 in. long and used for heavy work. Its thin blade is ground to a 25-degree angle and is used for precision work (Fig. 8.15).

Cold: A strong, heavy steel chisel in four general types; flat, cape, round nose, and diamond point. They are effective with metals and masonry. Size is 3/4 in. in diameter and 7 in. in length (Fig. 8.15).

FILES

Wood Rasp: Flat sides or one rounded side. Coarse teeth used for rough shaping. Ten and 12 in. long. Handle is detachable.

Wood File: Has smaller teeth than wood rasp. Like the rasp, it is 10 and 12 in. long and has a detachable handle.

Metal File: Usually 8 and 10 in. in length, its teeth range from coarse to fine. It is used only on metal.

Surform Tools: Trademarked tools with thin blades that have holes with sharpened edges. Works as a grater against wood, plastic, and metals.

VISES AND CLAMPS

Machinist's Vises: These are either clamp-on or bolt-on variety. The bases have regular or pipe jaws with at least a 3 1/2 in. opening, and are used to clamp wood for planing, shaping, drilling, and sawing. These vises are generally mounted on the edge of a workbench or table and flush with the top (Fig. 8.15).

C-clamp: Used to clamp two or more pieces of lumber together tightly after gluing or to hold

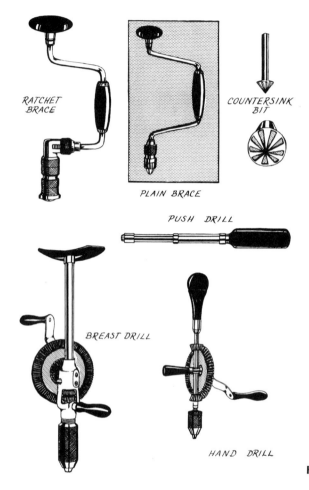

RATCHET
BRACE

COUNTERSINK
BIT

PLAIN BRACE

PUSH DRILL

BREAST DRILL

HAND DRILL

Figure 8.14   Braces and drills.

them together for sawing. The clamp opening should be 1–4 in. Pieces of plywood should be inserted between the jaws to protect the lumber surface. A most versatile tool for any shop (Fig. 8.15).

Woodworking Vises: These vises are mounted at the edge of a bench, and the top of the jaws should be flush with the bench top. The jaws of the vise are lined with wood for protection of the work (Fig. 8.15).

Adjustable Wood Clamp: Generally used for a secure hold on flat and angled work. These clamps can be adjusted to an angle, which can be a distinct advantage (Fig. 8.15).

Bar and Pipe Clamps: Also called cabinet or furniture clamps, these clamps have jaws that are

mounted on a flat steel bar in 12- and 48-in. lengths. The pipe is usually 1/2 in. or 3/4 in. steel pipe and can be any length. The clamp is tightened by a crank handle (Fig. 8.15).

MISCELLANEOUS TOOLS

Compression Stapler: Using 5/32-in. to 9/16-in. staples, this tool is for attaching muslin or canvas to flats and for attaching other thin materials, such as cardboard, to other wooden units. Also known as a staple gun or hand stapler (Fig. 8.16).

Sand Block: This is a block of wood wrapped with sandpaper, which can range from very coarse to fine. Depending on the type of abrasive,

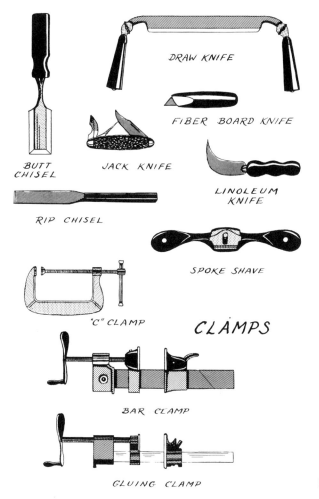

Figure 8.15 Chisels, knives and clamps.

Figure 8.16 Stapler.

sandpaper can be used on wood, plastic, fiberglass, and metals.

Staple Hammer: A handle tool with a tacker head used for stapling platform coverings, ground cloths, and other materials to the appropriate surfaces.

Scissors: Heavy-duty scissors for cutting canvas, muslin, and paper.

Utility Knife: Generally 6 in. long with a 2 1/2-in. double-ended blade used for trimming muslin, canvas, corrugated cardboard, and other stock.

Crowbar: Also called a pinch bar. This heavy steel tool is used for prying boards. One end is slightly bent and flattened for prying, while the other end is notched for pulling nails.

Grommet Setting Dies: This tool involves a small anvil-type base and a straight 4-in. heavy metal tool that inserts into the base for crimping the No. 2 brass rings that reinforce the holes in stage hangings such as drapes, curtains, and ground cloths.

Electric Glue Gun: A tool that supplies hot glue to a surface by squeezing a trigger. The quick drying quality of the glue makes it a very useful tool for any scene shop.

Sharpening Stone: Also called an oilstone, this item is made of abrasive compounds such as silicon carbide that can be coated with lubricating oil and used to sharpen planes, chisels, and knives. It usually has a coarse side and a fine side, for specific uses.

Tin Snips: Steel shears for cutting sheet metal are available in 7, 10, and 12-in. lengths.

Power Tools

It is difficult to imagine turning out the quantity and quality of work that has come to be associated with theatre technicians without the help of power tools. It may not be necessary to equip a scene shop with all the power tools described here, but the following descriptions of various tools will give the designer and the technician an estimate of the efficiency and capabilities of these tools.

Power tools can be as dangerous as they are helpful. Contrary to first impression, an electric saw requires more skill and care than a hand saw. Some educational scene shops will allow only qualified staff members or a professional shop supervisor to operate the power equipment. Students of scene construction should be carefully instructed in the care and operation of power tools, if they are to use them.

Cut-Awl. The cut-awl is a portable tool consisting of a motor-driven blade or chisel,

that can be slowly pulled or drawn along penciled lines. The blade moves up and down at a rapid rate, cutting through the material. With different blades, the cut-awl will make fine cuts through fiberboard, plywood, and even 1-in. white pine stock. The material that is to be cut must be placed on a sturdy work bench covered with a sheet of fiberboard. The flat surface of the cut-awl is placed on the work and then guided slowly over the outline. Since the cut-awl is portable, it can cut any size surface and is especially useful executing difficult, scroll details. This tool needs to be stored in a dust-free case when not in use and kept well oiled at all times (Fig. 8.17).

Heavy-duty Sewing Machine. Similar to the family machine, except larger and faster, the heavy-duty machine is clutch-driven, which makes for faster starting. Some machines are self-oiling and need little attention. This tool is used for sewing drapes, curtains, ground cloths, drops, and properties. The machine should be carefully stored and covered when not in use.

Sabre Saw. A portable, hand-held saw with a rigid blade, the sabre saw executes both straight and curved cuts. Different blades are used for different types and thicknesses of materials.

Circular Saw. The portable circular saw is a dangerous power tool that must be handled with care. It contains a motor enclosed in an aluminum frame held at the top by a handle with a trigger switch. There is an extra knob on the side for two-handed use. The circular blade is protected on the top and bottom by metal guards. Blade size can range from 6–8 in., but 7 1/2 in. is usual. The saw must be checked and lubricated regularly and stored in a protected case when not in use.

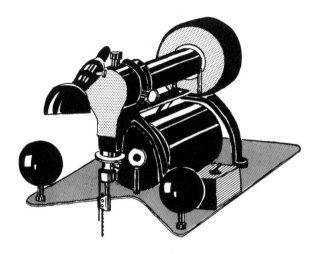

Figure 8.17 Cut-Awl.

Power Electric Drill. This tool, with a pistol-grip handle and a trigger switch uses several drill sizes, the most useful of which are 1/4 in., 1/2 in., and 3/8 in. The variable-speed model provides the greatest efficiency. Twist drill bits for countersinking and screwdriver bits are also extremely useful. The drill should be unplugged when not in use and stored in a safe place (Fig. 8.18).

Radial Arm Saw. Sometimes known as the pullover saw, this power tool works on a horizontal arm above the lumber and is pulled over the lumber manually. The arm has a 90-degree swivel, allowing the saw to make rip cuts, crosscuts, and angle cuts. The smallest model uses a 10-in., circular, all-purpose blade, and the largest model takes a 16-in. blade. The saw should be mounted in the center of a bench with a minimum length of twenty-eight feet to allow for ripping fourteen-foot lengths of lumber. This saw, the most versatile of power saws, is the most expensive, but it is well worth its cost if the shop has a heavy production schedule.

Table Band Saw. The table band saw uses a continuous saw blade running on two wheels with the blade intersecting the horizontal table plate. The wheels' sizes govern the length of the arm supporting the top section. Used for cutting single, thick pieces of lumber or a combination of pieces in single or double curves or in a combination of curves, this tool is extremely useful in the building of scenery (Fig. 8.19). A protective guard encloses most of the saw blade. The guard must be kept closed when the saw operates. Like most power tools, the band saw must be kept clean and checked monthly for oil and lubrication. The oil used is SAE 10 machine oil.

Bench Drill. This table drill or drill press is mounted on an upright column with a minimum diameter of 2 3/4 in. Attached to the column is a flat, metal table that is adjustable in height. The drill lowers down toward the table where the object to be drilled rests. A table drill can be converted into a combination tool by adding accessories. Accessories create the ability to mix paint, rout, sand, cut joints, and perform many other functions. The primary use of the table drill, however, remains the drilling of holes in metal and wood. Lubricate and oil this tool to keep it in efficient working order.

Wood-turning Lathe. A lathe is a long, narrow tool of heavy steel. At one end is the

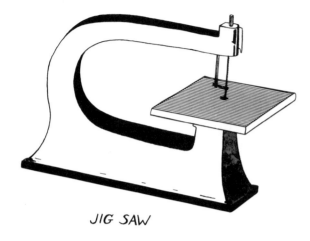

JIG SAW

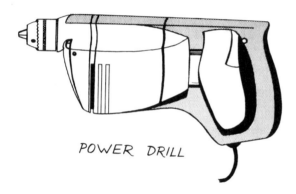

POWER DRILL

Figure 8.18 Jig saw and Power drill.

headstock, a solidly cast frame attached to the bed or bottom framework of the lathe. The headstock contains four wheels or pulleys that govern the speed of the lathe. A belt attached to a motor turns the pulleys in the headstock. The other end of the lathe has an adjustable tailstock that can move along tracks toward the headstock. Lumber that is to be turned is placed tightly between these two stocks and revolved. A sharp chisel is held against the wood to shape it into a design as it revolves. The lathe is used for making stair railings, table legs, and so on. Like all power tools, the lathe needs to be kept lubricated according to the manufacturer's instructions. It should be kept clean and covered when not in use. The chisel used with this must be kept sharp for best results (Fig. 8.20).

Portable Staple Gun. This tool gives the technician the fastest and most economical means for building the basic flat unit. It also comes in air-driven models. Operated by hand, the stapler has a trigger lever in the handle that, when depressed, drives one sta-

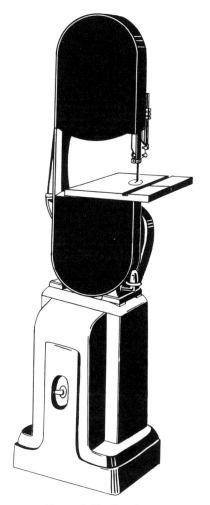

Figure 8.19 Band saw.

ple at a time into the material. Heavy-duty staples are required for this power-driven tool.

Electric Sander. This hand power tool is used to smooth rough wood and requires sandpaper discs and belts. Because sandpaper wears quickly, the tool requires frequent replacement of discs and belts for highest efficiency.

Metalworking Tools

During recent years, the use of metal has become extremely important in scene designing, not only as a functional replacement for lumber structures and supports, but also for pure sculptural effect, emphasizing form, texture, and color. Many scene shops now contain metalworking areas with welding equipment under the careful supervision of qualified technicians.

The designer may choose from three kinds of welding: gas, electric arc, and gas-metal arc. All three need careful safety precautions, and any equipment operators must be thoroughly instructed in handling welding tools, which must always be maintained in first-class condition. Local fire regulations need to be checked carefully before installation, and precautionary protective clothing as well as goggles must be worn while operating the equipment.

Gas welding involves igniting a mixture of oxygen and acetylene in a torch to produce a flame that burns at 6,000° F. The flame is controlled by adjustable valves on the torch itself. The two gases are kept in steel storage tanks under pressure, and regulators on the tanks control the amount of gas flow into flexible hoses connected to the hand-held torch.

Electric arc welding utilizes an electric spark arcing between an electrode or rod and the metal to be welded. The electric arc generates an intense heat of approximately 13,000° F and comes from a welding transformer. A cable from the transformer is connected to the metal material, and when the electrode is introduced to complete the circuit, a fusion results.

Gas-metal arc welding is a one-handed operation that makes welding easier to accomplish. This process uses a wire-fed electrode and a flexible hose leading to a nozzle. Some systems use a tungsten electrode in the

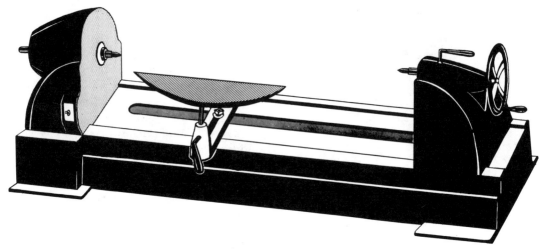

Figure 8.20 Lathe.

nozzle instead of the wire electrode. This equipment is quite heavy and not particularly portable, which may present some problems in smaller shops.

The scene designer who wishes to use the capabilities of metal in a design needs to consult thoroughly with the technical director or the shop foreman concerning the limitations of the available equipment. Those who design in the educational theatre and whose shops or budgets do not permit the purchase of welding equipment should check with the art department's sculpture professor. Nearly every college art department sculpture program has welding capability, and some accommodation on use of that equipment may be reachable.

MATERIALS

Lumber

Northern white pine and Douglas fir are the most practical for scenery (Fig. 8.21). Pine probably is the best, because it is rela-tively soft, strong, and lightweight. Fir is heavier, harder, and splintery. Choice grades are called select grades, and less choice grades are called common grades. Select grades are classified as A, B, C, and D and are judged on the basis of amount of knots, blemishes, and pitch marks. Generally, common grades are numbered 1 and 2. Lumber can be obtained in stock lengths in even numbers from eight feet to sixteen feet. Widths range from two inches to twelve inches. Thickness is labeled 1 in. or 2 in. However, lumber does not actually measure the exact dimension of either its width or thickness. That is, 1 inch thick lumber such as a 1 by 3 will actually measure only 3/4 in. by approximately 2 3/4 in. Lumber is priced by either the board foot or the linear foot. Moldings and trim strips are sold by the linear foot. Molding is available in quarter-round, half-round, cove, bed, crown, picture, and casing, and is used for paneling effects, door trim, handrail trim, mantle trim, cornices, and wainscoting. Dowel rods, poles, and handrails also are useful.

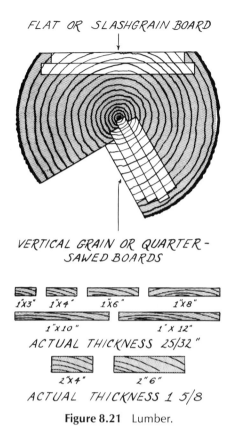

FLAT OR SLASHGRAIN BOARD

VERTICAL GRAIN OR QUARTER-
SAWED BOARDS

1"x3"   1"x4"   1"x6"   1"x8"

1"x10"   1"x12"

ACTUAL THICKNESS 25/32"

2"x4"   2"6"

ACTUAL THICKNESS 1 5/8

Figure 8.21 Lumber.

Douglas fir plywood is a sheet of thin, bonded, layered wood with the grain of each layer running in the opposite direction. Standard-size sheets are 4 by 8 ft., with thicknesses ranging from 1/8 in. to 3/4 in. Plywood comes in two types: interior and exterior. The difference lies in the bonding agent, which is moisture-resistant in the exterior type. Each type comes in grades A-B or C-D and is priced by the square foot.

Hardboard or Masonite, which is a trade name, is made of wood fibers and particles and comes in sizes similar to plywood. It also is sold by the square foot. Available in two degrees of hardness, the untempered board is softer than the tempered board. Tempered board is frequently used for a stage floor overlay because of its durability.

Fabric

The scene designer needs to be familiar with the various types and qualities of fabrics used for flat building, drops, curtains, draperies, floor coverings, upholstery, property construction, and other purposes. Some materials may be available at local stores, whereas others will need to be secured from stage equipment companies. The following is a listing of the more popular types of cloth materials used for stage purposes.

Bobbinet. Bobbinet is a cotton mesh material frequently used for curtain scrim. It is available in many different grades and widths. It can be secured in local stores in 36 in.- 42 in.- and 48 in.-widths and from theatre supply houses in 30 ft. widths. It will stretch under weight, but it takes paint and dye well. It is used for scrim and mist effects and as a base for glued or sewn applique, prop curtains, and so on.

Broadcloth. Broadcloth is a tight and plain woven cotton available in five or six different grades. It can be obtained locally in both white and colors in 36 in.- and 30 in.-widths. It is used primarily for properties and decor, such as curtains. It dyes easily.

Canvas. Canvas, also known as duck, is a tightly woven cotton that is stiff and firm. It is graded according to ounce weight and is obtainable in 8-, 10-, and 12-ounce weights. The 8-ounce weight is generally preferred. It is available in 36 in.-, 48 in.-, 60 in.-, and 72 in.-widths and is used primarily for covering flats, making drops and ceiling pieces, and for covering surface areas to be painted. The heavier weights are used for ground cloths and tents. Canvas takes paint well and dyes fairly well, depending on the amount of dressing in the cloth. Many scene shops buy this material in 100-yard rolls to avail themselves of the price discount.

Carpeting. Carpeting is a floor covering made of wool, cotton, or synthetic materials in clipped pile, woven jute, or burlap. The Wilton weave is the most serviceable for a stage cover, especially to deaden noise. Carpeting can be cut to fit the tops of platforms, stair treads, and so on. It also can be used as set dressing for realistic interiors and dyed various greens to resemble grass for exterior scenes. Usually plain neutral colors are preferred.

Carpet Padding. Carpet padding frequently is used on stage floors, stair treads, and platform tops to deaden noise. It requires covering by a rug or a tightly woven cloth, such as a canvas ground cloth, to prevent wear. Available in 6- to 9-ft. widths, it can be pieced together with tape.

Duvetyne. Duvetyne is a twill-weave cotton with a raised nap surface on one side. Scenery or fabric stores carry duvetyne in several grades, in widths up to 50 in., and in a large range of colors. Draperies, curtains, and cycloramas form its major uses in the theatre. However, repeated cleaning will flatten the nap of this fabric.

Flannelette. Flannelette is a soft, fleecy cotton fabric with a soft nap surface. Available in three grades and two widths, 27 in. and 36 in., it dyes well, but the nap will not withstand many washings. It can serve as an inexpensive substitute for duvetyne.

Gauze. Gauze comes in several types of weaves and weights. The more popular types are shark's tooth scrim, theatrical scrim, and bobbinette. Scenic netting, not unlike tennis netting, can also be included in the family of gauzes. Shark's-tooth scrim, available in 30 ft. widths and in three colors—sky-blue, black, and white—is the scene designer's most useful fabric because of its excellent opaque quality as well as its transparency. It takes dye very well and is easily painted.

Theatrical scrim, sometimes known as linen scrim, is limited in widths and is less opaque than shark's tooth scrim. Its natural linen color may influence the hold of dye colors. Bobbinette is a very lightweight gauze and consequently is very fragile, which limits its use. It is available in 30 ft. widths and in three colors—black, white, and sky-blue. Its delicacy calls for special handling. Scenic netting is usually found in 1-in. squares and in widths of 30 ft. Also known as fishnet, it is used to connect cutout areas in drops and legs and glued on the back of a unit. Generally, gauzes are available only from scenic supply houses.

Monk's Cloth. Monk's cloth is a heavy basket-weave cotton fabric available in natural (light tan) or colors. It has an interesting texture under stage lighting. It comes in three grades, according to the number of threads in the weave: two-ply, four-ply, and eight-ply. This fabric takes dye readily and can be purchased at theatrical supply houses and local stores in 36-in. and 48-in. widths. It is used mainly for draperies, curtains, and cycloramas.

Unbleached Muslin. Muslin is a firm, plain-weave cotton cloth graded according to the number of threads per square inch. No. 1 grade is the heaviest and averages 140 threads per square inch. No. 2 grade has 128 threads to the square inch, and No. 3 grade has 112 threads per square inch; it is the lightest weight. No. 2 is the preferred weight. Muslin comes either bleached (white) or unbleached (light cream). Only unbleached muslin should be used on the stage. Muslin comes in many widths from 36 in. to 108 in. Many of these widths can be purchased from local dealers, but it is possible to purchase unbleached muslin in 30-ft. widths from theatrical suppliers. It also can be ordered flame-proofed. Unbleached muslin probably is the most versatile and serviceable material for the theatrical shop, because it can be used for covering flats, three-dimensional units, curtains, drops, ceiling pieces, and various property pieces. It takes dye very well and has a fine painting surface.

Plush. Plush is a deep-pile, rayon fabric available in three grades and two widths; 36 in. and 50 in. It usually can be purchased in local drapery and upholstery stores. Generally, it can be used for properties, curtains, and upholstery.

Repp. Repp is a durable, strong fabric of silk, rayon, or cotton with a finely corded surface. Usually available in only one grade, it comes in two widths: 36 in. and 48 in. It can be purchased locally or ordered from a theatrical supplier in a wide variety of colors. It is used for curtains, upholstery, cycloramas, and draperies.

Sateen. Sateen is a cotton fabric with a satin weave and is available in three grades and three widths: 36 in., 45 in., and 50 in. Used for draperies, properties, curtains, and curtain linings, it can be purchased in many colors at local stores as well as from theatrical jobbers.

Satin. Satin is silk, nylon, or rayon fabric with a smooth glossy surface and a dull backing. There are three popular grades and widths from 36 in. to 50 in. Satin is used for upholstery, properties, curtains, and draperies and can be obtained in many colors from local fabric stores and theatrical supply houses.

Taffeta. Taffeta is a rayon or silk fabric that is thin and rather stiff with a slight surface sheen. Two grades vary with the size of the yarn, 180 denier and 300 denier. Taffeta comes in 45-in. widths and in many colors. Use it only for decor purposes.

Teddy Bear Cloth. Teddy bear cloth is a cotton-backed, rayon-faced fabric with a deep pile. Obtainable in three grades, it comes in 36-in. and 54-in. widths. Difficult to purchase locally, it normally comes from theatrical suppliers. It comes in many colors and takes dye exceedingly well. It can be used for curtains, cycloramas, draperies, and properties.

Terry Cloth. Terry cloth is a cotton fabric covered with loops on one side or both sides and available in two grades. It has only one width, 36 in., but it comes in many colors, as well as white, which dyes easily. It usually can be purchased locally as well as from theatrical suppliers and is used for curtains, draperies, and inexpensive cycloramas. Because of its interesting texture, it frequently passes for more luxurious material.

Tobacco Cloth. Tobacco cloth is a plain-weave, low-thread-count cotton. It is, in reality, unbleached cheesecloth and comes in three grades and three widths: 36 in., 42 in., and 46 in. Because tobacco cloth is unbleached, it is light cream in color. It will dye easily and can be used for inexpensive draperies of a temporary nature. This fabric is carried by local stores in some regions, but usually it must be ordered.

Velour. Velour is a soft, tightly woven, smooth cotton or rayon with a short, thick pile. Velours come in three popular grades and in a 54-in. width. It can be obtained in white as well as many colors from local stores and theatrical jobbers. It takes dye and paint very well and has an excellent texture for the stage. Many professional scene painters prefer velour to canvas as a painting surface. The commercial theatre frequently uses velour for covering flats, although that is usually too expensive a practice for educational and amateur theatres. Velour also is used for cycloramas, curtains, draperies, drops, upholstery, and decor.

Velveteen. Velveteen, a cotton fabric with a close, thick pile, is made to resemble velvet. There are two grades, straight-back and twill-back. Twill-back is the better grade. Velveteen can be obtained in many colors from local stores and theatrical supply houses in 36-in. and 50-in. widths and is used primarily for upholstery and decor.

Webb Binding. Webb binding is a strong, closely woven narrow cotton or jute material. It is obtainable in four 1–4-in. widths, in its natural color, at local upholstery and canvas stores. It is used for reinforcing the tops of cycloramas, draperies, drops, curtains, and the edges of ground cloths. It also is useful in upholstery work. It can be painted or dyed and used for borders and trim on curtains.

Plastics

Although the process of creating plastics was discovered before the turn of the century, the plastic process industry did not begin to develop until after World War II. Defined as a material that changes shape when pressure is applied and retains its new shape when the pressure is removed, it was originally an innovative chemical produced for industrial use. It is a major material in today's society. New items and uses are developed each year. Contemporary designers were quick to discover the advantages of plastics, which are strong, lightweight, inexpensive, and quickly and easily constructed. They have the ability to be transparent and reflective in addition to possessing interesting three-dimensional surfaces.

There are two basic types of plastics: thermosetting and thermo plastics. The former are materials that can be permanently shaped by heat and pressure. Thermoplastics can be reshaped when softened by heat and will harden when they are cooled. This process can be repeated. Essentially, plastic is a chemical compound produced by various combinations of the elements of carbon, hydrogen, chlorine, fluorine, nitrogen, and oxygen. Plastics can be created in several forms, among which are liquids, powders, pastes, foams, sheets, pipes, and rolls. Originally available only to industrial organizations, plastic products and materials are now found in hardware stores, hobby shops, and plastic supply stores and are available from theatrical equipment suppliers and building and lumber retailers.

Some types of plastics that have possible application in the scene shop are as follows:

Urethane (Styrofoam). It is available in four by eight ft. sheets, various-sized blocks, and in white, light blue, which is flameproofed, and green. It has several thicknesses, but the 1/2-in., 3/4-in., 1-in., and 3-in. thicknesses are the most useful. It can be layered by using white glue, rubber cement, or plastic adhesive. It is easily cut with the usual shop tools. Sharp, serrated knives and hot wire cutters will give smoother cuts. The more common uses for this plastic are architectural details, carved surfaces, and sculptures.

A trade name for urethane is Styrofoam, and it is available in several densities, depending on the needed strength. The finished product surface needs to be covered with cheesecloth attached by glue before it can accept scene paint. Styrofoam is available from plastic suppliers, insulation dealers, and lumber retailers.

Acetate. Acetate, a transparent plastic, can be secured in rolls in 40 in. by 12 ft. lengths and in sheets 40 in. by 24 in. Vinyl is similar but is available in roll widths of 36 in. and 48 in. by 100 ft. Both can be cut with scissors and used as a glass substitute. This product is available at hardware stores and lumber supply houses, and from plastic distributors and artist products retailers.

Polyethylene. This sheeting is available in black and clear, 20 in.–36 in. wide and 50–100 ft. in length. It is ideal as dropcloths to protect floors and other surfaces while set units and drops are being painted. Ethafoam, a trade name, is obtainable in rods or sheets and is an extremely flexible polyethylene that can be glued easily to other surfaces. However, it, too, needs to be covered with cheesecloth before painting. Ethafoam is extremely useful for three-dimensional moldings and architectural trim. The product is readily available from local building and hardware suppliers as well as from plastic manufacturers.

Celastic. Celastic is a trade name for material made of cotton flannel in rolls of 40 in. widths. A solvent is used to soften the material and thereby to allow it to be formed. It will harden into a solid. Celastic replaces papier-mâché, which is less efficient. Celastic must be ordered from theatrical supply houses that deal in plastics.

Mylar. A trade name for a saturated polyester from the group of thermoplastics, it presents a reflective or mirrored surface similar to glass or highly polished metal and comes in sheets and rolls of various widths and lengths. It is especially useful for striking visual effects. Theatrical suppliers are the best sources for this material.

Thermoplastic Sheets. These can be molded into panels for three-dimensional details such as brick, stone, paneled walls, or bas-relief carvings. Its use does require thermoforming equipment for the vacuum-forming process. Although commercially manufactured machines can be purchased, most scene shops prefer to build their own at less expense. The plastics most suited to vacuum formings are sheets of vinyl, acrylic, cellulose acetate, butyrate, and polystyrene. Commercial products of molded-relief surfaces such as stone, brick, and so on can be secured from local stores. However, these are generally intended for small areas and are rather expensive for use over large areas of scenery.

Many varieties of plastic materials are available to the contemporary scene designer and offer almost unlimited opportunities for experimentation. Today's artist must be aware of the possibilities for the use of plastics in the theatre and make a concerted effort to keep informed of the most recent developments in the industry. Work with plastics will present safety problems that ordinarily are not common to scene construction, and every effort must be made to avoid any health hazards.

Paper and Fiber Materials

Designers have resorted to using papier-mâché to produce properties and three-dimensional effects on stage since the 1800s, but with the increase in required realistic effects, the low cost of paper materials has led to increased usage. Wood is the base for paper products, and they are readily available from local suppliers.

Brown Kraft Paper. A heavy, course paper product, Kraft paper is available in 3 and 6 ft. rolls and is used for ground cloths, for edge masking, and for reproducing full-scale drawings on scenery and drops using the ponce method.

Fiberboard. Known by the trade name of Celotex, this is a soft, porous material available in four by 8 ft. sheets and in various thicknesses. One side is brown and the other is white. Curved shapes require the thinnest board, while profile work is best accomplished with 3/16-in. and 1/4-in. thicknesses. Fiberboard cuts easily with knives, small saws, and electrical cutting tools, which produce the cleanest edges.

Paper Tubing. Cylindrical paper tubes can be secured in a variety of lengths and diameters and are extremely effective in creating structural pillars and bas-relief representations.

Corrugated Board. Available in 4- by 8-ft. sheets from local paper suppliers, this board is very lightweight and can present problems when painted with scene paint. It can be used when strength is not an important consideration.

Upson Board. A hard-surface board used for covering flats for added stability, it can be used for contouring edges of flats and some curved thicknesses. Upson board cuts easily with utility knives, cutawls, and saws. This material is available at lumber supply stores in 4 by 8 ft. sheets, in thicknesses of 1/8 in., 3/16 in., and 1/4 in. Upson board is extremely useful when strength is not a factor.

Metals

Metal is steadily increasing in importance as a material for stage scenery. Originally used as structural support for platforms, as we mentioned earlier, it is now replacing wood as the material most often used in the construction of scenery. This has evolved because of the rising cost of lumber, the superior strength of metal, its nonflammable quality, and its delicate and decorative visual properties.

Sheet Metals. These include aluminum, galvanized iron, and black iron, all of which are available in 3 by 8-ft. sheets in a variety of thicknesses. Aluminum is lighter in weight than iron, but it is more expensive.

Mesh and Screen. The types of metal most generally used for property and scenery construction are steel mesh chicken wire and window screening. Steel mesh is sold in rolls with a width of six feet. The openings are 6 in. by 6 in., and it is easily formed and bent into interesting shapes. Chicken wire is available in a variety of widths from 18 in.– 5 ft., in rolls with either small or large openings. Like steel mesh, it is easily shaped around forms to provide a base for papier-mâché or Celastic work. Window screening can be obtained in steel or aluminum in widths beginning with 2 ft. and going up to 4 ft. The mesh is usually 1/16-in. and can be worked by hand to form irregular shapes for tree or rock forms.

Pipe. Three types of pipe are used in the scene shop. The most useful is black iron pipe, which can be obtained in 18-ft. lengths and in 1 in. to 1 3/4 in. diameters. Pipe is used for hanging battens on stage as well as for structural set pieces. Steel pipe, which can be galvanized, is available in lengths up to 21 ft. and 1 in. to 1 3/4 in. diameters. It is used for railings, scaffolding, and platforms. Electrical conduit comes in 1/2 in. to 1 in. diameters and in lengths of 10 ft. It is easily bent for non-weight-bearing structures.

Strap Iron. Made of cold rolled and mild steel in 1/8-in., 3/16-in., and 1/4-in. thicknesses and a variety of widths, it can be bent by hand; however, best results emerge from securing the iron in a vise for bending. This metal has a number of uses, but it is essential for door units. Perforated strap iron, with holes evenly spaced, can be bent easily and used to reinforce joints.

Channels, Angle Iron, Tubes, and I-Beams. Known by Unistrut, Telespar, and Dexion trade names, channels come in preformed angle and square shapes, 1 in. to 2 in. in size, which can be bolted together in specific lengths and used for braces, platform legs, and scaffolding. I-beams are preformed beams designed as supports for platforms and stage wagons.

Wire and Cable. Various wires and cables are frequently used to suspend scenery, construct properties, and connect objects. The most important is the flexible steel or hoisting cable used for flying systems. Bailing wire, generally sold by the roll, is the most useful in twelve or fourteen gauge. Piano or spring steel wire can be used to support items where it is necessary for the wire not to be visible. Piano wire is sold by the pound, and the most common sizes for stage use are nos. 13, 20, and 26. Remember that kinks in wire weaken it and make it dangerous to use.

HARDWARE

The remainder of this chapter comprises an inventory of essential stage hardware which every designer needs to know in order to address problems in construction and rigging—problems that will dictate, in practical terms, whether or not the design will work as the designer has envisioned it. Some readers may view this material as the province of the technician and outside the responsibility of the designer. So be it. For those who need a more comprehensive picture, this material will be of benefit. Because this book is designed for those just entering the discipline, this material also may be viewed as an inventory list for initially stocking the scene shop.

The hardware used in constructing scenery can be divided into two groups: that which can be purchased easily from local distributors and that which must be ordered from stage hardware supply houses. In reality, although special stage hardware might be more efficient, the ingenious technician will frequently have to make do with a substitute found at the nearest hardware store. The prevalence of such a condition in the practice of theatre technology across the country is one of the reasons we have chosen to include this material in a book on design. Ultimately, the designer must be able to assist if not decide outright whether the hardware that will make the design work *can* be substituted. Purity of job function just is not as precise a situation as some might wish it to be, especially in the forums in which *most* designers in this country must work.

To prevent running out of stock items during a heavy building period, the shop technician must keep a careful check on supplies and replenish them before they are completely gone. Most hardware, with the exception of nails and staples, can be used over and over. You must remember to remove, sort, and save all hardware after the show has closed and before scenic units are returned to storage. Hardware can be a major item in a shop budget if carelessly handled, and waste in hardware often causes the budgetary constraints that limit the creative, artistic aims of the scenic designer. This is especially true in the educational and community theatres.

Bolts

Bolts should be used for all heavy assembly where the greatest strength is necessary. Washers are used in connection with bolts to extend the thickness of the wood and to prevent the bolt from pulling through the wood. Plain nuts and wing nuts are also used with bolts. Sold according to diameter and length, bolts can be purchased at all hardware stores.

Carriage Bolts and Nuts. Carriage bolts have a round head, a square shoulder under the head, and a partially threaded stem. They range in diameter and length, up to 10 in. Nuts are made to fit each size. Carriage bolts are used for attaching legs to platforms, for assembling large hardware pieces, for assembling framed drops, and for roll and book ceilings. Wing nuts frequently are used with carriage bolts for fast assembly. Because of its square shoulder, the carriage bolt locks in place when the nut is fastened.

Stove Bolts and Nuts. Stove bolts have a flat head with a slot; the entire stem is threaded. They vary in diameter and length, up to 3 in. These are used in place of screws where extra strength is needed and are used for attaching small or medium pieces of stage hardware. The stove bolt should be held in place with a screwdriver when the nut is tightened.

Machine Bolts and Nuts. Machine bolts have a square head and a partially threaded stem and are obtainable in various diameters and lengths, up to 10 in. They are used for special construction and are particularly valuable in connecting metal pieces. To tighten the nut, hold the machine bolt with pliers.

Casters

Casters are rollers that enable units to be moved easily, quickly, and silently. There are three different types of casters, rigid, swivel, and brake. Made of steel, casters are usually attached with bolts to ensure maximum strength and wear. Local hardware stores usually keep them in stock.

Truck Casters. *Truck casters,* which can be either rigid or swivel, is the generic term for casters acceptable for stage work. Rigid casters turn in a free swing of 360 degrees. Rigid casters can move in only two directions, backward and forward. The wheels of both types should be rubber-tired to reduce backstage noise and should move on ball bearings for easy action. Casters are ordered according to wheel diameter, which varies from 2 in. to 6 in. Anything smaller than 4 in. is not dependable for stage use. The truck caster should be used for any type of horizontal shifting, called rolling, where any weight is involved (for example, on wagons, dollies, and tip jacks).

Brake Casters. These casters are equipped with a brake to lock the wheel in place to prevent the unit from rolling.

Gliders

Gliders, sometimes called the "dome of silence," are polished metal discs that, when attached to a unit, will allow it to be pushed or pulled across the floor with a minimum of noise and effort. Manufactured primarily to be used on furniture legs, and often called furniture glides, they can serve in other capacities. They serve to protect hardwood floors if scenery needs to be placed on such a floor. They can be substituted for truck casters if the latter are not available. Gliders do not work efficiently on rough surfaces, and because they are merely tacked onto the wood, they are easily knocked off. They can be obtained at local variety stores.

Air Casters

Air casters are not casters at all, but represent a technology whereby, by means of compressed air jets, a scenic unit is raised onto a cushion of air and floated across the stage. This technology is silent and efficient, but it requires an absolutely smooth stage floor under the unit. Air casters are tremendously expensive.

Hinges

Three types of hinges are used in stage construction. They are loose-pin, tight-pin, and strap; the latter are sometimes called barndoor hinges. Hinges are sold by the dozen and can be secured from local hardware stores. They are used more as fasteners than as actual hinges.

Loose-pin Backflap. These hinges are square and have removeable pins. Available in various sizes, the most popular for stage use are 1 1/2 in. by 2 in. Hinges are attached to the wood with either wood screws or bolts. Loose-pin backflap hinges are used for the temporary fastening of units.

Strap Hinges. The strap hinge has two long triangular flaps, each tapering from the pin to the end. This hinge is available in various sizes, with 6- and 8-in. sizes being most applicable to stage use. They are used to fasten together heavy units such as wagons, platforms, and so on, and to support heavy door shutters or other swinging units. They also can hold door units in place in a door flat.

Tight-pin Backflap. This hinge is exactly like the loose pin hinge, except the pin is not removeable. Available in the same sizes as the loose-pin hinge, tight-pin hinges are used for folding parallels, book ceilings, twofold and threefold flat units, and door and French window units.

Metal Plates

Angle Irons. Constructed of flat steel, angle irons are made to fit on the inside corner of a frame. The size, which is the measurement of the length of one arm, ranges from 1 in. to 6 in. The width increases correspondingly with the length of the arm. Holes in the arm are countersunk for No. 9 wood screws. Angle irons are used to reinforce corners and strengthen joints. They can be purchased locally.

Corner Plates. Corner plates are similar to angle irons; they can be purchased locally and are available in the same sizes as angle irons. However, unlike angle irons, corner plates are flat. They serve as reinforcement on the right-angle joints of wooden frames and are attached with No. 9 wood screws.

Crate Corner Plates. This plate is made of steel 2 1/2 in. wide and 3 in. by 3 in. long, with three countersunk screw holes on each face. It is used for reinforcing corners of crates, chests, and heavy units that must be shifted frequently.

Mending Plates. This plate is available in three sizes or it can be made to order with little effort from shop technicians with proper metalworking tools. These plates also can be ordered from theatrical equipment houses. Mending plates are used to mend or reinforce wooden battens or frames.

Shoe Plates. The shoe plate is similar to the crate corner plate. The difference is that it has a third side so that the metal piece fits snugly over a wooden corner. Three countersunk holes for No. 9 wood screws are used to secure this piece of hardware, whose main use is to protect corners of crates and chests that accompany traveling companies.

Sill Iron. The sill iron is made of rolled steel and has countersunk holes for No. 9 wood screws. It can be used in place of a saddle iron and can be made easily in the scene shop. A long, thin bar with 9-in. angles on each end, it is used on door flats. It must be countersunk. The door flat fits into the sill iron, which can remain permanently on the flat.

T-Plates. T-plates are another form of reinforcing plates. They are made of steel and are available in 6 by 6 and 7 by 7-in. sizes. The *T* shape makes the device useful for reinforcing butt T-joints. The plate has countersunk holes for No. 9 wood screws and can be purchased at local hardware stores.

Nails

Nails are graded according to their length, which is indicated by the term *penny*—for example "tenpenny" or "10d". This term originated from the price per hundred in England.

Blue Lath Nails. These are 3d-size nails that are blue and can be used as a substitute for clout nails. They are used for attaching plywood and fiberboard to flat frames.

Box Nails. Box nails have a regular flat head and a slender stem. Available in various sizes, they can be substituted for common nails, and they can be used for nailing plywood and fiberboard to wood frames.

Brads. Pyramid-pointed, flat-headed nails of a small diameter, brads range in length and are used for cabinet work or in place of a larger nail that might split the wood.

Clout Nails. Clout nails are made of a softer metal than other nails, and thus they clinch or bend back on themselves more easily. They have a square stem and a flat head and can be ordered in various lengths. Clout nails are generally restricted to attaching plywood corner blocks and keystones to flat frames. They must be ordered from a stage hardware company.

Common Nails. Common nails have flat heads and pyramid-shaped points. Used for all general construction, they are available in sizes from 4d to 20d.

Double-headed Nails. Double-headed, or duplex-head, nails are normally used for concrete molds and temporary scaffolding but can be very helpful for nailing temporary structures that must be taken apart.

These nails come in all standard sizes according to length.

Finishing Nails. These nails have small, round heads, slender stems, and pyramid-shaped points. Available in sizes from 4d to 10d, they are used for general construction projects that require nail heads that cannot be seen. They are used also for building up moldings and as a substitute for a common nail when the latter would be too large.

Galvanized Shingle Nails. Shingle, or roofing, nails are short with a large flat head and thick stem and come in two lengths: 3/4 in. and 1 in. Sometimes they can be substituted for clout nails, but they are used more frequently for attaching fiberboard to wood and for tacking down ground cloths and floor padding.

Tacks. Carpet tacks are made of sterilized black iron in two sizes. They are used for upholstery and properties, for covering flat frames, and for attaching drops to battens (if a staple gun is not used). They also are used for hanging draperies and for tacking down floor cloths.

Pins

Wire. Wire pins are used to hold loose-pin hinges together. They can be purchased commercially, or they can be made easily in the shop of 14-guage wire. They can even be made from coat hangers. If the pins are homemade, they should be approximately 6 in. long and made of wire that is easily bent. After inserting the wire in the hinge, bend the two ends so that the wire will not slip out. In an emergency, an 8d nail can be used as a loose pin, but it cannot be removed quickly.

Hinge. These pins are the pins holding the two flaps of a tight-pin hinge together. Similar in shape to a bolt, they fit snugly but do not have threads. If the pins are removed to change a tight-pin hinge into a loose-pin hinge, the pins should be saved and reused.

Screws

Flat-head Wood Screws. The screws most used in scenery construction are flat-head bright steel screws, which are available in a variety of sizes. All screws are purchased by the box, each box containing a gross of 144 screws. The most useful sizes are No. 6 and No. 9 screws that are either 7/8-in. and/or 1 1/2-in. in length. They are used to attach plywood corner blocks and keystones, all types of stage hardware, for assembling units, in repairing broken lumber, and for fastening two battens together when extra strength is needed.

Lag Screws. A lag screw has a square head and a round neck and is threaded over halfway up the stem. Lag screws are sized according to length and range in diameter from 1/8-in. to 1/2-in. They are used for heavy-duty work that cannot be handled by a bolt of the same size. A wrench instead of a screwdriver is needed for lag screws.

Phillips Screws. The Phillips or Phillips-type screw has a flat head with an indented cross slot instead of a single slot, and it can only be used with a Phillips screwdriver. Available in a variety of sizes, the Phillips screw is used for machinery and certain cabinetwork.

Screen-Door Hooks and Eyes. Made of steel, they are made in two parts: a small screw eye with a long hook attached to it and a separate screw eye that fits the hook. Sizes are determined by the length of the hook; for stage work, the largest size is preferred.

Screw Eyes. Screw eyes are made of steel, usually zinc-plated, in the shape of a circle with a projecting screw point. Sizes are ac-

cording to the overall length. These can be used as substitutes for lash-line eyes, stage brace cleats, and stage screws.

Screw Hooks. Like screw eyes, screw hooks are made of zinc-plated steel in the form of a hook with a screw end. They range in size and are used as a substitute for other hardware, for hangers, and so on.

Specific Stage Hardware and Equipment

Much of the special stage hardware is manufactured specifically for stage use and is available only from theatrical supply houses. Thus, the technician should keep a sufficient supply on hand to prevent unnecessary emergencies. Stage hardware is strong and sturdy and can be used again and again, a characteristic that makes it less expensive in the long run.

Brace Cleat. The brace cleat is a small flat steel plate with countersunk holes for No. 9 wood screws and has a large hole into which a stage brace is hooked. Approximately 2 in. by 4 in. the brace cleat is used to brace a flat.

Ceiling Plate. Made of galvanized steel in one size only, the plate measures 7 in. by 2 1/2 in. and has a metal ring attached slightly off-center. One end of the plate has five countersunk holes for screws; the other has two holes and 3/8 in. carriage bolts and wing nuts. The ceiling plate holds together the butt joints of the wooden ceiling frame and thus allows a flying line to be attached to the ring.

Foot Irons

Flat. Twelve in. long by 7/8 in. wide and 3/16 in. thick, the flat has three countersunk holes for No. 9 wood screws. It must be countersunk when attached to the underside of a unit. The large hole at one end is used to fasten the iron to the stage with a stage screw.

Solid. This iron is 8 in. high by 1 in. long and 1/4 in. thick. It has three countersunk holes for No. 9 wood screws. It has a short arm with a large hole for a stage screw. It is used to fasten units securely to the stage floor.

Hinged. This iron is 8 in. high by 4 in. wide and has four countersunk holes for No. 9 wood screws on the upright flap and one large hole on the short flap for a stage screw. This iron is used for securing the bottom batten of a flown drop to the stage floor.

Hanger Irons

There are two kinds of hanger irons: straight and hooked. The straight iron is approximately 7 1/2 in. long, 1 1/8 in. wide, and 1/4 in. thick, with a metal ring at one end. It has three countersunk holes for No. 9 wood screws and is attached to the top of the scenery units for flying. Hooked irons are only 4 1/2 in. long, with a metal ring at one end and a hook formed by the iron at the other. This hardware has two countersunk holes for No. 9 wood screws and is attached to the bottom of the scenery unit. The hooked iron is used only if the unit is especially heavy. Lines to the bottom iron must pass through the rings at the top of the straight iron.

Other Hardware

Lash Cleat. This is a small iron or steel cleat with one countersunk hole for No. 9 wood screws. It is attached to the inside frame of the flat. It is available in two sizes and is used for lashing flats together.

Lash Line Eye. It is made of steel and is approximately 3 1/2 in. long. It has one countersunk hole for a No. 9 wood screw

and a hole at one end through which a cord or line can be threaded. It is used for attaching the lash line, which in turn lashes two flats together by hooking around the lash line cleats.

Picture-frame Hanger and Socket. It is composed of two units, the hook and the socket, and is available in two widths. Each unit has countersunk holes for No. 9 wood screws. The socket is attached to the front of the flat, and the hook is attached to the back of the picture to be hung. Two units should be used if a picture is to hang straight.

Pulleys. Pulleys are available in many styles and sizes. The pulleys used in conjunction with normal stage tasks are not the heavy-duty ones used with steel cable for rigging stage flying systems. Rather, they are used for spot lines, special flying work, temporary rigging, small traverse curtain units, and so on. They can usually be obtained from local sources. Awning pulleys are available in single and double wheels, or sheaves. They are identified by the size of the wheel. Made of cast iron, they can be used for small curtains. Tackle blocks generally are used for hoisting and can be helpful at various times. They are equipped with a large steel hook for hanging or holding and have wheel diameters of 2, 3, and 3 1/2 in. They are made with single, double, and triple sheaves.

S Hooks. Keepers, or S hooks, are made of galvanized steel to fit 1 by 3 lumber and are used to stiffen lashed or hinged flats.

Saddle Irons. These are long, thin steel bars with two upright angle irons at specified distances from each end of the bar. Both the bar and the angles have countersunk holes for No. 9 wood screws. Saddle irons are used as reinforcement at the bottom of door flats. The angles fit inside the door opening.

Sash Cord. Sash cord or clothesline is a lightweight cotton cord (1/4 in. diameter) used for lashing flats and used where strength is most important. It can be purchased at local hardware stores.

Manila Hemp Rope. A strong, flexible rope with long-wearing qualities, Manila hemp is available in various diameters. It is sold in lengths of 100 ft. and is used for the majority of all stage rigging. It can be purchased locally.

Snap Hook. Sometimes referred to as a harness hook, the snap hook is made of galvanized steel and has a spring or snap closing. Its size depends on the inside diameter of the hook, which can range from 7/16 in. to 1 1/4 in. It can be used to attach lines to rings or as a chain for flying.

Stage Brace. Stage braces are used to brace and support flat scenery in an upright position. Made of hardwood and steel, they can be extended in length. A double metal hook is attached to the flat by means of the brace cleat, and the bottom is secured to the stage floor with a stage screw. An iron set screw in the middle of the brace adjusts it.

Stage Screw. Floor pegs or stage screws are made of either forged steel or malleable iron and are used to fasten scenery to the stage floor. They have a handle for easy gripping and a sharp, pitched screw that can be screwed into softwood stage floors.

Steel Chain. Long lengths of steel chain are used in the bottom hems of curtains for weight. Shorter lengths are made up as trimming chain, with a snap hook at one end and a metal ring at the other. These are used for attaching units to pipe battens for flying. Steel chain can be secured locally.

Stop Cleat. The stop cleat is a flat steel plate approximately 7/8 in. by 2 3/4 in. with countersunk holes for No. 9 wood screws. It is placed at the back of the flat to keep the flat flush with its neighbor when the two are lashed together to form a corner of the set. A stop cleat can be made in the shop or purchased locally.

Turnbuckles. Turnbuckles consist of an open steel frame with a screw hook set in one end and a screw eye in the other. The screws move into the frame. Turnbuckles are used in adjusting the tension of cable or wire.

Wire Rope. Two basic types of wire rope are useful for stage work. The first, hoisting rope, is used for counterweight systems and is made of steel wire wound around hemp, and is available in various diameters. Aircraft cable, because of a slightly different construction, is more flexible. Diameters of 3/16 in. and 1/4 in. are used for rigging where flexibility is needed.

Wire Rope Clip. A curved piece of malleable iron, wire rope clip is threaded on both ends with two fitted hex nuts. When the nuts are tightened, an additional piece of iron, threaded on the two ends of the curve, is forced against the rope, holding it in place. Clips are available for all standard rope sizes.

Wire Rope Thimbles. Wire rope thimbles are curved metal channels used to prevent wear on wire rope. Local hardware stores frequently stock this item.

Washers. Washers are metal discs with a hole in the center. Available in brass, iron, and steel in many different sizes, washers are used with bolts to prevent the nut from gouging into the lumber. They also may be used for weighting curtain hems. Local hardware stores carry them in all sizes.

CHAPTER NINE

SCENE PAINTING

The scene designer must have a thorough knowledge of scene painting to execute the design accurately. Most professional designers are excellent scenic artists because of their training and apprentice work in the field. Practically all designers, professional or not, will work as scene painters on their own sets unless union regulations will not permit this. Professional scene painters can be scarce, if not prohibitively expensive, and a good designer needs to be especially careful of trusting inexperienced personnel to produce the desired effects. Even in the educational theatre, where the development of student talent is important, the designer needs to supervise carefully the execution of painting to assure accuracy and quality.

Scene painting requires skill in several specialized techniques not found in other painting forms. Most stage designs are "larger than life" in color, line, and mass, so that details will carry to the audience. When compared to other types of graphic art, the techniques and scale of scene painting can be described as broad. Anyone who wishes to become a proficient scene painter should realize that this skill will require a good deal of practice and experimentation before success can be expected.

The art of scene painting reached rather astonishing heights during the nineteenth century, when theatre art began competing with two-dimensional landscape art. Much use was made of painted perspective to give a three-dimensional effect to standard wing and drop settings. Stage lighting was limited to general illumination until after the turn of the century, and the scenic artist was relied upon to paint shadows and highlights on the scenery's two-dimensional, flat surfaces. Present-day designers must take into consideration effects achieved by highly developed stage-lighting techniques. In spite of the increasing importance of three-dimensional scenery, there remains a necessity to make frequent use of the illusionary elements of perspective to trick the vision of the audience.

Scene painting was a rather mysterious art that remained a highly specialized field until the 1950s. Early books on stagecraft and design gave very little information on various techniques and materials, because such information was closely guarded by skilled European artisans. Practically no information on the use of aniline dyes for drop painting appeared in textbooks until the 1960s, although these dyes had been used to great effect in Europe for a number of years.

Today, most professional productions, including television and motion pictures, employ the services of a scenic studio equipped with all the tools, materials, and space necessary to reproduce the design. The designer must meet initially with the studio's head painter to discuss the desired style and interpretation for sketches, drawings, and models.

Some organizations, such as regional and educational theatres, have their own paint shops to develop their designs. Some are required to utilize the actual stage for painting when shop space will not allow a trial setup of the constructed setting. Using the stage as a paint area is not a recommended procedure because of the obvious problems it creates in maintaining a clean, orderly area.

Scene painting is essentially a developed skill, not unlike typing or playing the piano—that is, the technical part of playing the piano. To perform the act of scene painting, you must understand the characteristics of scenic paint materials, the paints to be used, the application, and the reproduction of the color elevations. As with any skill, it is essential to devote a reasonable amount of time to the actual practice of the craft.

DESIGN TRANSFER

The visual color composition of the design sketch or paint elevation can be reproduced in a variety of ways. An accomplished scene painter must be able to identify the colors on the sketch, achieve them with the pigments available in the shop, and, through careful analysis, estimate the proportions of pigments in a combination necessary for a reasonable duplication.

This may be easier said than done, because transparent watercolor sketches allow the paper color to influence the effect of a color, and opaque watercolors do not always match available scene colors. You should always mix samples of the scene paint, and, after allowing a reasonable time for drying, compare the results with the designer's sketches. Then you can adjust the pigment proportions, if necessary, before mixing the required amount of paint.

SCENE PAINTS AND PIGMENTS

The selection and use of the many different types of paints and their preparation will vary according to the individual production, the designer's preference, the painters' familiarity with the paint, the availability of the materials, and the budget restrictions. The best pigments and paints for scenery must be obtained from scenic paint suppliers, although some comparable items can be obtained from local outlets. When ordering supplies, order more than is needed to cover emergencies, which are unavoidable in any shop organization.

Six basic colors compose the color spectrum. They are the primary colors—red, yellow, and blue—and the secondary colors of orange, green, and violet. These colors can be combined into six intermediate colors of red-orange, yellow-orange, yellow-green, blue-green, blue-violet, and red-violet. The result is twelve principle colors. *Hue* is the term used to define a color classification and its relationship to other colors on the color wheel. Colors opposite each other on the wheel are called complementary colors.

At the center of the color wheel is a gray or neutral color that is either a combination of white and black or a combination of two colors opposite each other on the wheel. The addition of white to a color will produce a tint, whereas the addition of black will produce a shade or a lower value. *Saturation* refers to the amount of white in a color, and *brilliance* and *intensity* refer to a color's degree of purity. A color atlas can assist you in easily and accurately selecting pigments and in making judgments. Using a color atlas also reinforces your color memory (see Chapter Two).

Scene paint has three basic parts: (1) the pigment, which is the coloring matter; (2) the size or binder, which binds the pigments to the surface; and (3) the medium, which holds the pigment and the binder in suspension for application and then evaporates. Easier to prepare and use than ordinary commercial paint, scene paint is relatively pure and mixes readily, yielding strong finishes.

Types of Scenic Paints

Dry Pigments. Dry pigments are obtainable in powdered form in one-, five-, and fifty-pound units from scenic paint supply houses. Some local hardware, lumber, and art supply stores may stock some earth-tone

pigments, but the intensities will be less than those of the more desirable scenic pigments. Since dry pigments are mixed in the theatre paint shop as needed, there is a minimum of waste or leftover mixed paint. Dry pigments also are less expensive than ready-mixed paints. The binding agent also is made up in the theatre shop, further reducing the cost of manufacture and shipment. Dry pigments have been the staple item of theatrical paint shops for many years. They continue as the dominant choice of many designers, who are impressed with the excellent range of colors available.

Because some dry pigments are not easily suspended in water, they are available in wet or pulp consistency, which allows them to mix more readily with the binding medium. Wet pigments are obtainable in five-pound containers and are particularly useful for making a color wash or glaze, which is a transparent coating applied to a painted surface to modify its tone or quality. Keep in mind that wet pigment will change color upon drying, so you must test for the final color.

Dry and pulp pigments are divided into three categories: earth-tone colors, high-intensity colors, and neutral colors.

Earth-tone Colors:

French Yellow Ochre. Dry—mixes very well and has a slight chalky quality. Inexpensive.

Golden Ochre. Dry—rich and slightly transparent.

Burnt Turkey Umber. Dry—rich brown with walnut tones. Inexpensive.

Raw Turkey Umber. Dry—not a good mixer and slightly opaque. Greenish in tone. Inexpensive.

Burnt Italian Sienna. Dry—warm reddish brown tone. Inexpensive.

Italian Raw Sienna. Dry—rich tan tone. Inexpensive.

Brown Lake. Wet—similar to Van Dyke Brown. Rich. Expensive.

Imported Van Dyke Brown. Dry—not good mixer but a very deep, rich brown. Useful for wood effects.

High-intensity Colors:

Yellow

Milori Yellow Medium. Dry—strong and brilliant yellow. Close to primary yellow.

Milori Yellow Light. Dry—strong and cool yellow.

Chrome Yellow Light. Dry—lemon yellow. Inexpensive.

Chrome Yellow Medium. Dry—warm, golden yellow. Inexpensive.

Hoyt's Yellow Lake. Wet—rich yellow, slightly transparent.

English Dutch Pink. Dry—rich yellow with greenish tone.

Milori Yellow Orange. Dry—strong yellow-orange.

Orange

French Orange Mineral. Dry—strong orange with a slight red tone.

Chelsea Vermilion. Dry—strong red-orange. Very brilliant.

English Vermilion. Dry—strong red-orange similar to a geranium color. Expensive.

American Vermilion. Dry—deep red-orange.

Red

Bulletin Red. Dry—brilliant red. Close to primary red.

Turkey Red Lake. Dry and wet—very rich red. Closest to primary red. Expensive.

Light Maroon. Dry—strong red. Expensive.

English Venetian Red. Dry—a good mixer but slightly opaque.

Terra Cotta. Inexpensive.

Dark Maroon. Dry—deep, rich, dark red. Expensive.

Magenta Lake. Dry—strong red with blue tones. Expensive.

Solferino Lake. Dry and wet—strong red-violet. Makes an excellent pink. Expensive.

Violet

Purple Lake. Dry—strong, warm violet with a red tone. Expensive.

Violet Lake. Dry—cool, strong violet. Expensive.

Royal Purple. Dry—very strong violet. Very saturated. Expensive.

Blue

French Ultramarine Blue. Dry—strong, warm blue with a slight reddish tone.

American Ultramarine Blue. Dry—similar to French Ultramarine Blue but not as strong.

French Cobalt Blue. Dry—strong blue. Close to primary blue.

Italian Blue. Dry—very strong blue with turquoise overtones.

Prussian Blue. Dry—deep, intense blue with greenish tones. Not a good mixer.

Antwerp Blue. Wet—very intense blue, similar to Prussian Blue. Expensive.

Celestial Blue. Dry—very dark turquoise blue.

Green

Chrome Green Light. Dry—good basic green. Inexpensive.

Emerald Green. Wet and dry—very strong and brilliant green.

Chrome Green Medium. Dry—less-saturated green. Inexpensive.

Chrome Green Dark. Dry—darker, less-saturated green.

Hanover Green. Dry—warm and bright green. Good for foliage effects. Expensive.

Saphite Green. Dry—warm green similar to Hanover Green.

Malachite Green. Dry—cool, dark, and very rich green with blue tones. Good for foliage effects.

Royal Green Lake. Dry—warm, strong, rich, dark green with blue tones. Expensive.

Neutral Colors

Permanent White. Dry—also known as Zinc White, this is very opaque and excellent for highlights.

Danish Whiting. Dry—heavy but soluble and opaque.

Ivory Black. Dry—slightly transparent but very rich.

Hercules Black. Dry—very strong and brilliant black. Extremely long-lasting.

Lithaphone. Dry—very opaque. A mixture of zinc sulfide and barium sulfate. Good for priming woods. Inexpensive.

Dry and pulp pigments require a medium for binding that is known as size or sizing and is made by combining an animal glue solution with hot water. There are two types of animal glue: gelatin and carpenter glue. The gelatin glue needs to be covered with cool water and allowed to soak for at least four hours before being heated in a double boiler or electric glue pot. The hot glue can then be slowly added to sixteen parts of water to provide the binding agent for the dry and wet pigments. Suppliers of scene paints also carry prepared scenic liquid size, sold by the gallon, which can be of help for technicians faced with limited facilities but few budget constraints.

Protein Scene Paints. Premixed, opaque scene paints with a casein base are able to be thinned with water and will dry to a flat finish. They are nonflammable, and their metal containers are easily stored. The casein-based paint is a milk derivative and is available in quart, gallon, and five-gallon cans. An excellent range of brilliant colors not available in commercial casein paints can be secured from theatrical suppliers. Among these colors are

White	Dark red
Black	Orange
Raw white	Chrome oxide green
Raw umber	Emerald green
Yellow ochre	Lemon yellow
Raw sienna	Golden yellow
Ultramarine blue	Dark green
Red	Navy blue
Bright red	Turquoise blue
Magenta	Burnt umber

Casein colors mix very well with dry and pulp pigments; latex, acrylic, and vinyl paints; and metallic powders, as well as with other casein colors. This paint is water-repellant after it dries and has a desirable matte finish, which makes it an excellent choice for outdoor scenery units. It is extremely effective at covering all types of surfaces, both porous and nonporous, including wood, plastic wallboard, and fabrics. Casein is not as susceptable to spoilage as are dry-pigment paints, and that is a strong advantage in high humidity. Casein paints should be stored in tightly closed containers and kept in a relatively dry place. This will reduce the development of caking or lumps. Another protein-based paint is soya-protein premixed paint. It is available in paste form and is sold in quarts as well as one-, two-, and five-gallon tins.

Latex Paints. Latex, a water-based paint with a synthetic rubber plastic binding agent, covers well and is usually flexible. Reasonable in cost, latex paint can be purchased locally in limited colors; its primary use is for interiors. It can be used for primer coats or mixed with more color-saturated, casein paints as well as other scene paints and dry pigments. Some manufacturers do produce a wider range of colors, but they are not readily available from local distributors.

Vinyl Acrylic Paints. Vinyl acrylic paints have acrylic resin as a binder, and although the color range is not quite equal to that of casein paints, they have some definite advantages in that they will not spoil. These paints dry without luster and have excellent adhesive qualities. This can be most important for today's designs, in which metals and plastics are widely used. In addition, some contemporary scene materials have surfaces that are flexible, and vinyl acrylics do not crack or flake, as do casein and dry-pigment paints. Vinyl can also be adapted for use on fabrics for costumes and drops. Outdoor settings often present problems in durability, but this paint is waterproof and particularly durable for extended performance runs. The colors can be mixed and stored indefinitely. There are some fourteen colors available for scene paint:

Iron red	Chrome green
Yellow ochre	Green-shade blue
Burnt umber	Thalo green
Raw umber	Magenta
Burnt sienna	Spectrum red
Red	Chrome yellow
Ultramarine blue	Moly orange

Colors are sold in units of two quarts, whereas black-and-white bases and separate gloss and flat mediums are obtainable in one- and five-gallon containers.

Aniline Dyes. A completely different coloring agent for scene design use is aniline dye, which, with the exception of white, is available in the same colors as dry pigments and casein scene paints. Dyes come in powdered form and can be dissolved in alcohol or water. As opposed to covering the surface of scenery, as does paint, dye enters the fabric and changes its color. The fabric surface needs to be covered with a sizing of liquid starch to prevent bleeding. Dye can be controlled to achieve translucent effects, such as stained glass, by adding a binding agent to the liquid dye.

Additional Paint Materials

Several additional materials frequently are needed to aid in achieving some particular effect. Bronze, silver, copper, and gold powders mixed with bronzing liquid, which is a varnish, produces a metallic appearance on woods or fabrics. Other binding agents, such as white shellac, clear gloss latex, and vinyl, can be used. The luster of the paint will be improved if dextrine is added to the binding agent. Test metallic paints to ascertain the correct amount of binder to use on the selected surfaces. Aerosol spray cans of metallic finishes can also be used, but not as effectively.

At times, the scene painter will be required to create a hard gloss finish to simulate wood, tile, or marble. A flat paint will not represent finished or highly polished woods adequately. Varnish or white shellac thinned with denatured alcohol will give the surface a reasonable luster without too much shine, which could reflect light. Test the final result, because sometimes the painted graining may be obscured by too heavy a coat. Lacquers and gloss vinyl paints are also capable of producing overly shiny surfaces.

Some spray paints can be helpful at times, but generally their use should be reserved for work on properties. These paints include spray enamel, upholstery dyes, leather dyes, oil rubbing stains, and liquid wax. They also are too expensive to use for any large area of work. At times, fluorescent paints are used for special effects. These need to be activated by black light to glow in the dark. Luminous or phosphorescent paint will glow after exposure to any light.

Mixing

Paint needs to be mixed in an area specifically designed for the activity. The area should be equipped with running water, a large sink, incandescent lighting, electrical outlets, reasonable storage space for paints, brushes, and various other materials. The area should also contain space for additional safe storage for flammable paint materials, work tables, and a reasonable assortment of paints.

The actual mixing of paint ingredients can be reduced to three basic steps:

1. Combining the dry-color pigments including whiting or black pigments, if necessary. When dry pigment is mixed, the resulting color is exactly as it will appear after drying. When you add water, the color will darken significantly.

2. The binding agent of animal glue is mixed with water to form size water. The usual formula is sixteen parts water to one part glue.

3. The size is mixed with the dry pigments to form the liquid scene paint.

Although the part-mixing procedure is simple, the refinements are many. Dry-pigment colors vary in strength; consequently, it is frequently necessary to control the strength of the mixture by adding other colors, black, or white. Some pigments do not mix well with water and will need to be suspended in alcohol or a liquid detergent to facilitate their blending with sizing and other pigments. Whenever possible, mix dry pigments together, as we just noted, before adding the size, to see the actual dry color.

Write down the exact formula for each mixed color to make certain you can duplicate the mixture if necessary. Before adding the size water to the dry mix, make sure you have available several clean pails or containers and paint paddles for handling the finished mix. Always be certain that enough paint is prepared for the required job so as to avoid the necessity of having to attempt to remix and match the previous colors.

Size water is made of animal glue and water. The dry glue crystals are placed in an electric glue pot, covered with water and allowed to soak overnight. Note that an elec-

tric, thermostatically controlled glue pot provides a better device for handling glue than does the antiquated double-boiler arrangement that frequently allows the glue to burn, if not watched constantly. When glue burns, it creates an obnoxious and lingering stench that is difficult to dispel.

After the glue is thoroughly dissolved, it can be combined with water, using one part glue to sixteen parts water, as just mentioned. Galvanized trash cans of the twenty- or thirty-gallon variety are used for mixing the size water. A small amount of Lysol or carbolic acid, available from local lumber or hardware stores, as well as scenic supply houses, should be added to retard spoilage. Prepared scene size in liquid form can also be ordered from scenic suppliers in gallon cans. Other binders available are flexible glue, cold water glue, and cold water size. Because of cost, these items should be considered only for limited scenic work.

When adding the size water to the dry pigment mix, begin by adding only a small amount at a time and carefully stirring until the mixture reaches the consistency of heavy cream. Make certain that all lumps are dissolved. Remember that the mixture will tend to settle if not stirred frequently. This condition could affect the color of the paint, which might result in uneven variations of surface color. If you use several pails of the same color, remember to mix each container frequently so that color consistency is maintained across the lot. If you use a mechanical paint mixer, a compressed air mixer is preferable to an electric tool because of the hazard involving a possibly damp floor in the shop area.

The amount of mixed dry pigment used should approximate one part pigment to one and one-half parts size water, but this can vary slightly, depending on the compatibility of the dry pigments. You probably should not mix all the prepared dry pigment at one time, but only enough for the work to be done at the time. In addition, keep some of the dry mix in reserve until the end of the performance run to handle possible repairs to the scenery. Leftover paint mixed to alter the color can be used for other paint jobs on the setting, such as base colors for backings, trims, floors, and back painting of flats.

Premixed scene paints such as casein, latex, and acrylic vinyl can be stored indefinitely if left unopened. However, when casein paint is opened, it eventually spoils. Remember that scene paint, when not in use, needs to be carefully contained and stored to prevent evaporation, spilling, and accidental disposal. When estimating the amount of paint to mix for a particular job, consider the surface to be painted; more paint is needed for textured wood or napped fabric than for a smooth surface, and more is needed for an open-weave surface than for a net surface.

Paint mixing is a learned skill and an individually cultivated craft. Just a few of the procedures and techniques have been touched on here, but the serious theatre artist will be able to find many ways to elaborate on these basic techniques and thereby improve his or her performance.

BASIC PROCEDURES IN SCENE PAINTING

Scenery may be painted using two methods: vertical and horizontal. The vertical method should employ some form of paint frame. Ideally the frame is constructed of wood and suspended by a pulley system that allows the frame to be lowered into a slot in the floor. The frame has a ledge at its base to allow two-dimensional pieces of scenery to be supported with the help of a few strategically placed nails. This system allows the painter to stand on the shop floor while the scenery is slowly raised or lowered as needed. Some-

times, if the building's construction will not permit a floor slot, the wooden framework can be attached permanently to the wall, and scenery pieces can be attached to the framework. In this situation, the painter must use boomerangs, various stepladders, and movable scaffoldings to reach all the parts of the scenery. Drops can also be laid out, stapled to the outside battens of movable paint frames, and painted vertically. The vertical method, of course, applies to any situation in which the scenery is painted in an upright position. A paint frame of either variety may not be available, and so the designer, using ladders or whatever is available, will simply have to do the best that circumstances will allow. Because some theatres have limited shop space, the setting may need to be painted in position on stage. This is not generally recommended, however, for reasons of proper stage maintenance.

Horizontal painting requires a large area of floor space to lay out the two-dimensional scenery for the work involved. This method requires painting with long-handled brushes and involves a different set of skills than vertical painting. Large scenic studios equipped for horizontal painting employ a series of catwalks above the floor on which the painters stand to work, thereby avoiding any necessity of walking on the scenery. Both methods have advantages and disadvantages, and decisions must be made according to personal preferences if the shop facilities are equally adaptable.

Fireproofing

We mentioned in the previous chapter that municipal safety regulations require the use of a flame retardant. Inasmuch as many scenic fabrics can be purchased from supply houses already fireproofed, it may be necessary to treat only the wooden frames with a proofing solution before covering. Since the solution is usually mixed in the paint shop and applied with spray or brush, we consider it a part of the basic painting procedure.

The usual method is to apply the solution to the unit after the covering has been attached to the frame, assuming that the fabric has not been treated previously. However, a color change can develop when a base coat is applied after the proofing solution. If this presents a problem, tests should be made. One way to solve this dilemma would be to apply the flame-retardant solution to the back of the scenery after the painting is completed on the front.

If draperies or stage hangings are to be fireproofed, use complete immersion and allow the fabric to dry in a hanging position. The flameproofing treatment is not permanent, and so it will not remain in effect for much longer than a five-year period, which means it would be necessary to retreat the items within reasonable time limits to comply with safety regulations.

The Prime Coat

Because scenery surfaces vary widely, depending on whether they are formed of wood, fabric, or metal, and on whether they are new or used, a variety of surfaces must be prepared to accept successive coats of paint uniformly. New woods can be coated with opaque shellac, and translucent drops can use liquid starch effectively as a prime coat. The prime coat should be economical, and so inexpensive whiting is a good choice. By adding a bit of color pigment, you can easily match the brush strokes. When using large priming brushes, make sure to use crisscross strokes to avoid directional marks. "Feathering" the edges may reduce harsh boarders. A spray gun or paint roller may serve as alternate application methods.

The Base Coat

The next step in the painting process is applying the base coat, which provides a foundation for the desired final intensity and color for the setting. With the color sketch as a reference, you may choose to make the base coat the lightest, darkest, or a medium tone. The paint mixture should not be too thick or the surface of the unit will be overloaded with paint. Proper consistency can be achieved by using more pigment and less whiting in the paint mixture.

The same crisscross brush technique should be used for the base coat. Start at the top of the scenery and avoid scrubbing or overpainting. You can use several different techniques for base coating to achieve desired effects. Usually an even, flat appearance is required, but occasionally a shaded appearance may be needed. Degrees of the same hue can be used and carefully blended while the colors are moist. This will avoid a freshly painted look, which a flat, even base would convey. Several colors can be worked together using separate brushes to give a variegated effect and to provide an excellent background for foliage, masonary, brick, and stone. A rougher result can be achieved by dribbling several brushes charged with different colors over the surface and then using a straw broom to work the colors together. The last technique can only be used if the scenery is placed in a horizontal position on the floor.

Texture Coats

Used to provide a dimensional quality to a setting, texturing techniques produce certain emotional variations to a setting that are not created by flat, single tones. Texturing can add depth to a surface and enhance the style of execution. Stage lighting tends to dispel shadows and any reflected light. Carefully painted texturing can restore that dramatic element. The scene painter needs to determine which technique is most appropriate to the emotion and style of the particular play. Most texturing techniques are achieved through skill and practice. Considerable experimentation and testing must take place before final application. This step of the painting process is apt to be time-consuming and rather untidy. However, when the proper results are achieved, the rewards are gratifying.

Spattering, or hand splashing, as it is called in England, is the most common of texture techniques (Fig. 9.1). Relatively faster than most procedures, it can provide a rich character to an otherwise flat color or sur-

face. It also can improve errors made in an unsuccessful application of base coat. It can correct and tone down mistakes and is very useful in emphasizing the actors by effecting a darker coat at the top of the set and, thereby, controlling audience focus. Sometimes spattering is used to tone down designs such as wallpaper or graining and similar details too definite in execution. The technique can be used to simulate pitted surface textures such as plaster, stone, or brick.

To apply, use a laying-in brush and dip only slightly into the paint. Drain off excess paint on the edge of the bucket, and, with the brush in one hand, hit the ferrule against the heel of the other hand. This will cause the brush bristles to flip drops of paint onto the scenery. The size the drops will

Figure 9.1 Spatter

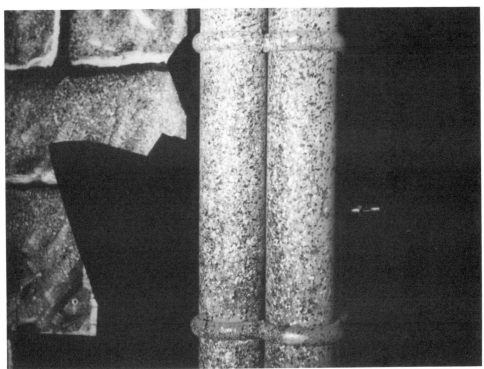

depend on the type of brush, the distance from the surface, the amount of paint on the brush, and the force of the impact against the hand. As with most texturing techniques, the usual test samples need to be made to control the process. Paint spots should be approximately 3/16 in. in diameter and executed at a distance of some three feet or more from the surface for maximum coverage and the best effect.

Dry Brushing. A very effective method of reproducing wood grains and blending color over a base coat, dry brushing is sometimes referred to as scumbling or combing, since the basic tools and eventual effects are reasonably similar. It is a fairly easy technique to use, but like many other painting techniques, it cannot be reworked (Fig. 9.2). If mistakes occur, the areas will have to be treated to a second coat. The effect is ob-

tained by using an old laying-in brush with bristles that are bunched up. String or rubber bands can be used to bind the sections together when necessary. The brush is dipped into the paint and wiped against the sides of the bucket to remove as much paint as possible, and then drawn lightly over the base-coated scenery. It may be necessary to research actual pictures of various wood grains to achieve an accurate reproduction.

Stippling. Stippling produces a heavier and coarser effect than spattering, but it is more subtle than sponging (Fig. 9.3). Stippling brushes, with appropriate, stiff bristles, are available from scenic paint suppliers, but some older, stiff brushes may work as well. Both natural and artificial sponges are used for stippling, and they can be cut or sculptured into uneven shapes that produce interesting patterns. Rags, fabrics, and tur-

Figure 9.2   Dry brushing

Figure 9.3 Stippling

key feather dusters are also employed with excellent results (Fig. 9.4). The brush or applicator is dipped lightly in the paint and daubed on the base-coated surface. To add variety to the pattern, the applicator is turned each time. The most desirable effects are achieved by using two or more colors.

Rolling. This technique makes use of paint rollers that can be trimmed or shaped to produce a pattern if lightly charged with paint (Fig. 9.5). Special rollers with specific design patterns are also available at local commercial paint stores. These rollers should be charged lightly with paint and then gently applied to the surface. This is a time-saving technique when handled correctly. Paint rollers are the fastest means of covering large surfaces, such as floors, platform tops, and so on. Some experimentation

may be needed, but the results are worth the effort.

Applique. When a more realistic texture is desired, it can be achieved by making some additions to the base coat paint. Wood chips and sawdust are effective as long as a bit more glue is added to the size to give more adhesion to the mixture and to prevent the material from shedding. Commercial preparations, which contain actual plaster, will also work if handling or moving will not cause them to crack or shed.

Rag Rolling. This process, although time-consuming, is extremely effective in presenting a rough, textured finish similar to stucco and plastered surfaces (Fig. 9.6). Rag rolling uses burlap, approximately 18 in. square, with fringed edges. It is dipped in paint and

Figure 9.4   Feather dusting

rolled, keeping the fringe on the outside. The surplus paint is squeezed out as the burlap is rolled on the surface of the unit. The direction of the roll is changed with each application, and a different roll is used for each new paint color.

Sponging. A fast and effective method of application, this technique uses either large, natural or artificial sponges charged with paint and lightly applied to the surface in a rolling motion (Fig. 9.7). The position of the sponge imprint must be changed to avoid duplicating the pattern.

Spraying. Various mechanical devices can be used to create textured patterns on scenery, and although they are a fast means of application, they do not necessarily give the most effective results. The Hudson tank sprayer is the most efficient and easiest to use. The spray gun, with its air compressor, has more control over the types of spray required. For more delicate work, such as small details and shadowing, an airbrush gun can be used. However, these mechanical applicators need constant and thorough cleaning to keep them operational.

Flogging. Cloth such as muslin, monk's cloth, netting, or corduroy, can be dipped in paint, rung out, and then slapped or flogged against the scenery surface. The resulting patterns can resemble coarse plaster and rough stonework.

Stamping. This technique is especially useful for creating repeated patterns with differences in color intensities. The stamp is made by cutting a design in a piece of foam

Figure 9.5 Rollers

Figure 9.6 Rag Rolling

Figure 9.7 Sponging

rubber or plastic and, through the use of several colors, can be very helpful in producing foliage and leaf effects.

Stenciling. Stenciling creates repeated patterns and is especially useful for wallpaper designs inasmuch as the designs found in actual wallpaper are too small and intricate to be effective on stage. This technique is frequently used for border designs or patterns on drapery fabric (Fig. 9.8). Stencil paper is available at local art and paint stores in 20 in. by 24 in. sheets that are impregnated with heavy oil. The stencil design pattern is cut out of the board with a single-edged razor blade or an X-Acto knife, stapled to a 1 in. by 2 in. wood frame, and nailed together on edge. The paper is then covered with shellac or a clear acrylic spray to aid in protecting the stencil from the de-

bilitating effects of the water content in the paint. It may be advisable to have additional stencils on hand. Paint can be applied by spray gun, with a brush, or with a sponge, depending on the desired effect. The stencil should be wiped clean of paint after each application to prevent a buildup of paint on design edges.

Detail Painting

This particular technique involves the decoration of a two-dimensional surface so it will resemble three-dimensional details. Architectural moldings require the most exacting analysis and subsequent execution to create a realistic representation. Often referred to as lining, the procedure involves special lining brushes of high quality in a variety of widths, along with several straight-

Figure 9.8 Stenciling

edges with handles and beveled edges to en-sure accuracy in control of the painted lines. A cross-section of the molding or paneling to be duplicated needs to be carefully deter-mined to ascertain the width and type of lines to be drawn. Determining sources of light aids in the establishment of highlights, shades, and shadows, and in choosing colors. Some architectural details will involve curved and decorative carvings that can best be produced by first drawing the design in correct scale on brown Kraft paper, and then perforating it with a tracing wheel. A pounce bag of cheesecloth filled with dry pigment or powdered charcoal is then used to transmit the design onto the scenery. After using charcoal or a pencil to complete the design, paint in highlights and lowlights to give a three-dimensional effect.

Another type of detail painting is used to achieve the look of foliage. Several general tones of green are scumbled on the surface to provide a background. When the back-ground is dry, the individual leaflike forms are applied in several hues and intensities, using short, leaf-size strokes. Liners usually work well for this effect; feather dusters can then be used for a casual appearance.

Glazing

This process can be used to blend fin-ished colors on scenery and produces a more subtle effect. It also can be employed to give an "antique" look to particular areas and to contribute a "polished" finish to woods and marble reproductions. Almost any paint product can be converted into a workable glaze through the addition of a thinner and sometimes by adding binding. Shellacs, dyes, water-based paints, and clear latex can be used.

Back Painting

Opacity must usually be given to the fin-ished scenic units to ensure that backstage lights cannot bleed through. Some translucent drops may bleed in certain areas and need to be opaqued if backlighting is involved. Backpainting can also provide an opportunity for flameproofing, if that has not been accomplished previously.

PAINT SHOP ORGANIZATION

An efficiently organized and carefully planned shop arrangement will contribute greatly to quality production. Unfortunately, most paint shops are woefully inadequate in space, ventilation, lighting, and accessibility. Horizontal and vertical space should be considered when planning for work space. Approximately 8 ft. of work space needs to be allowed in front of the paint frame so that painters can move easily in the area. If possible, enough space should be allowed so that patterns can be projected onto units for painting. Projections provide immense help in layout for drops and smaller units as well. Twenty to thirty feet should be adequate. An electric winch system in the paint shop also provides invaluable assistance.

If horizontal painting is employed, the floor will need to be constructed of softwood, inasmuch as drops need to be stretched taut and tacked down before sizing. In addition, the floor should be free of depressions or paint and water will collect in those areas. Ideally, a catwalk should be constructed over the area, as noted earlier. The size of the largest drop to be painted usually determines the size necessary for the paint shop floor. Good, general incandescent illumination in the shop should be located so that shadows of the scene painters will not interfere with their work. Proper ventilation, with adequate temperature and humidity controls, will facilitate reasonable drying times for newly painted scenery. Storage areas need to be planned to accom-

modate a full range of dry colors, with large-sized bins for the most-often used colors, such as ochre, umber, sienna, black, chrome green, and ultramarine blue. The other dry colors can be stocked in smaller amounts. Caseins, vinyls, and latex paints, as well as aniline dyes, can be stored in their original containers. Brushes should be stored in a hanging position in well-ventilated cabinets. Metal cabinets need to be supplied for all flammable materials.

The paint-mixing area needs to be conveniently close to the storage bins, the water supply, and container or paint bucket storage areas. A large work table surface should be readily available for mixing paint and should be located in close proximity to the electric glue pot and stove. A large utility sink, with hot and cold running water, will need a wide drain to handle all the washing requirements for brushes and containers. A shelf above the sink should be stocked with cleansers and paper towels.

Because the painting of scenery requires the mixing of pigments and the use of various application techniques, such as spraying and spattering of large surface areas, it is essential that the area be thoroughly cleaned with great frequency. Good management will save both time and money and will help achieve more artistic results.

Equipment and Care

Proper equipment for work in a theatre paint shop is essential to allow the scene designer to use the full range of painted effects needed to achieve the final desired result. For example, a different texture can be achieved only by using a different application method. Consequently, a large priming brush cannot be used to get a foliage effect. Scene painters, like most graphic artists, develop a dependence on specific favorite tools, and many maintain a personal collection of these special tools for their private use.

A well-equipped paint shop will undoubtedly have most of the following items.

Brushes:
Priming—6 in. to 8 in. in width
Laying-in—3 in. to 5 in. in width (Fig. 9.9)
Stippling—9 in. by 3 1/2 in. with 3 in. bristles
Fitch—1 1/2 in. to 2 1/2 in. wide
Decorating—2 in. to 3 in. wide
Lining—1/4 in., 3/8 in., 1/2 in., 3/4 in., 1 in., and 1 1/2 in. (Fig. 9.10)
Sash—1 in. to 3 in. wide
Several small, inexpensive brushes
Poster brush for combing (Schlepitchka technique)
Additional Paint Appliers:
Sponges—natural and plastic
Turkey feather dusters
Brooms—standard and push
Spray gun and air compressor
Hudson compression sprayer—2-, 3-, and 4-gallon size

Figure 9.9 Laying-in-brushes

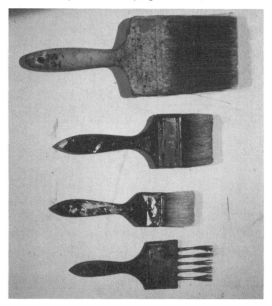

Layout Tools:
Charcoal sticks and holder
Yardstick
Straightedges—6 ft. and 3 ft.
Felt-tip pens and markers
Chalk snap line—50 ft.
Bow snap line—6 ft.
Tracing wheel
Large compass—36 in.
Bamboo drawing sticks—4 ft. long
Plumb bob
Steel measuring tape—50 ft. long
Miscellaneous Items:
Masking tape
Electric glue pot (Fig. 9.11)
Electric opaque projector
Small electric stove or hot plate
Gaffer's tape
Paint carrier with handle large enough to hold several small tins of paint for horizontal painting (Fig. 9.12)
Scrub brushes
Heavy-duty tack hammer
Low dolly cart with wheels for mobile paint palette
Stepladder—6 ft. to 10 ft.
Metal strainers
Stencil paper
Cheesecloth
Chalk
Sinks—large and deep with running water
Gray Kraft paper—50 ft. rolls
Storage bins and work table
Brown wrapping paper—50 ft. rolls
Cabinets of metal for flammable items
Large metal dippers
Dust masks
R-spirator
Wooden paddles for paint mixing
Metal scoops
Containers:
Galvanized tins—20- to 30-gallon size
Buckets—1-, 5-, and 10-gallon size
Tin containers—8-oz. size
Glass jars with lids—1-gallon size

To ensure that the equipment will perform effectively when needed, you need to use it properly and clean it thoroughly and carefully after you use it. Adequate storage facilities for protection and ventilation need

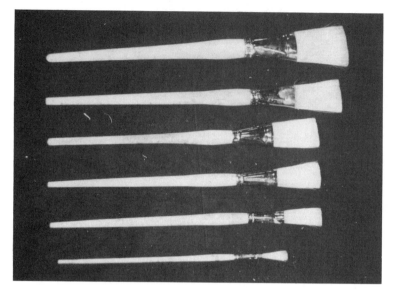

Figure 9.10   Lining brushes

to be provided. Liquids should be tightly capped to reduce evaporation. Every designer realizes the importance of a watercolor brush to create an effective color sketch. Scene painting brushes are equally important, regardless of their size. They require the same care and treatment to produce repeated results over a long period of time.

Here are some important points to remember when working with brushes:

1. Always use the proper brush for the task; for example, do not use watercolor brushes for oil-base paints, do not use liners for laying in, and so on.

2. Do not use a brush to stir paint. Use a

Figure 9.11   Electric glue pot

Figure 9.12 Paint carrier

paint paddle. Do not allow the brush to rest on its bristles while soaking in water or paint.

3. Do not use a brush with a scrubbing motion. Lightly stroke the surface to be painted.

4. Clean the brush thoroughly as soon as possible after using. Shape the bristles after cleaning to allow drying in the original form.

5. Hang the brushes up to dry in a well-ventilated cabinet. Liners can rest carefully in a flat position.

Because the characteristics of the materials used in scene painting do not lend themselves to tidiness and spotlessness, you must control the conditions of cleanliness in the paint area. Failure to do so will lessen your efficiency. Paint buckets should be thoroughly cleaned after use. Floors should be swept and washed down frequently. Brushes should be cleaned and put away. Premixed paint should be tightly capped. These and other similar activities will improve the shop's operation.

DROP PAINTING

The use of backdrops as backgrounds for actors is almost as old as recorded theatre history. Certain elements trace back to the early Greeks, but the actual painted scene did not take on its true importance until the Italian Renaissance. A backdrop will fulfill a number of production requirements: It can hide undesirable backstage views from an audience; it can influence acoustics; it can unify a design; it can represent distance through perspective; it can identify a specific location and time of day; and it can establish the mood and intention of the playwright. Drops, which English designers refer to as back cloths, are made in varying sizes which depend on use, stage size, production budget and dimensions of the paint area, as well as design requirements. Radio City Music Hall uses drops 90 ft. wide by 45 ft. tall, while a neighborhood theatre group may need one no more than 18 ft. by 12 ft.

Several types of hanging pieces are used in the theatre, depending on the particular requirements of the production. The most familiar drops comprise gathered fabric curtains used as a front curtain, side legs, borders, or background curtains. Hanging pieces can be made of velvet, velour, duvetsyn, satin, or muslin as well as other materials. They can be stenciled, sprayed, appliqued, and painted. Asbestos safety curtains and straight-front curtains may have attractive scenes and designs painted on them. Cycloramas, which are large curved hangings, can be gathered or straight. If straight hanging, they are generally carefully lighted to represent sky.

Small painted drops are sometimes used outside doors and windows in realistic settings and, of course, dimensional-appearing backgrounds are almost a requirement for any present-day musical. Designers in the nineteenth century made great use of rollers for raising and lowering curtains and drops, mainly because of the absence of stage houses for flying. Some designers have used side rollers to slowly move the painted scene horizontally and to suggest an opposite movement in the foreground. A plain, unpainted backdrop can also serve as a screen for slide projections and motion pictures composed as elements of the production.

Painting a backdrop is challenging but ultimately rewarding to the scene painter. It requires careful preparation and execution. If the drop is to be painted horizontally, a position preferred by most professional scene painters, care must be taken not to soil the new muslin. Use gray bogus paper to cover the floor before spreading and smoothing out the drop. Next, snap off lines on all four sides to the exact measurements of the drop, and then nail or staple the drop to the floor.

A sizing preparation is applied to the new muslin with a Hudson sprayer and brushed into the fabric with long-handled, clean brooms or brushes. The sizing comprises liquid starch, the formula for which is 1 lb of Argo gloss laundry starch dissolved in 1/2 gallon of cold water and then poured into 3 gallons of boiling water. Allow the mixture to cool before using. The sizing process should be continuous, so be certain to mix enough of the size to handle the job.

If the drying process is prolonged because of climatic conditions, it can be hastened by the use of electric fans and heaters to shorten waiting time. To avoid having the muslin adhere to the protective paper under the drop, circulate air under the material. While the drop is still damp, the staples and nails can be removed from the two sides of the drop, and wooden triangles, 2 in. in height and 4 in. in length, can be placed carefully under the drop, thereby elevating it and preventing it from sticking.

After the starch is dry, again attach the sides to the floor and then establish a centerline on the drop. Using either a chalk snap line or a black cotton thread, create 2- or 3 ft. squares on the drop to correspond to a grid, which you have established on the painting elevation. Cartoon in the squares with a felt-tipped pen or charcoal stick. If you use charcoal, dust away excess dust with a feather duster.

When mixing colors for the drop, remember to separate them into distant, middle, and foreground areas by color intensities. This will aid in achieving perspective effects of space and distance.

The first paint applied should be the sky, if there is one in the design. Use a Hudson sprayer for this, lightly but carefully spreading the paint. Clouds can be created by masking areas with cutout patterns; they can be painted in later with a spray gun or brush. After the sky is dry, fill in other opaque areas, beginning with the distant details first.

So-called mistakes possibly can be corrected by using one part chlorine bleach to two parts water and a reasonable drying time. When the painting is finished and thoroughly dry, remove the nails and staples and attach the drop to a batten, fly it, and adjust it to hanging position. Old drops sometimes can be bleached or washed out and repainted. If a drop is primarily painted with dye, you may be able to do opaque painting on the drop to create a different appearance. However, opaque paints diminish a drop's ability to travel and store. Certainly retouching old drops, which makes them appear fresh and new, can save money.

Cut drops should be completely painted and thoroughly dried before they are cut and trimmed. Sometimes, because of the intricate design of the cutting, you will need to use netting glued to the back of the drop to support the trimmed edges and help them to hang properly. The netting should be dyed black and attached to the back of the drop with white, flexible glue.

Scrim drops are generally dyed a specific color and may have cutout material appliqued on them; they are subsequently painted. Some scrim drops have complete scenes painted on them in the same manner as opaque muslin drops. A properly executed drop is the most economical method a designer has for covering a large area artistically—a fact that undoubtedly accounts for the continued popularity of the drop over the years.

SPECIAL-EFFECTS PAINTING

Special-effects scenery painting generally refers to a multitude of techniques the scene painter can use to represent realistic patterns and three-dimensional objects on two-dimensional surfaces. The techniques depend on careful observation and research of the objects to be reproduced.

Foliage

Foliage is difficult to do well, because this effect involves several textures and a variety of patterns to simulate living trees, shrubs, branches, bushes, and other plant life (Fig. 9.13). Research from actual color photographs, master landscape painters, and life itself will offer background material to help the scene painter achieve the required results.

Figure 9.13 Foliage

First, three basic areas should be sketched out in charcoal. They are the distant, middle, and foreground elements. The distant areas are filled in first, followed by the middle areas, and then the foreground. Each area's base coat should consist of two colors, one light and one dark, and be applied in what might be termed a "casual" fashion. You can use a number of painting techniques, including puddling, scumbling, stippling, and even dry brushing for tree trunks and branches. Leaf shapes and forms can be executed with a 2 1/2-in. or 3-in. Fitch brush or more boldly with a feather duster. Keep leaf tone colors in the same distant, middle, and foreground relationships and add lighter shades and highlights last. Establish a direction for a light source so highlights and shadows can be established consistently. Work with a selected and sparing pattern; consider foliage as an accent rather than a copiously duplicated leaf form. Allow sections of sky to show through the foliage for a more natural effect. A light spatter coat will produce a subtle blending of various colors and techniques.

Wood Graining

The appearance of wood is almost as diversified as natural foliage, and, like foliage, it requires examining and researching in detail. Wood colors, grains, and patterns have tremendous differences, and you must know exactly what you are trying to achieve if you are to create an acceptable finished product (Fig. 9.14).

Several painting techniques apply to wood graining. The two most often used involve flat painting combined with dry brushing, and glazing. The former procedure works fairly well for rough, unpolished woods and requires a wet blending of two or three colors, using some basic middle values of the particular type of wood to be reproduced. A two-color (one light, one dark) dry brush technique is applied then to the base, carefully detailing the direction and patterns of the grain of the specific wood. After the graining is completed, add highlights and shadows for joints and knots. If necessary, use a straightedge to ensure trimness.

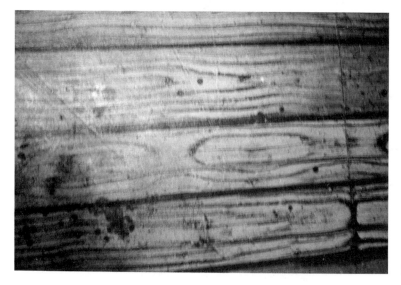

Figure 9.14 Wood graining

If a polished appearance is required, shellac with some thinner or apply a gloss vinyl glaze.

The second method uses shellac thinned with alcohol and tinted with woodlike dry pigments. Generally, two coats will be needed to produce an acceptable flat coat. Regular oil stain can then be used for graining. Some experimentation with brush work in combing the oil stain will give you the effect you want. A less popular, third, method involves painting the surface with a flat white base and then dry-brushing the graining effect in ultramarine blue. After drying, a glaze of orange shellac, thinned and tinted with pigments approximating the desired wood color, is brushed on. This method is quick and effective, but it does require some testing.

Stones

Like everything else in life, stone comes in many varieties of color and texture. Its use also affects its appearance; that is, cutting and masonry techniques influence the way stone looks. Know what you are trying to achieve before you start. There are stones, and then, again, there are stones (Fig. 9.15). The base coat is wet blended or scumbled using shades of gray. Sponging, ragging, and some spattering will dispel the smooth surface of the base for the texture coat. Mortar divisions are detailed by lining and accenting with highlights and shadows. If the stone is laid in an orderly fashion, use a straightedge. Otherwise, a freehand technique probably is best.

Brick

Because they usually fall in even patterns, bricks can be stenciled. If a stencil is used, the base coat should be the mortar color. If a stencil is not used, the base can be wet-blended. Three or four tones of brick color should be used to give variety. Bricks can be smooth or rough textured, and the amount of stippling, spongeing, and spattering you do will be determined by the surface texture desired. Detailing involves the use of a snap line and straightedge to lay out mortar lines. Highlighting and shadowing the bricks give them further definition. Additional spatter

Figure 9.15 Stones

Figure 9.16   Brick

coats and glazes increase the appearance of depth (Fig. 9.16).

Marble

Again, various types of marble exist, and their patterns and colors differ considerably. Do your research carefully. Marble grain, like wood grain, has a definite direction that will need to be emphasized to carry to the audience. The base coat uses a minimum of two colors scumbled or blended. The colors need to flow together, and so you should assist the blending by using brushes charged with water. Veins can be applied with small liners or with a cotton cord dipped in paint and dragged over the surface while the base coat is still wet. Vary the widths of the lines, which can be crisscrossed for a more realistic appearance. A final coat of dye glaze, clear shellac with thinner, or clear gloss vinyl will add the polished appearance necessary (Fig. 9.17).

Draperies

Unlike other special effects that deal with the reproduction of nature, cloth draperies

and tapestries are manufactured by humankind and usually are painted with highly realistic detail (Fig. 9.18). Foliage, for example, is next to impossible to portray in absolute realism, and so some degree of stylization is not only needed but fully acceptable to an audience. Theatre conventions more or less acknowledge that "only God can make a tree." Draperies are quite another matter. Consequently, your observation and painting technique must be flawless. After the base coat is applied in a reasonably even fashion and allowed to dry, draw in the folds of the material. Sheer fabric hangs in narrow folds; heavier materials such as velvets hang in stiff, large, and thick folds. If curved draperies are at issue, use rope or cotton cord as the pattern for hanging when working vertically. When working horizontally, you can make a string compass to aid in freehanding the outline.

Use two darker and two lighter tones of the base coat for laying in the folds. The direction of light is a most important consideration at this time. Highlights and shadows are critical in making painted drapery appear real. Brush the first dark color into the

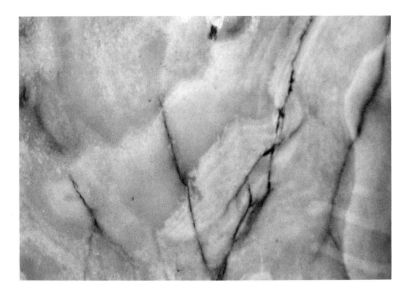

Figure 9.17 Marble

folds; follow this with the first light color; then comes the darkest color followed by the highlight or lightest color. Once the vertical folds are completed, add whatever details you desire, such as ropes and tassels, fringes, and fancy borders.

Although most painting of draperies is done dry, you can work while the paint is wet, as one might while doing a watercolor sketch. However, we do not recommend this method without a good deal of experimentation ahead of time.

Figure 9.18 Tapestry drapery

Experienced scene designers always look forward to the challenge created by the application of paint to the constructed settings. The design takes on visual qualities only suggested by sketches or diminutive models. Most designers relish the challenge of selecting and mixing scenic colors and delight in the results that various painting techniques achieve. The entire process stimulates the imagination and encourages creativity.

CHAPTER TEN

RUNNING THE SHOW

Theatre is a cooperative art, and it cannot be created by a single artist. A play can be read, but it comes to life only in performance. A scene design sketch cannot be considered a work of art, because it is only a suggestion of the actual finished product on the stage. Collective wisdom states that, for every actor who walks on stage to perform, there are forty individuals working in various backstage capacities. Writers, designers, technicians, publicists, stage managers, dressers, electricians, and many others work together to present a single actor to an audience. The scene designer is, of course, one of those cooperative people who must function in an organization dedicated to presenting a successful production.

Good communication is a vital factor in any producing company. Without it, no one functions well, and chaos reigns. With it, the varied talents of each participant grow and contribute to the success of the venture. Good communication requires a number of presentations, conferences, meetings, and discussions with the persons who have responsibility in the creative development of the production. The designer must be aware of the other personnel involved and their particular responsibilities in order to secure the cooperation and assistance necessary to operate within the group successfully.

In previous chapters we discussed the professional designer's contractual responsibilities and gave an overall view of the design process from first reading of the script to final painting. In addition, we must examine actual operational procedures, staff, and others' responsibilities.

JOB ASSIGNMENTS

Producer

The producer organizes the production, beginning with solicitations to investors, setting up budgets, and securing peformance and rehearsal spaces (Fig. 10.1). This person brings together the script, the theatre, the director, the designers, and the actors. He or she ultimately is responsible for the production's finances. In educational theatres, the department chairperson normally fulfills this function, but in the professional theatre the producer may be anyone (preferably one who has strong business and artistic inclinations).

Director

This artist controls the actors, and, in a less direct fashion, controls the designers, stage manager, and technical director. The amount of authority varies according to the organization. Educational theatre directors often exert more control in their instructive situation than is necessary in the professional theatre. However, ultimate decisions must sometimes be made by the director after careful consideration. That authority for a production often riles scenic designers, who do not take kindly to another's decisions that affect their work and livelihood. Nonetheless, such authority is a fact of contemporary theatre, and the designer must learn how to live productively with it.

Stage Manager

The stage manager has complete control of all elements of the performance. He or she is responsible for all the cues, which coordinate the actors and the production technicians. To accomplish this, the stage manager must have been associated with the production from the earliest meetings. In the professional theatre, the stage manager is a member of Actors Equity. As a member, the stage manager is allowed to replace a cast member if an emergency should arise. The stage manager has complete authority over all backstage and onstage operations. After the opening performance, the professional stage manager is responsible only to the producer. A stage manager's prompt book is used to record script changes, shifting instructions, actors' stage movements, and light, sound, special effects, curtain, and activity cues.

Technical Director

The technical director is responsible for supervising all aspects of the technical production, including budgets and schedules. The technical director directs assembly of all the elements, such as scenery, lights, and properties for the production.

Construction Head

He or she sometimes is called the shop foreman or master stage carpenter and takes responsibility for construction, rigging, and assembly of all scenery. Order and safety are the watchwords for this job.

PROPERTY HEAD

Often referred to as the property manager, he or she assumes responsibility for constructing, assembling, and organizing all set properties, hand props, and decor items required by the script, the designer, and sometimes, even the actors. This job also involves running the show during the production and returning properties to lenders or storage when the run closes.

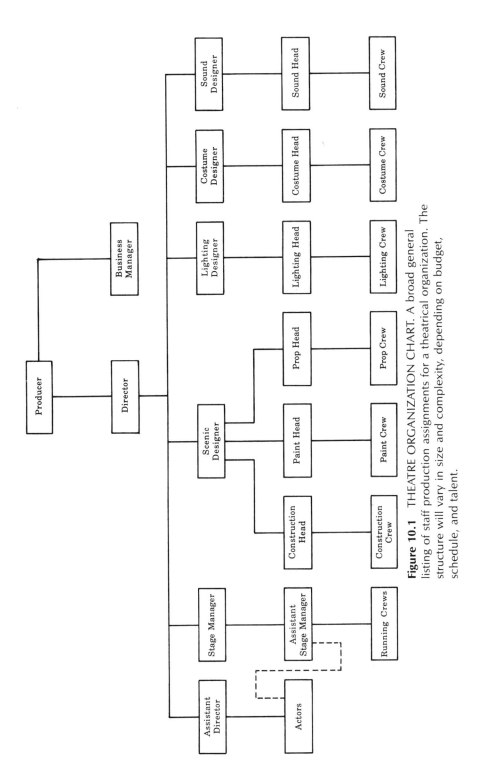

Figure 10.1 THEATRE ORGANIZATION CHART. A broad general listing of staff production assignments for a theatrical organization. The structure will vary in size and complexity, depending on budget, schedule, and talent.

Lighting and Costume Designers

These are artistic functions on an equal level with the scenic designer, and both artists function with procedures similar to those of the scene designer. The lighting and costume designers need frequent conferences with the scene designer to make certain that coordination exists between all the visual elements of the production. Each of the three designers is dependent on the other two, and a failure in concept, communication, and procedure by one can have a disastrous effect on the others.

PROCEDURAL ELEMENTS

The scene designer must concern himself or herself with procedures beyond the actual creative design process of model making, sketching, and drafting. A production calendar needs to be created. A production calendar is as important for the designer as a rehearsal schedule is for an actor. Reasonable deadlines and assignments must be established and agreed upon by all concerned. The designer must remember that schedules are not imposed; they are agreed upon. They may differ in many respects from one production to another, depending upon the working habits and styles of the people involved. Above all, schedules must be realistic. Design artistry often depends not upon what one would *like* to do, but upon what one has *time* to do.

Many creative individuals are unable realistically to estimate time, which is absolutely vital in a well-organized production. Unlike the graphic artist, hidden away in a garret, the scene designer has definite deadlines that involve numerous other persons and their jobs. For example, the lighting designer cannot do his or her job if the setting is not assembled and painted when the time comes

for focusing and selecting the color media for the lighting instruments. Opening night presents the final product to the audience. Undoubtedly, compromises may be needed, but once an agreement is reached on the schedule, production work can begin. Actually, the schedule will break down into two, very important deadlines. The first is the move-in date, which involves several different crews working in several different areas of production: paint, building, properties, costume construction, and so on. The second deadline comprises the first actual technical run-throughs or technical rehearsals. When this occurs depends upon the working style of the production team and the complexities of the show. Here occur the coordination and integration of all production elements (Fig. 10.2).

As mentioned earlier, communication within groups and with other area groups must be maintained to facilitate working relationships. Individual areas may need daily meetings to plan the day's work and review progress. Other meetings, involving several areas or even all production areas, can be held weekly or whenever needed. These include design presentations, budget discussions, move-in plans, work assignments, and other important matters.

The designer must work closely with the stage manager, construction personnel, and the technical director in planning the shifting plot, the mechanics involved, and the number of stagehands required. These factors can influence the final design. Setup plans follow a basic arrangement of sequence and must be carefully prepared in advance of the work. All flown scenery is set up first. This includes lighting instruments, ceilings, scenery pieces, backdrops, and masking draperies. Next, the floor cloth is laid down and attached to the stage floor, and then scenic pieces are assembled and platforming put in place. Finally, the total

SUGGESTED CALENDAR FOR SCENIC DESIGNERS

1ST WEEK	Feb. 30	Monday	Production meeting with director, designers and business manager.
	Mar. 1	Tuesday	Reading and research.
	2	Wednesday	Same.
	3	Thursday	Same.
	4	Friday	Thumbnail sketches. Conference with director.
	5	Saturday	Compose color sketches and/or model.
	6	Sunday	Same.
2ND WEEK	Mar. 7	Monday	Production meeting with director, designers and all production heads. Sketch and/or model presentation. Crews announced.
	8	Tuesday	Begin drafting and initiate ordering of needed materials.
	9	Wednesday	Same.
	10	Thursday	Same.
	11	Friday	Same. Begin paint elevations.
	12	Saturday	Same.
	13	Sunday	Same.
3RD WEEK	Mar. 14	Monday	Production meeting. All plans and drawings finalized and presented to director, construction, paint, property, light, sound and running crew heads.
	15	Tuesday	Construction begins. Short presentation of sketches and/or model to cast at start of rehearsal.
	16	Wednesday	Construction continues.
	17	Thursday	Same.
	18	Friday	Same.
	19	Saturday	Dark.
	20	Sunday	Dark.
4TH WEEK	Mar. 21	Monday	Production meeting. Reports from crew heads. Construction continues.
	22	Tuesday	Construction continues.
	23	Wednesday	Same.
	24	Thursday	Same.
	25	Friday	Same.
	26	Saturday	Dark.
	27	Sunday	Dark.
5TH WEEK	Mar. 28	Monday	Production meeting. Reports from crew heads. Paint begins.
	29	Tuesday	Paint continues.
	30	Wednesday	Same.
	31	Thursday	Same.
	Apr. 1	Friday	Same.
	2	Saturday	Same.
	3	Sunday	Same, if necessary.
6TH WEEK	Apr. 4	Monday	Production meeting. Load in on theatre stage. Designer is required.
	5	Tuesday	Setup: lights and sound.
	6	Wednesday	Setup: scenery, lights and sound.
	7	Thursday	Setup: props, scenery, lights and sound.
	8	Friday	Paint touch up. Technical rehearsal.
	9	Saturday	Technical rehearsal.
	10	Sunday	First dress.
7TH WEEK	Apr. 11	Monday	Production meeting. Second dress.
	12	Tuesday	Picture call. Third dress.
	13	Wednesday	Final dress.
	14	Thursday	Preview.
	15	Friday	Opening night.

Figure 10.2 Suggested calendar for designers.

settings are brought into place on- or off-stage. The setting may require some touching up with paint or slight repair to damage created in the move. This is a most important time for the designer, because it will be the first time the design is completely set up in the theatre where it will be used. Sometimes this provides unexpected problems, especially if one discovers any inaccuracies in the plans for the theatre, on which the design was based.

After the setup, the designer must be concerned with set props and their location on the ground plan and with set dressing elements that help to unify the total visual appearance.

The next few days are occupied with adjusting lighting instruments, technical rehearsals (with and without cast), and shifting problems. The usual procedure is to work on the technical problems during the day and work with the cast in the evenings. However, one is advised to have at least one rehearsal, complete with cast, where the action is stopped each time a problem is found, and suspended until a solution is achieved. Actors normally hate this rehearsal, and the designer is advised to wear a thick skin and a cheerful countenance, trying to be oblivious to the satiric comments that inevitably crescendo from seemingly everywhere in the theatre. This rehearsal can be frustrating, but it will uncover solutions and alternatives that cannot be arrived at by any other means. The stage manager and the director play key roles in this anxiety-ridden practice,

but the end results are rewarding and reassuring. After this baptism by fire, the remaining rehearsals should proceed smoothly.

Dress rehearsals acquaint the actors with their costumes and allow them to adjust to movement in them. At some time during the several dress rehearsals, the publicity department will schedule photo calls, which can come before or after a rehearsal and sometimes even during, if action shots are needed. The photo call should be scheduled carefully, because it will generally involve the entire company, including stagehands, electricians, and wardrobe personnel.

The final dress rehearsal should be conducted as if there were an audience in the theatre. Essentially its purpose is to help the actors adjust to any final problems and to give a sense of performance formality. In reality, it is a performance without audience. Many theatres now present a series of preview performances for audiences at reduced ticket prices. These allow the actors to perform and adjust to audience reactions. Occasionally, minor dialogue changes occur at this point, based on audience reactions. The opening performance, of course, plays to an audience that has paid full ticket price and to critics who are guests of the management. At this point, the stage manager is in complete control of the production. The designer is free to turn to the next project, assuming that the next project and several others, for that matter, have not already been started.

CHAPTER ELEVEN

A DESIGN ANTHOLOGY

This chapter presents a visual anthology of scenic design for you to study without benefit of text. In the following examples, you will find a wide variety of creativity, style, and practical application. The dozens of renderings and production photographs provide a rich resource for broadening your horizons.

SUMMARY

When we began examining the scene designer's role, we discussed the creative insight and individual dedication necessary to the development of a theatre artist. Given a written work of someone else's vision, the scenic designer must produce a visual mood, theme, and environment that will enhance the meaning of that vision. In later chapters we began to move the designer into a more collaborative position as the design began to take shape. Eventually we discussed the designer's emergence as part of an intricate arrangement of plans, dreams, ideas, labor, and creativity.

Theatre, like a stained glass window, is a cooperative creation. The range of its composition has given challenges to the designer from the Renaissance to the present. We can teach the steps and the techniques inherent in designing scenery for the theatre. That is what this book is about. However, the creativity that makes all the difference between a great designer and ordinary mortals cannot be taught. It can be enhanced, perhaps, but true creativity comes from the inside. We can nurture and coax. You, ultimately, will discern whether to ignore it or set it free into the glorious light of day.

Figure 11.1 Hawes Craven, scene design for *A Midsummer Night's Dream* (wood scene), 1901. Courtesy of the Victoria and Albert Museum.

Figure 11.2 Hawes Craven, scene design for *Cymbeline,* act 4, scene 2. Cut scene and backcloth, forming model design. Lyceum Theatre, 1896. Courtesy of the Victoria and Albert Museum.

Figure 11.3 Hawes Craven, scene design for *Quo Vadis,* Lyceum Theatre, 1900. Courtesy of the Victoria and Albert Museum.

Figure 11.4 The Grieve family, scene design for *The Wrecker's Daughter,* Drury Lane, 1836. Courtesy of the Victoria and Albert Museum.

Figure 11.5 The Grieve family, scene design for *Harlequin and Old Grammer Gurton,* Drury Lane, 1836. Courtesy of the Victoria and Albert Museum.

Figure 11.6 The Grieve family, scene design for *Shakespeare's Early Days,* Covent Garden, 1829. Courtesy of the Victoria and Albert Museum.

Figure 11.7 The Grieve family, scene design for *Rob Roy the Gregarch,* Drury Lane, 1818. Courtesy of the Victoria and Albert Museum.

Figure 11.8 The Grieve family, scene design for *Nigel* or *The Crown Jewels,* Covent Garden, 1823. Courtesy of the Victoria and Albert Museum.

Figure 11.9 Clarkson Stanfield, design for *Henry V,* Battle of Agincourt, early nineteenth century. Courtesy of the Victoria and Albert Museum.

Figure 11.10 R. F., design for *Columbus,* by Ernst August Friedrich Klingemann, first 1/4, nineteenth century. Courtesy of the Victoria and Albert Museum.

Figure 11.11 John Henderson Grieve, design for *Ali Pasha,* by Howard Payne, Covent Garden 1822. Courtesy of the Victoria and Albert Museum.

Figure 11.12 John Henderson Grieve, design for *Harliquen and the Magic Rose,* 1825. Courtesy of the Victoria and Albert Museum.

Figure 11.13 William Telbin, design for *Ivy Hall,* adapted by J. Oxenford, Princess' Theatre, 1859. Courtesy of the Victoria and Albert Museum.

Figure 11.14 Thomas Grieve, design for *Henry V,* Princess' Theatre, 1859. Courtesy of the Victoria and Albert Museum.

Figure 11.14 *(continued)*

Figure 11.15 William Telbin, design for *Othello,* Princess' Theatre, 1860. Courtesy of the Victoria and Albert Museum.

Figure 11.16 William Telbin, design for *Hamlet,* Lyceum Theatre, 1864. Courtesy of the Victoria and Albert Museum.

Figure 11.17 Hawes Craven, design for *MacBeth,* Lyceum Theatre, 1888. Courtesy of the Victoria and Albert Museum.

Figure 11.18 Hawes Craven, design for *Henry VIII,* Lyceum Theatre, 1892. Courtesy of the Victoria and Albert Musuem.

Figure 11.19 Hawes Craven, design for *Becket* by Tennyson, act 3, scene 1, Lyceum Theatre, 1893. Courtesy of the Victoria and Albert Museum.

Figure 11.20 Hawes Craven, design for *Olivia,* by W. G. Willis, Lyceum Theatre, c. 1900. Courtesy of the Victoria and Albert Museum.

Figure 11.21 C. Ricketts, design for *Salome* by Oscar Wilde, Covent Garden, 1906. Courtesy of the Victoria and Albert Museum.

Figure 11.22 Frederick Cayley Robinson, design for *The Bluebird* by Maurice Maeterlinck, scene in act 4, The Kingdom of the Past, Haymarket, 1909. Courtesy of the Victoria and Albert Museum.

Figure 11.23 Chris Dyer, scene design for *Macbeth,* Royal Shakespeare Company, England, 1982–1983. Directed by Howard Davis; Costumes by Peggy Mitchell; Photo by Donald Cooper/ Photostage.

Figure 11.24 John Gunter, scene design for *All's Well that Ends Well,* Royal Shakespeare Company, England, 1982. Directed by Trevor Nunn; Costumes by Lindy Hemming; Photo by Donald Cooper/Photostage.

Figure 11.25 Sally Jacobs, scene design for *A Midsummer Night's Dream*, Royal Shakespeare Company, England, 1970. Directed by Peter Brook; Photo by Donald Cooper/Photostage.

Figure 11.26 Sally Jacobs, scene design for *A Midsummer Night's Dream*, Royal Shakespeare Company, England, 1970. Directed by Peter Brook; Photo by Donald Cooper/Photostage.

Figure 11.27 Bob Crowley, scene design for *The Comedy of Errors*, Royal Shakespeare Company, England, 1983. Directed by Adrian Noble; Photo by Donald Cooper/Photostage.

Figure 11.28 Bob Crowley, scene design for *As You Like It,* Royal Shakespeare Company, England, 1985. Directed by Adrian Noble; Photo by Donald Cooper/Photostage.

Figure 11.29 Ralph Koltai, scene design for *Much Ado About Nothing,* Royal Shakespeare Company, England, 1982. Directed by Terry Hands; Photo by Donald Cooper/Photostage.

Figure 11.30 Maria Bjornson, scene design for *Hamlet,* final scene, Royal Shakespeare Company, England, 1984. Directed by Ron Daniels; Photo by Donald Cooper/Photostage.

Figure 11.31   Hawes Craven, scene design for *A Midsummer Night's Dream* (wood scene), 1901. Courtesy of the Victoria and Albert Museum.

Figure 11.32   Hawes Craven, scene design for *Cymbeline,* act 4, scene 2. Cut scene and backcloth, forming model design. Lyceum Theatre, 1896. Courtesy of the Victoria and Albert Museum.

Figure 11.33 Tom Macie, scene design for *Appear and Show Cause.*
Hillberry Repertory Theatre.

Figure 11.34 Jonathan Sabo, scene design for *A Streetcar Named
Desire.* Hillberry Repertory Theatre.

Figure 11.35 Ming Cho Lee, scene design for *Roberto Devereaux*, New York State Opera. Courtesy of University of Arizona Theatre Collection, Tucson.

Figure 11.36 Robert C. Burroughs, scene design for *Peer Gynt*. University of Arizona, Tucson.

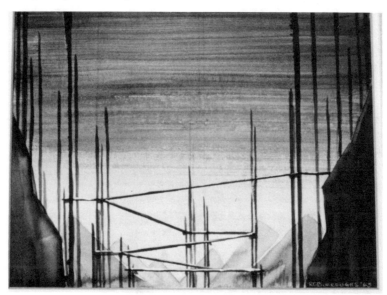

Figure 11.37 John Wright Stevens, scene design for *Norma,* act 1. Houston, Cincinnati, and Philadelphia Opera Companies. Photograph by John Wright Stevens.

Figure 11.38 Mark Donnelly, scene design for *Cyrano de Bergerac.* Act 4. Denver Center Theatre Company, Denver, Colorado.

Figure 11.39 Tom Benson, scene design for *Richard III*, Utah Shakespeare Festival, Cedar City.

Figure 11.40 John Wareing, scene design for *Who's Afraid of Virginia Woolf?* Playbox Community Theatre, Tucson, Ariz.

Figure 11.41 Robert C. Burroughs, scene design for *The Royal Family*.
University of Arizona, Tucson.

Figure 11.42 Douglas W. Schmidt, scene design for *Over Here!*
Shubert Theatre, New York City. Courtesy of University of Arizona Theatre
Collection, Tucson.

Figure 11.43 Hal Tiné, scene design for *The Gin Game,* Buffalo Arena Stage. Buffalo, New York.

Figure 11.44 Mark Donnelly, scene design for *My Fair Lady,* act 1 scene 1. Pacific Conservatory of the Performing Arts, Santa Maria, California.

Figure 11.45 James T. Singelis, scene design for *Faust*. Cincinnati Opera Company, Cincinnati, Ohio.

Figure 11.46 John Wareing, scene design for *Merlin,* University of Arizona, Tucson. Courtesy of University of Arizona Theatre Collection, Tucson.

Figure 11.47 Robert C. Burroughs, scene design for *The School for Husbands,* University of Arizona, Tucson.

Figure 11.48 John Wright Stevens, scene design for *Le Roman de Fauvel.* The Waverly Consort, New York City. Photograph by John Wright Stevens.

Figure 11.49 John Wareing, scene design model for *Romeo and Juliet.* University of Arizona, Tucson.

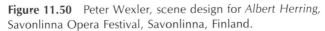

Figure 11.50 Peter Wexler, scene design for *Albert Herring,* Savonlinna Opera Festival, Savonlinna, Finland.

Figure 11.51 Thom Gilseth, scene design for *The Foreigner,* Phoenix Little Theatre, Phoenix, Ariz.

Figure 11.52 Peggy J. Kellner, scene design model for *The Petrified Forest.* University of Arizona, Tucson.

Figure 11.53 Mark Donnelly, scene design for *Picnic*. Cerritos College, Cerritos, Calif.

Figure 11.54 Vicki Smith, scene design model for *Taking Steps*. Arizona Theatre Company, Tucson.

Figure 11.55 Robert C. Burroughs, scene design *Under Two Flags.*
University of Arizona, Tucson.

Figure 11.56 James T. Singelis, scene design for *Flight of Devils.* Long Island Stage Company, Long Island, N.Y.

Figure 11.57 Thom Gilseth, scene design for *Brighton Beach Memoirs.* Phoenix Little Theatre, Phoenix, Ariz.

Figure 11.58 Jeffrey L. Warburton, scene design for *The Rimers of Eldritch.* University of Arizona, Tucson.

Figure 11.59 Peggy J. Kellner, scene design for *Nobody Loves an Albatross*. Old Globe Theatre, San Diego, Calif.

Figure 11.60 Charles O'Connor, scene design for *The Greeks*. University of Southern California, Los Angeles, Calif.

Figure 11.61 John Wareing, scene design for *Butterflies Are Free*. Playbox Theatre Company, Tucson, Ariz.

Figure 11.62 Robert C. Burroughs, scene design *Misalliance*. ACTF Festival, Fords Theatre, Washington, D.C.

Figure 11.63 John Wright Stevens, scene design for *The Duchess of Gerolstein.* (bridal cottage scene). San Francisco Opera Company, San Francisco, Calif. Photograph by John Wright Stevens.

Figure 11.64 Mark Donnelly, scene design for *Love's Labour's Lost.* University of Arizona, Tucson.

Figure 11.65 Hal Tiné, scene design for *A Christmas Carol*. Syracuse Stage Company, Landmark Theatre, Syracuse, N.Y.

Figure 11.66 Thom Gilseth, scene design for *The Amorous Flea*. Phoenix Little Theatre, Phoenix, Ariz.

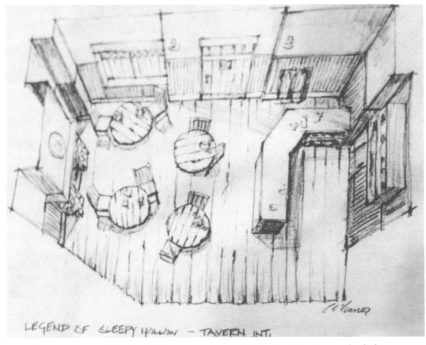

LEGEND OF SLEEPY HOLLOW – TAVERN INT.

Figure 11.67 Charles O'Connor, scene design for *The Legend of Sleepy Hollow*. Tall Tales T.V. Platypus Productions, Los Angeles, Calif.

Figure 11.68 Robert C. Burroughs, scene design for *Dinny and the Witches*. University of Arizona, Tucson.

Figure 11.69 Lee Watson, scene and lighting design for *Carmen*. New Jersey State Opera, Newark.

Figure 11.70 John Wright Stevens, scene design for *La Bohème,* act 2. Cincinnati Opera Company, Cincinnati, Ohio. Photograph by John Wright Stevens.

Figure 11.71   Tom Buderwitz, scene design for *Great Expectations.*
Arizona Theatre Company, Tucson. Photo by Tim Fuller.

Figure 11.72   John Wareing, proposed design for *Aida,* University of
Arizona, Tucson.

Figure 11.73 Charles O'Connor, scene design for *Fabriola*. Ensemble Studio Theatre, Los Angeles, Calif.

Figure 11.74 Peter Wexler, *The Matter of J. Robert Oppenheimer.* Repertory Theatre of Lincoln Center, New York City.

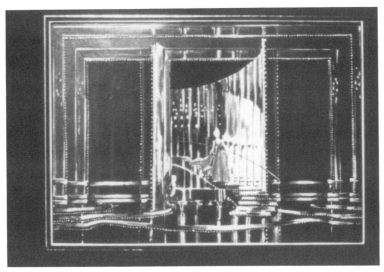

Figure 11.75 Hal Tiné, scene design for *Jerry's Girls*. National Tour and St. James Theatre, N.Y. U.S.A.

Figure 11.76 Peter Wexler, scene design for *The Devils,* Center Theatre Group, Mark Taper Forum, Los Angeles, Calif.

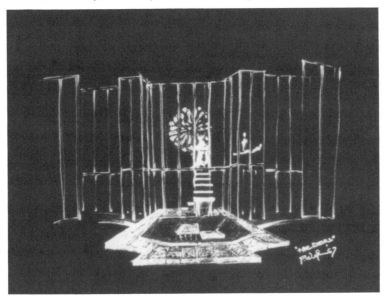

Figure 11.77 Tom Benson, scene design for *Cabaret,* Mainstage, University of Arizona, Tucson.

GLOSSARY

Act curtain Curtain hung at front of stage behind a proscenium arch. Used to separate act changes.

Acting area Performance areas for actors.

Aniline dye Water-soluble dyes available in transparent colors of exceptional brilliance. Used for painting drops, inking, glazing, as well as dying materials. Can be mixed with water-based paints.

Animal glue A substance composed of crude gelatin made from animal parts and used as an adhesive.

Apron Part of the stage area that projects into the auditorium beyond the proscenium or curtain line. Also called the forestage.

Arbor A metal frame housing the counterweights. Used to contain the counterweights when suspending scenery.

Arena stage The acting area surrounded by the audience.

Asbestos curtain A safety curtain made of asbestos used in proscenium theatres to separate stage from auditorium in the event of emergencies. Also called a fire curtain.

Backdrop A painted cloth hung at the back of the stage. Also called a backcloth.

Backing A unit of scenery used to mask backstage areas from the audience. Used outside doors, windows, and other openings to finish the scenic effect.

Backstage Stage areas beyond the acting areas usually defined by the scenery placement. Also called offstage.

Batten A length of pipe (usually 1 1/2 in. in diameter) or lumber hung from above the stage area to support drops, lights, or scenery pieces. Also used to stretch the bottom and top of drops.

Black box theatre A flexible theatre space with movable seating facilities, usually painted black to minimize visual distractions.

Blacks A set of draperies including teasers, legs, and curtains. Usually considered standard proscenium stage equipment.

Bleeding Previously painted surfaces may bleed through to a second coat if not sufficiently sealed with a size base.

Block The framework, metal or wood, for a pulley or sheave.

Bogus paper Gray heavyweight paper in rolls. Used to provide a smooth, absorbent surface for horizontal painting of flats and drops.

Book flat Two flats, hinged together, that can be folded.

Boomerang A mobile, multilevel platform.

Border A narrow horizontal curtain or flat hung parallel to the proscenium to mask lights or hanging scenery from view of the audience.

Box set A setting composed of three walls enclosing the acting area. Usually realistic in design.

Boxing Mixing paint together by pouring from one container to another.

Brace An angled adjustable support for scenery attached to the floor with a stage screw.

Bridge A catwalk built across the stage or auditorium.

Butcher paper Brown wrapping paper available in 3 ft and 6 ft rolls. Used for drawing and masking and for protecting scenery. Also known as brown Kraft paper.

Casein paint A water-soluble paint in paste form with a milk protein base. Easier to use and more permanent than dry pigment paints.

Center line An imaginary line bisecting stage-right from stage left. Drawn on ground plans and used as a basis for measurement in setting up scenery on conventional stages.

Clinch plate A steel plate used under joints during flat assembly to clinch the nails as they are driven through the wood.

Continental seating The arrangement of audience seats in single continuous rows allowing for only two aisles in the auditorium. Originating in Europe, this seating arrangement is becoming increasingly acceptable in recent theatre planning in America.

Counterweight system A mechanical system of flying scenery balanced by weights.

Cue sheet An organized sequence on paper of changes of any kind such as sound, lights, or movements during a performance.

Curtain line A horizontal imaginary line on the stage floor defined by the position of the front curtain. Drawn on ground plans used and as a basis for measurements in setting up scenery on conventional stages. A proscenium line could be an alternative.

Cut drop A backdrop with cutout areas to present a more interesting or realistic effect such as foliage or building silhouettes.

Cyclorama A backdrop painted or lighted to give the effect of sky or space. Usually curved and hung at the back of a stage. Occasionally constructed of plaster or wooden panels.

Dead hung A unit hung permanently above the stage.

Dope An adhesive solution composed of animal glue, whiting, and water. Used to glue muslin and canvas to wood or to create certain textures.

Downstage Area of stage nearest the audience.

Dress rehearsal Final rehearsals complete with sets, lights, costumes, sound, and, of course, actors.

Dutchman A narrow strip of material, usually cloth, used to cover the joining of two flats.

Elevations Mechanical drawings, in scale, of the vertical views of scenery, properties, theatres, and the like.

Escape Offstage step units leading from onstage levels.

Facing Masking pieces for edges of steps and platforms.

False proscenium A unit of scenery shaped like a proscenium. Used to change the size or shape of the permanent proscenium. Usually placed behind the permanent proscenium.

Flood A lighting instrument not usually adjustable that provides a wide distribution of light.

Floor plan A mechanical, scaled drawing of a setting as it appears on the stage floor when viewed from above.

Fly floor A narrow platform along an offstage side wall above the stage floor containing a pin rail from which flown scenery can be operated.

Forestage See **Apron.**

Flipper A narrow flat or jog hinged to a wider unit and set up at an angle.

Grid Metal framework above the stage area, a few feet below the stage house ceiling, which supports the flying system of lines and pulleys.

Grommet A metal eyelet that prevents fraying

and tearing of cloth drops and curtains when they are tied off to battens for hanging. Also called a grummet.

Ground cloth   A stage floor covering of canvas frequently painted as part of the set design. Also called a floor cloth or in England, a stage cloth.

Ground plan   See **Floor plan.**

Ground row   A profile flat placed upstage of the acting area used to mask lighting equipment and the bottom edge of drops or cycloramas.

Hand prop   Small properties used or carried by the actor.

Hanging iron   Stage hardware used for flying scenery. Consists of a metal plate with a ring that can be attached to flats, ceilings, and framed drops.

Hanging plot   A mechanical scale drawing showing the hanging arrangement of the scenery to be flown.

Header   A small flat attached between two standard flats to form an archway or doorway.

House curtain   The main curtain in a proscenium theatre. Also referred to as the act curtain or front curtain.

In one   A setting placed downstage generally within or in front of a larger set. Most frequently used in multiscene musicals.

Jack   A brace for standing scenery.

Jackknife stage   A castored wagon designed to pivot on one corner, which allows it to swing on- or offstage easily.

Jog   A narrow flat used as a wing or an offset in wall.

Keystone   A piece of plywood in the form of a keystone used to join toggle bars to stiles in a flat.

Kraft paper   See **Butcher paper.**

Lash line   The rope attached to a flat and used to secure one flat to another.

Latex paint   A water-soluble paint in liquid form with a rubber base. Compatible with caseins and dry pigments.

Left stage   The left side of the stage when the audience is faced. In England, it is called the prompt side.

Leg   A narrow piece of scenery such as a flat, a piece of canvas, or a curtain that is hung vertically to mask the sides of the stage.

Level   A stage platform.

Lip   A narrow strip of beveled plywood used to mask scenery joints.

Loading bridge/gallery   A platform above the fly floor used to load counterweights for the flying system.

Mask   The use of scenic units to hide backstage areas from the view of the audience.

Offstage   Areas not in the view of the audience.

Olio curtain   An elaborately painted curtain usually placed downstage. Used for backing for vaudeville acts in melodramas.

Onstage   Stage areas in view of the audience.

Paint frame   A large wooden frame to which scenery or a drop can be attached for vertical painting. It is advantageous if the frame can be raised or lowered.

Parallel   A folding platform with a removable top.

Pin rail   A railing of metal or wood on the fly gallery holding pins to which rope lines used for flying scenery can be attached.

Plug   A small flat used to cover an opening in scenery.

Portal   See **False proscenium.**

Priming   The preparation coat of size or paint on new scenery.

Props   Items used onstage that are not costumes or scenery.

Proscenium   An archway or opening in the wall that separates the stage from the audience in a conventional theatre structure.

Rail   The horizontal parts of a flat frame.

Rake   An angled position of a stage floor or platform top. Can also be applied to scenery set on an angle.

Return   Flats set at angles leading offstage. Sometimes used to appear as thickness.

Reveal   Any material used to give the effect of thickness on a piece of scenery.

Right stage   The right side of the stage when the audience is faced. In England it is called opposite prompt side.

Riser   A step, or the vertical face of a step.

Saddle iron   A narrow metal strip of strap iron used to connect the legs of a door flat for stability. Also called a sill iron.

Scale rule   A ruler with the conversion of dimensions into several scales for drafting accurate mechanical drawings. Also called an architect's rule.

Scene dock   A storage area for flats.

Scrim   A loosely woven fabric that can be painted and can be made transparent or opaque by lighting.

Set dressing   Decoration of the setting for visual effects rather than actual use.

Shutter   The door panel of a door unit.

Sightlines   The lines of vision from the most extreme seating positions of the audience that will affect the placement of the scenery on the stage.

Size   The glue and water mixture used to prepare the surface of scenery for paint. Also used as the binding agent for dry pigment.

Smoke pocket   A track or slot on the inside edge of the proscenium in which the asbestos fire curtain runs.

Spot line   A single line from the grid to a specific spot on the stage floor.

Stage screw   A large metal screw with a handle for securing scenery to the stage floor.

Stiffener   A length of lumber on edge used to stiffen several flats hinged together.

Stile   The vertical parts of a flat frame.

Straightedge   A bevel-edged strip of metal or wood, preferably with a handle, used in drawing or painting straight lines on scenery.

Tab curtain   Two separate curtain panels on a track that can be opened or closed. Sometimes rigged to open diagonally for a special draped effect.

Teaser   A short horizontal curtain used for masking at the tip of the stage opening. Similar to a border.

Technical rehearsal   Rehearsal in which scenery, properties, lighting, sound, and shifting is introduced and integrated. The actors are not necessarily involved.

Template   A work table designed to aid in the more accurate construction of flats.

Thickness piece   See **Reveal.**

Thrust stage   The acting area surrounded by the audience on three sides.

Toggle rail   The horizontal center rail or rails of a flat frame.

Tormentor   A flat or curtain used for side masking behind the proscenium and used with the teaser.

Trap   A section of the stage floor that is removable.

Traveller   A track on which curtains can be hung parallel to the proscenium and then opened and closed.

Trim   The planned height of a unit of hung scenery. Also can involve masking. In England, the term used is *"dead."*

Tripping   A system of folding scenery while it is being flown. Used when the stage house height does not allow storage from audience sight.

Tumbler   A length of 1 in. by 3 in. lumber hinged between two flats of a threefold flat unit to allow more efficient handling.

Turntable   A platform that revolves. Frequently built into the stage floor. Used to change scenery units.

Valance   A decorative drapery used at the top of a draped opening.

Vinyl   A water-soluble paint in liquid form with acrylic resin as a base. Fast-drying and durable.

Wagon   A castored platform used for shifting scenery units.

Wainscoting   Decorative wood paneling usually found on the lower portion of a room.

Webbing   A woven jute fabric in narrow width. Used to strengthen and reinforce the tops of curtains and drops.

Winch system   A mechanical system for moving heavy scenic units. Usually power-driven.

Wing and drop   A setting made up of legs, borders, and drops to be used in the early proscenium theatres.

Wings   Right and left offstage areas.

Work light   Minimum lighting used for rehearsals and security.

BIBLIOGRAPHY

ALLPORT, ALAN J., *Model Theatres,* New York: Charles Scribner's Sons, 1978.

ARNOLD, RICHARD L., *Scene Technology,* Englewood Cliffs, N.J.: Prentice-Hall, 1985.

ARSON, JOSEPH, *The Encyclopedia of Furniture,* New York: Crown Publishing, 1965.

ASHWORTH, BRADFORD, *Notes on Scene Painting,* New Haven, Conn.: Whitlocks Inc., 1952.

BAKER, JAMES W., *The Elements of Stagecraft,* Sherman Oaks, Calif.: Alfred Publishing Co., 1978.

BAY, HOWARD, *Stage Design,* New York: Drama Book Specialists, 1974.

BELLMAN, WILLARD F., *Scene Design, Stage Lighting, Sound, Costume and Makeup* (Rev. ed.), New York: Harper and Row, 1983.

BOYLE, WELDON F., *Central and Flexible,* Berkeley: University of California Press, 1956.

BRIDGES-ADAMS, W., *The British Theatre* (3d ed.), London: Longmans, Green and Co., Ltd., 1948.

BROCKET, OSCAR G., *History of the Theatre,* Boston: Allyn and Bacon, Inc., 1968.

BURDICK, ELIZABETH B., PEGGY C. HANSEN, and

BRENDA ZANGER, (eds.), *Contemporary Stage Design USA,* Middletown, Conn.: Wesleyan University Press, 1974.

BURRIS-MEYER, HAROLD, and EDWARD C. COLE, *Scenery for the Theatre* (Rev. ed), Boston: Little, Brown, 1971.

BURRIS-MEYER, HAROLD, and EDWARD C. COLE, *Theatres and Auditoriums,* New York: Reinhold, 1949.

BURRIS-MEYER, HAROLD, and EDWARD C. COLE, *Theatres and Auditoriums* (2d ed.), New York: Reinhold, 1975.

CARTER, CONRAD, A. J. BRADBURY, and W. R. B. HOWARD, *Production and Staging of Plays,* New York: ARC Books, Inc., 1963.

CARTER, PAUL, *Backstage Handbook,* New York: Broadway Press, 1988.

CLIFFORD, JOHN E., *Educational Theatre Management,* Skokie, Illinois: National Textbook Co., 1972.

COLLINS, JOHN, *The Art of Scene Painting,* London: Harrup Ltd., 1985.

DRYDEN, DEBORAH M., *Fabric Painting and Dyeing*

for the Theatre, New York: Drama Book Specialists, 1981.

ELDER, ELDON, *Designs for the Theatre,* New York: Drama Book Specialists, 1978.

EVERETT, HERBERT E., and WILLIAM H. LAWRENCE, *Freehand and Perspective Drawing* (4th ed.), Chicago: American Technical Society, 1946.

FREEDLEY, GEORGE, and REEVES, JOHN, *A History of the Theatre,* (3rd ed.) New York: Crown Publishers, 1968.

FRIEDERICH, WILLARD J., and JOHN H. FRASER, *Scenery Design for the Amateur Stage,* New York: Macmillan Co., 1950.

FUERST, WALTER R., and SAMUEL J. HUME, *Twentieth Century Stage Decoration,* Vol. 1 text, Vol. 2 ill., New York: Dover Publication, 1968.

GASSNER, JOHN, *Producing the Play,* New York: Dryden Press, 1941.

GILLETTE, A. S., *An Introduction to Scene Design,* New York: Harper, 1967.

GILLETTE, A. S., and J. MICHAEL GILLETTE, *Stage Scenery, Its Construction and Rigging* (3d ed.), New York: Harper and Row, 1981.

GILLETTE, J. MICHAEL, *Theatrical Design and Production,* Palo Alto, California: Mayfield Publishing Co., 1987.

GORELIK, MORDECAI, *New Theatres for Old,* New York: Samuel French, 1940.

HAINAUX, RENE (ed.), *Stage Design Throughout the World Since 1960,* New York: Theatre Arts Books, 1972.

HAINAUX, RENE (ed.), *Stage Design Throughout the World Since 1935,* New York: Theatre Arts Books, 1964.

HARTNOLL, PHYLLIS, *The Oxford Companion to the Theatre,* (3rd ed.), London: Oxford University Press, 1967.

HEFFNER, HUBERT, SAMUEL SELDEN, and Hunton Sellman, *Modern Theatre Practice,* New York: Appleton Century-Crofts, 1959.

HELVENSTON, HAROLD, *Scenery, A Manual of Scene Design,* Stanford, Calif.: Stanford University Press, 1931.

JACKSON, ALBERT, and DAY, DAVID, *Tools and How to Use Them,* Alfred A. Knopf: New York, 1978.

JONES, LESLIE A., *Scenic Design and Model Building,* Boston: Walter H. Baker Company, 1939.

JONES, ROBERT EDMOND, *The Dramatic Imagination,* New York: Theatre Arts Books, 1941.

JONES, ROBERT EDMOND, *Drawings for the Theatre,* New York: Theatre Arts Books, 1978.

JOSEPH, STEPHEN, *Scene Design and Painting,* London: Sir Issac Pitman and Sons, Ltd., 1964.

KATZ, JUDITH A., *The Business of Show Business,* New York: Harper and Row Pub., 1981.

KERNODLE, GEORGE and PORTIA, *Invitation to the Theatre,* New York: Harcourt Brace Jovanovich, Inc., 1971.

KOMISARJEVSKY, THEODORE, and LEE SIMONSON, *Settings and Costumes for the Modern Stage,* New York: Benjamin Blom, 1966.

KORNERUP, A. and J. H. WANSCHER, *Reinhold Color Atlas,* New York: Reinhold, 1962.

LANGLEY, STEPHEN, *Theatre Management in America* (Rev. ed.), New York: Drama Book Publishers, 1980.

LOUNSBURY, WARREN C., *Theatre Backstage from A to Z,* Seattle: University of Washington Press, 1967.

MELVILL, HARALD, *Stage Management in the Amateur Theatre,* London: Barrie and Rockliff, 1963.

MIELZINER, JO, *Designing for the Theatre,* New York: Atheneum, 1965.

MIELZINER, JO, *The Shapes of Our Theatre,* New York: Clarkson N. Potter, Inc., 1970.

MOTLEY, *Theatre Props,* London: Studio Vista, 1975.

MacGOWN, KENNETH, and ROBERT EDMOND JONES, *Continental Stagecraft,* New York: Benjamin Blom, Inc., 1964.

NICOLL, ALLARDYCE, *The Development of the Theatre* (Rev. ed.), New York: Harcourt Brace and World, Inc., 1967.

NISBET, HUME, *On Painting in Water Colours* (8th ed.), London: Reeves and Sons Ltd., 1927.

OENSLAGER, DONALD, *Scenery Then and Now,* New York: Russell and Russell, 1966.

OENSLAGER, DONALD, *Stage Design: Four Centuries of Scenic Invention,* New York: Viking, 1975.

PARKER, W. OREN, HARVEY K. SMITH, and R. CRAIG WOLF, *Scene Design and Stage Lighting,* New York: Holt, Rinehart, and Winston, 1985.

PAYNE, DARWIN REID, *Materials and Craft of the Scenic Model,* Carbondale: Southern Illinois University Press, 1976.

PAYNE, DARWIN REID, *Theory and Craft of the Scenographic Model,* (Rev. ed.), Carbondale: Southern Illinois University Press, 1985.

PECTAL, LYNN, *Designing and Painting for the Theatre*, New York: Holt, Reinhart and Winston, 1975.

PENDLETON, RALPH (ed.), *The Theatre of Robert Edmond Jones*, Middleton, Conn.: Wesleyan University Press, 1958.

PHILIPPI, HERBERT, *Stagecraft and Scene Design*, Boston: Houghton Miffin, 1951; Cambridge, Mass.: The Riverside Press, 1953.

PINNELL, WILLIAM H., *Theatrical Scene Painting*, Carbondale: Southern Illinois University Press, 1987.

PRAZ, MARIO, *An Illustrated History of Furnishings*, New York: Braziller, 1964.

REID, FRANCIS, *The Staging Handbook*, London: Pitman Publishing Limited, 1978.

ROWELL, KENNETH, *Stage Design*, Studio Vista, 1968.

SHERINGHAM, GEORGE, and JAMES LAVER (eds.), *Design in the Theatre*, London: The Studio, Ltd., 1927.

SIMONSON, LEE, *Part of a Lifetime*, New York: Duell, Sloan and Pearce, 1943.

SIMONSON, LEE, *The Stage Is Set*, New York: Theatre Arts Books, 1964.

SIMONSON, LEE, *The Art of Scenic Design*, New York: Reinhold, 1968.

SPELTZ, ALEXANDER, *The Styles of Ornament*, New York: Dover, 1959.

SPORRE, DENNIS, *The Creative Impulse*, Englewood Cliffs: New Jersey, Prentice-Hall, Inc., 1987.

SPORRE DENNIS, *Perceiving the Arts*, 3d ed., Englewood Cliffs, New Jersey: Prentice-Hall, 1989.

STEIL, W. JOSEPH, *Scenery*, New York: Richards Rosen Press, 1970.

SWEET, HARVERY, *Graphics for the Performing Arts*, Boston: Allyn and Bacon, 1985.

WARRE, MICHAEL, *Designing and Making Stage Scenery*, London: Studio Vista, 1966.

WELKER, DAVID, *Theatrical Set Design: The Basic Techniques*, Boston: Allyn and Bacon, 1969.

WOLANSKY, WILLIAM D., *Woodworking Made Easy*, New York: Charles Scribner's Sons, 1972.

WOLFE, WELBY B., *Materials of the Scene*, New York: Harper and Row, Inc., 1977.

INDEX

Absurdism, 75
Academia dei Confidenti, 14
Actor movement, 82–83, 91
Actors Equity, 254
Aeschylus, 4
   The Eumenides, 33
Aestheticism, 75–76
Albee, Edward, *104*
Alberti, 10
Aleotti, Giambattista, 14, *15*
Alswang, Ralph, 40–42, *41, 42*
American National Standards Insti-
   tute (ANSI), 160, 199
American National Theatre and
   Academy, 114
American Society of Safety Engineers,
   199
American Theatre Wing Award, 43
Anderson, Maxwell, 35
Antoine, Andre, 31–32
   naturalistic movement, 31–32
   Theatre Libre, 32
Appia, Adolphe, 32
   The New Stagecraft, 32
Architects, theatre, 13–14, 17, 36–37
Architectural principle of theatre de-
   sign (see Theatre design)
Architecture (*see* Theatre architec-
   ture)
Arena stage (*see* Stages, types of)
Ariosto, 10, 13
Aristotle, 2–3
   Poetics, 79
   theory of drama, 73
   theory of play analysis, 73–75
Aronson, Boris B., 43
Audience (*see* Theatre design)
Awards, theatrical and dramatic:
   American Theatre Wing, 43
   Maharram, 43
   New York Critics, 43
   Tony, 43
Ayers, Lemuel, 40,*40*

Bach, J. S., *76*
Bailey, James, *41–42*
Bakst, Leon, 34
Balance, as a principle of composi-
   tion, 57–58
   asymmetrical, 58, *60*
   radial, 58, *60*
   symmetrical, 58, *59*
     bilateral symmetry, 58,
Balzac, 79
Bancrofts, 29
Baroque theatre (*see* Theatre, types of)
Basic Building Code, 199
Bay, Howard, 42–44, *44,* 106
Beckman, Max, *78*
Belasco, David 32, 35
Bel Geddes, Norman, 35–37, *37*
Benois, Alexander, 34
Benson, Tom, *280, 300*
Betterton, 23
Bjornson, Maria, *275*
Booth, 31
Boston University, 45
Boucicault, Dion, 29
Brahm, Otto, 32
Breton, Andre, 81
Brick, painting techniques for (*see*
   Scene painting)
Broadway theatre (*see* Theatre, types
   of)
Brook, Peter, 41

Brotherhood of Painters, Decorators
   and Paperhangers of the
   United States and Canada,
   AFL-CIO, 107
Bruneticre, Ferdinand, 74
Bryson, Nicholas, 193
Buderwitz, Tom, *297*
Burbage, James, 17–19
Burlesque, 71, 96
Burletta, 71
Burris-Meyer, Harold, 89–90
Burroughs, Robert C., *117, 278, 281,*
   284, 295
Bury, John, 45

Capon, William, 25
Carnegie Tech, 45
Ceiling unit, 187
   book ceiling, 187
Charles, Emperor, 20
Charles I, King, 20
Chekhov, Anton, 32
   The Cherry Orchard, 32
   Three Sisters, 32
Chicago World's Fair of 1893, 31
Classicism, 76
Cochran, C.B. 38
Cole, Edward, 89–90
Color:
   as an element of composition, 51–
     55
   hue, 51–52, 228
     color wheel, 51–52, *54,* 55, 228
     spectrum, 51–53, 228
   intensity, 55–57, 228
     chroma, 55
   palette, 56
     warm and cool colors, 56
   pigments and paints, 227–33
   value, 52–55
     brilliance, 54–55, 228
     saturation, 53–55, 228
Comedy, 71
   types of, 10–11, 71–72
Community theatre (*see* Theatre, types
   of)
Composition:
   elements of:
     color, 51–57
     form, 50–51
     line, 47–50
     mass, 57
   principles of:
     balance, 57–58
     focal area, 58–61
     proportion, 61–62
     repetition, 57
     unity, 62–63
   additional factors:
     style, 64–67
     texture, 63–64
Computer Aided Drafting and Design
   (CADD)
   for scene design drawings, 169–75
   hardware:
     Apple II and IIG, 170
     IBM PC, 170–73
     Macintosh, 170
   software:
     MacPaint, 175
Concerts, 94–95
Connelly, Marc, 34
Constructivism, 34, 76
Copeau, Jacques, 34–35
Copyrighting designs, 122–23

Craig, E. Gordon, 32–33, 38, 76, 87
Craven, Hawes *260, 261, 269, 270, 276*
Crowley, Bob, *274*
Cubism, 76–77
Curtains, stage, 187–88
Cycle plays, 71
Cycloramas, 246

Da Bibiena family, 20–21
Dance, 96
De Hooch, Pieter, 57
   Interior of a Dutch House, 57, *59* (ren-
     dering)
Del Cogo, Nicollo, 11
De Loutherbourg, Philippe Jacques,
   25
Designers, costume, 256
Designers, lighting, 256
Design process, set (*see* Scene design,
   process)
D'Este, Duke Ercole, 10, 11
Devine, Jerry, 84, *85*
Diaghilev, Sergei, 34
Donnelly, Mark, *104, 105, 279, 282,*
   287, 293
Drafting for scene design, 141–82
   accessories, 151–53
   computers for, 169
   conventions of, 156–59
     types of lines, 156–59
   drawing media, 152–54
   equipment, 141–56
   reproduction, methods of, 154
   scale, drawing to, 165–66
   techniques, 154–56
   types of drawings, 166–69
Drama, legitimate, 94–95
Drame, 71
Drawings, types of, 166–82
   computer, 169–75
   isometric, 166–68, *167*
   oblique, 168–69, *170*
   orthographic projection, 166, *167*
   persective, 175–82
   sectional views, 169, *170*
Drops, 187–88
   painting of, 245–47
   sizing, 246
Dyer, Chris, *272*
Dyes, aniline, 227, 231

Eckart, William and Jean 40–41, *43*
Eclecticism, 77–78
Educational theatre (*see* Theatre, types
   of)
Edwards, Ben, 42
Eigsti, Karl, 45
Elizabeth, Empress, 20
Elizabethan Stage Society, 33
Elizabeth theatre, 17–20, 96
   architecture, 17–18
   masques, 20
   stage design, 18–20, 96
English Licensing Act of 1737, 71
English Restoration, theatre during,
   23
Equity Waiver theatre (*see* Theatre,
   types of)
Esslin, Martin, 75
Expressionism, 78
   effect scenery, 34

Farrah, 45
Fauvism, 78–79
Fechter, Charles, 27, 29

Fielding, Henry, 71
Flats, 184–86
  plain, 184–86
  profile, 186
Focal area, as a principle of composition, 58–61
  color, 61
  confluence of line, 61, *61*
  encirclement, 61, 62
Foliage, painting techniques for (*see* Scene painting)
Ford Grant, 43
Form, as an element of composition, 50–51
France, Anatole, 35
Frederich the Great, 21
Freud, Sigmund, 81
Futurism, 79

Galli da Bibiena, Antonio, 21
Galli da Bibiena, Carlo, 21
Galli da Bibiena, Ferdinando, 20–21, 25
Galli da Bibiena, Francesco, 21
Galli da Bibiena, Giuseppe, 21, *22*, 25
Galsworthy, John, 32
Garland, Judy, 94
Garrick, David, 25
Gilbert and Sullivan, 95
Gilseth, Thom, *118, 286, 290, 294*
Goethe, Johann, 28, 81
Goetsch, David L., 175
Goldoni, Carlo, *126–129, 136, 138–39*
Gorky, Maxim, 32
Graf, Herbert, 93
Greece:
  history of scene design in, 1–6
  stage machinery 4–6
  theaters, *2, 3, 4, 5*
Grieve Family, *261, 262, 263*
Grieve, John Henderson, *265*
Grieve, Thomas, *27, 85*
Ground plans, of stage settings, 135, *136*
Guggenheim fellowship, 43
Gunter, John, *272*

Handel, G. F., 76
Harris, Audrey, 42
Harris, Margaret F., 42
Hauptman, 32
Henslowe, 17–20

IBM computers, 170–73, *174*
Ibsen, Henrik, 32
Immerman, Karl, 31
Impressionism, 79
International Alliance of Theatrical Stage Employees (IATSE), 108
Irving, Sir Henry, 29, 31
Italian Renaissance theatre, 10–16

Jacobs, Sally, *273*
James I, King, 20
Jones, Inigo, 20, *21*, 23
Jones, Robert Edmond, 35, 37
Jung, Carl, 81

Kaufman, George S., 34
Kean, Charles, 26–28, 81, 84–85
  Richard II, 27, 28, 85
Kellner, Peggy J., *291*
Kemble, J. P., 25–26
King John, 26
Klingemann, Ernst August Friedrich:
  Columbus, 264
Koltoi, Ralph, 45, *275*

Lawson, John Howard, 35
League of New York Theatres and Producers, Inc., 107, 112

Lee, Ming Cho, 43–44, *278*
Legitimate Theatre Employees (LTE), 108
Lester Polakov School of Design, 45
Line:
  as an element of composition, 47–50
  types, 156–59, 163
Loquasto, Santo, 44–45

Macie, Tom, 126, 127, 128, 129, 134, *136, 138, 277*
Macintosh computer, 170
MacKaye, Steele, 31–32
  Spectatorium, 31–32
Maeterlinck, Maurice, 82, *271*
Maharram Awards, 43
Mamet, David, *134*
Mantegna, 11
Marble, painting techniques for (*see* Scene painting)
Mass, as an element of composition, 57
Massey, Raymond, 36
Matisse, Henri, 78
Mauri brothers, 20
Medieval theatre, 10–12
Melodrama, 72
Messel, Oliver, 38
Metropolitan Opera, New York, 35–36, 44
  Les Troyens, 44
  Ring Cycle, 35
Meyerhold, Vsevolod, 34, 76
Michelangelo, 11
Mielziner, Jo, 36–37, 42–43, 103
Miller, Arthur, 81
Miro, Joan, 48
Models of stage sets, 133–35
  materials for building, 133–34
  procedure for building, 134–35
Moiseivitch, Tanya, 41
Moliere, 34, 71
Montgomery, Bruce, 84, *85*
Montgomery, Elizabeth, 42
Morgan, Henry, 182
Motion pictures, 96–97
Musicals, 94–95
Musicals, titles of (*see* Theatrical works)

Naguchi, 34
Napier, John, 45
National Association of Broadcasting Engineers and Technicians (NABET), 108
National Board of Fire Underwriters, 199
National Building Code, 199
National Endowment for the Arts, 114
National Fire Protection Association, 199
National Institute for Occupational Safety and Health, 199
National Safety Council, 198
Naturalism, 79
Nemiravich-Danchenko, Vladimir, 32
Neoclassicism, 79–80
Neorealism, 80–81
Nestroy, Johann, 31
New School for Social Research, 34
The New Stagecraft, 32–34
  apprentices in, 36–37
  expressionist effect on scenery, 34
New York Critics Awards, 43
Nicholas V, 10
Night club cabaret, 94–95

Occupational Safety and Health Administration (OSHA), 199
O'Connor, Charles, *291, 295, 298*
Oenslager, Donald, 36–39, 42–44
Off-Broadway theatre (*see* Theatres, types of)

Olympic Academy, 11, 13
O'Neill, Eugene, 34–35
Opera, grand, 92–3
Orchestra, 2, 6–7

Pageants, 92–93
Paints, (*see* Scene design)
Paint shop, theatre:
  equipment and its care, 242–45
  organization and layout, 242–45
Palladio, Andrea, 13, 20
Papp, Joseph, 43
Parsons, Terry, 45
Payne, Howard, *265*
Perspective drawing, 175–82
  center of vision, 177
  drop-point, 177–82, *178, 179, 180*
  grid-method perspective, *181*, 182
  linear perspective, 175
  observsation point, 177
  picture plane, 177
  tormentor plane, 177
  vanishing point, 177–82
Peruzzi, Baldessare, 13
Piaf, Edith, 94
Picasso, Pablo, 34, 76, 77
Pigments (*see* Scene painting)
Pinero, Arthur Wing, 32
Pirandello, 75
Piscator, Erwin, 34
Planche, J. R., 26, 29
Platforms, types of, 188–90
  folding, 188–90
  metal, 188–90
  rigid, 188–90
  wagons, 189–90
Plautus, 11
Play analysis, 68–86
  Aristotle's concept, 73–75
  facts or story, 70
  genre, 70–73
  mood, 72
  plot, 73–75
  production demands, 82–86
  reading the play, 68–70
  research, 84–86
  setting, 70
  style, 75–82
Plays:
  genre:
    autos sacramentales, 70–71
    burlesque, 71
    burletta, 71
    comedy, 71
    cycle plays, 71
    drame, 71
    farce, 72
    history plays, 72
    melodrama, 72
    miracle plays, 72
    morality plays, 72
    mystery plays, 72
    pastoral, 72
    tragedy, 72–73
  religious, 1, 10
    autos sacramentales, 70–71
    cycle plays, 71
    Medieval theatre, 10
    miracle plays, 72
    morality plays, 72
    mystery plays, 72
Plot, in play analysis, 73–75
  complication, 74
  denouement, 74–75
  exposition, 73–74
Poel, William, 31, 33, 38
Pollock, Jackson, *50*
Pollux, 4, 6, 10
Pompey, 7
Portfolio, development of a design, 118–19
Presentation, 97

Production, elements that impact
  scene design, 82–86
  actor movement, 82–83
  audience needs, 88–93
    acoustics, 90–91
    lack of distractions, 91
    safety, 92
    seating comfort, 92–93
    vision, 89
  furniture, 83
  property, 83–84
  scene changes, 84
Productions, theatrical, types of:
  burlesque, 71, 96
  concert, 94–95
  dance, 96
  grand opera, 92–93
  legitimate drama, 94–95
  motion pictures, 96–97
  musicals, 94–95
  night club cabaret, 94–95
  pageant, 92–93
  presentation, 97
  vaudeville revue, 92–93
Property, stage, 83, 193–97
  decor items, 194, 196–97
  Elizabethan, 20
  exteriors, 196–97
  floor covering, 196
  furniture, 195–96
  naturalistic, 31
  nineteenth-century English, 25
  obtaining, 195
  property head, 254
  researching, 194
  special effects, 197
  types, 193–96
    breakaway, 194
    hand, 194
    set, 193–96
  window treatments, 196
Proportion, as a principal of composition, 61–62
  scale, 61
Puppets, 97

Raphael, 11
Realism, 81
Regional theatre (see Theatre, types
  of)
Reinhardt, Max, 33–34, 36, 77
  eclecticism, 77
Renaissance, Italian, theatre, 10–17
Renderings, color, 128–33, 175
  materials for watercolors, 129–31
  perspective drawing, 175–82
  techniques of watercolor painting,
    131–33
Repetition, as a principle of composi-
  tion, 57
  harmony, 57
  rhythm, 57
  variation, 57
Resume, composition of, 120–22
Riario, Cardinal, 10
Rice, Elmer, 34, 35
Ricketts, Charles, 32, 33, 271
Robertson, Tom, 29
Robinson, Frederick Cayley, 271
Roman Academy, 11
Roman theatre, 6–10
Romanticism, 81
Rorke, Richard, 115

Sabbatini, 16
Sabo, Jonathan, 277
Sachs, Curt, 75
Sainthill, Loudon, 41
Scamozzi, Vicenzo, 13–14
Scene design:
  for audience visibility, 89
  drafting, 141–82

employment in, 107–9
  assistant to designers, 108
  Broadway theatre, 107–9
  contracts, 122
  copyright, 122–23
  design portfolio, 118–19
  educational theatre, 116–17
  equity waiver theatres, 113–14
  off-Broadway theatre, 107–9
  outside the theatre, 109
  regional theatre, 114–16
  resume, 120–22
  showcase theatre, 113–14
  unions, 107–10
history of, 1–46
  American, 35–38
  in ancient and classical Greece,
    1–4, 3
  antiquarianism, 26–27
  British, 38–39, 45
  Elizabethan, 17–20, 96
  European, 32–35
  in France, 31
  Greco-Roman, 6
  in Hellenistic Period, 4–6
  in Italian Renaissance, 10–17
  Medieval theatre, 10
  in nineteenth-century England,
    25–31
  in Rome, 6–10
  since World War II, 39–46
  in Spain and Holland, 17
movements in:
  constructivism, 34
  expressionism, 34
  naturalism, 31–32
  New Stagecraft, 32–34
perspective drawings, 175–82
play analysis for, 68–86
production demands on, 82–86
  production calendar, 256–58
process, 124–40
  color renderings, 128–33
  ground plans, 135
  models, 133
  presentation sketches, 126–28
  sightline drawings, 135, 137
  thumbnail sketches, 125–26
university programs in, 37, 39, 45,
  106–7
as visual art, 47–67
  elements of composition, 47–57
  principles of composition, 57–63
working sketches, renderings,
  models and front elevations,
  125–39
Scene painting, 226–52
  back painting, 241–42
  base coat, 234
  detail painting, 240–41
  drop painting, 245–47
  fireproofing, 233
  glazing, 241
  horizontal method, 233, 242, 246
  mixing paints, 231–33
  pigments and paints, 227–31
  prime coat, 234
  scenic studio, 227
  special effects, 247–51
    brick, 249–50
    draperies, 250–51
    foliage, 247–48
    marble, 250–51
    stones, 249
    wood graining, 248–49
  texture coats, 234–40
    applique, 237
    dry brushing, 236
    flagging, 238
    rag rolling, 237–38, 239
    rolling, 237, 239
    sponging, 238, 240

spraying, 238
sputtering, 235–36
stamping, 238–40
stenciling, 240, 241
stippling, 236–37, 237
vertical method, 233
Scene pigments and paints, 227–33
  dry pigments, 228–30
  earth-tone colors, 228–29
  high-intensity colors, 228–29
  latex paints, 230
  mixing, 231–33
  neutral colors, 228, 230
  paint composition, 228, 232
  protein paints, 230
  size, 228, 230, 232
  vinyl acrylic paints, 230–31
  wet or pulp pigments, 228–30
Scenery:
  box set, 25, 27–29, 32
  building, 1–2, 4, 6–7
    frons scaenae, 7
    skene, 2, 4, 6
  derivation of term, 2
  devices, 20
  machinery, 6
  multiple sets, 101–3
  naturalistic movement, 31–32
  New Stagecraft, 32–34
  painted, 2–4, 10–17, 19–20
  simultaneous set, 30, 101, 103–4
  traps, 29
  units, 101, 103–4, 183–92
    curved units, 191–92
    three-dimensional units, 188–90
    two-dimensional units, 183–88
  wing and drop set, 20, 23, 25, 27, 32
Scene shop, 197–225
  location, 198
  materials, 212–25
    fabric, 213–16
    hardware, 219–25
    lumber, 212–13
    metals, 218–19
    paper and fiber, 217–18
    plastics, 216–17
  safety and security, 198–200
    fireproofing, 199–200
    OSHA regulations, 199
  size, 197–98
  tools, 200–212
    hand, 200–208
    metalworking, 211–12
    power, 208–11
Schmidt, Douglas, 45, 281
Schreyvogel, Josef, 26
Semper, Gottfried, 30
Seneca, 11
Serlio, Sabastian, 14, 16, 20
Sets:
  building the, 183–225 (see also Scen-
    ery)
    materials for, 212–19
      fabric, 213–16
      hardware, 219–25
      lumber, 212–13
      metals, 218–19
      paper and fiber, 217–18
      plastics, 216–17
  installing the, 256–58
  properties and furniture, 193–97
  scene shop, 197–212
  sculptured effects and textures,
    192–93
Shakespeare, William, 18, 25, 31, 34,
  72–73, 81–82
  All's Well That Ends Well, 272
  Anthony and Cleopatra, 19
  As You Like It, 274
  The Comedy of Errors, 274
  Cymbeline, 260, 276

Hamlet, 27, *29,* 31, 33, 35–36, *268,*
    275
Henry V, 264, 266–67
Henry VIII, 269
Julius Ceasar, 72
King John, 82, *83*
King Lear, 83
Macbeth, 269
A Midsummer Night's Dream, 34, *260,*
    273, 276
Much Ado about Nothing, 275
Oedipus Rex, 34
Othello, 268
Richard II, 27, 28, 85
Richard III, 19, 35
Romeo and Juliet, 285
Shaw, George Bernard, 32
Shops, theatre:
    construction head, 254
    paint, 242–45
    scene, 197–225
Showcase theatres (*see* Theatre, types
    of)
Shune, Larry, 74
Sightline:
    drawings, 135
    planning, 89–90
Simonson, Lee, 35, *36,* 37, 103
Singelis, James T., *111, 283, 289*
Sketches, *125–28, 175–82*
    perspective drawing, *175–82*
    presentation, *126–28, 127*
    thumbnail, 125–26, *126*
Smith, Oliver, 40, *41*
Smith, Vickie, *116, 287*
Society of Antiquaries, 26
Sophocles, 4, 73
Sporre, Dennis, *83, 85, 102*
Stages:
    apron or forestage, 19, 23
    history of 4, 6–7, 16, 19–23, 25–31,
        97
    machinery, 4–6, 20, 27, 29, 31–32
    types of:
        arena, 90–91, 96, *97*
        elevator, 31
        extended, 99
        jacknife, 6
        mansion, 10, *11,* 20
        open, 91, 98–99
        proscenium, 2, 20–23, 25–26, 89,
            98–101
        thrust, 90–91, 96, *97*
Stanfield, Clarkson, *264*
Stanislavski, Konstantin, 31–32
Stevens, John Wright, *110, 279, 284,*
    293, 296
Stones, painting techniques for (*see*
    Scene painting)
Style:
    in composition, 64–67
    in play analysis, 74–82
        absurdism, 75
        aestheticism, 75–76
        baroque, 76
        classicism, 76
        constructivism, 76
        cubism, 76–77
        eclecticism, 77–78
        expressionism, 78
        fauvism, 78–79
        formalism, 79
        futurism, 79
        hyperrealism, 79
        impressionism, 79
        naturalism, 79
        neoclassicism, 79–80
        neorealism, 80–81
        realism, 81
        romanticism, 81
        surrealism, 81–82
        symbolism, 82

Surrealism, 81–82
Svoboda, Josef, 45–46
Symbolism, 82

Tagg, Alan, 45
Technical Assistance Group (TAG),
    108
Telbin, 27, 29, *266, 268*
Tennyson, Alfred Lord, *270*
Texture, as a factor in composition,
    63–64
Theatre:
    architecture:
        history, 1–46
    design:
        history, 1–46 (*see also* Scene de-
            sign)
    forms (*see also* Stages, types of and
        Sets, types of)
    lighting, 16, 23, 25, 29–32, 91
    plans, 2, 4, 7
    seating, 2, 7, 10, 13–14, 18–19, 21–
        25, 92–93
    staff, 254–56, 258
        construction head, 254
        director, 254, 258
        lighting and costume designers,
            256
        producer, 254
        property head, 254
        stage manager, 254, 258
        technical director, 254
        theatre organization chart, *255*
    types of,
        Broadway, 107–12, 114
        educational, 116–17
        equity waiver, 113–14
        off-Broadway, 112–13
        regional, 114–16
        showcase, 113–14
    visual aspects of, 89–91
Theatres:
    ANTA Washington Square Theatre,
        43
    Arizona Theatre Company, *287,*
        297
    of Aspendos, 8–10
    Astely's, 24
    at Athens, 2–4
    Avery Fisher Hall, 38
    Bayreuth Festspielhaus, *30*
    Blackfriars, 18
    Brugtheater, Vienna, 26
    Buffalo Arena Stage, Buffalo, *282*
    Center Theatre Group, Mark Taper
        Forum, *299*
    Cincinnati Opera Company, *283, 296*
    Court Theatre, Mannheim, Ger-
        many, 28
    Covent Garden, 24, 29, 133, 262–63,
        265, 271
    The Curtain, 17
    Delacorte Theatre, 43, 196–97
    The Fortune, 18–19
    Garrick Theatre, 35
    Georgian theatre, 23–25
    Globe Theatre, 17–19
    Hartford Stage Company, 44
    Haymarket, 271
    Hillberry Repertory Theatre, 126–
        29, 134, 136, 138, *277*
    Hope Theatre, 18
    Hotel de Bourgogne, *24*
    John F. Kennedy Center for the Per-
        forming Arts, 38
    The King's Concert Rooms, 24
    La Scala, Milan, 22
    Long Island Stage Company, *289*
    Lyceum Theatre, 260–61, 268–70
    Madison Square Theatre, 31
    Mainstage, University of Arizona,
        300

    at Marcellus, 7
    at Megalopolis, 4
    Moscow Art Theatre, 31–34
    National Theatre Company, 45
    New Jersey State Opera, *296*
    New York Shakespeare Festival, 44
    New York Yiddish Theatre, 43
    Orange, France, Roman theatre at,
        8, 10
    Pacific Conservatory of the Per-
        forming Arts, *282*
    Pantheon Theatre, 24
    Paris Opera House, 30
    Phoenix Little Theatre, *290, 294*
    Piraeus, 4
    Playbox Community Theatre, *280,*
        292
    Potter's Little Theatre in Haymar-
        ket, 24
    Princess' Theatre, 266–68
    Purdue Music Hall, 87
    Radio City Music Hall, 97, 245
    Repertory Theatre of Lincoln Cen-
        ter, *298*
    The Rose, 17–18
    Royal Circus Theatre, 24
    Royal Shakespeare Company, 41–
        42, 45, *272, 273, 274, 275*
    Royalty Theatre, 24
    Savonlinna Opera Festival, Fin-
        land, *285*
    Saxe-Meiningen Players, 31
    State Opera House, Tbilisi, Georgia
        USSR, *26*
    State Theatre at Lincoln Center, 38
    at Stratford, Canada, 41
    Syracuse at Sicily, 4
    Syracuse Stage Company, Land-
        mark Theatre, *294*
    Teatro di Fano, 22
    Teatro d'Imola, 22
    Teatro di Torino, 22
    Teatro Farnese, Parma, 14–15
    Teatro Olimpico, Vicenza, 13–15,
        133
    Thalion Hall, Wilmington, NC, 87–
        88
    The Theatre, 17
    Theatre da Vieux-Columbier, 34
    Theatre Royal, Drury Lane, London,
        23
    Theatre Royal in Bridges Street,
        London, 23
    Thoricus at Attica, 4
    University of Arizona, *278, 281, 283,*
        284, 285, 286, 288, 290, 293, 295,
        297
    Utah Shakespeare Festival, *280*
    at Valenciennes, France, 10, 12
Tine, Hal, *282, 294, 299*
Toller, 34
Tony award, 43
Tools for set building, 200–212
    hand, 200–207
    metalworking, 211–12
    power, 208–12
Tragedy, 11, 72–73
Tragicomedy, 73
Tucker, Sophie, 94

Union:
    apprenticeship, 108
    designers, 107–8
    exams, 109–10
    membership, 108
    stage hands and technicians, 108
    theatrical unions, 108
United Scenic Artists of America
    (USA), Local No. 829, 107–8,
    112, 122
    exams, 109–110

United States Institute for Theatre Technology (USITT), 108
United States Institute for Theatre Technology Graphic Standards Board Recommendations for Standard Graphic Language in Scene Design and Technical Production, 156, 159–65
  conventions, 160
  dimensions, 161
  general description, 159
  ground plan, 159–60
  lettering, 160
  line weights, 160, 163
  symbols, 164–65
  title block, 160–61

Unity, as a principle of composition, 62–63
University of Indiana, 45
University of Iowa, 45

Vanbrugh, 23, 24
Van Gogh, Vincent, *49*
Vaudeville, 25
  revue, 92–95
Vestris, Mme., 28–29
Victoria and Albert Museum, 194
Visibility, audience, 89–90
  polychromatic vision, 89
Vitruvius, 2, 4, 10, 13–14

Wagner, Richard, 27, 30
Wagner, Robin, 45
Warburton, Jeffrey L., *290*

Wareing, John, *280, 283, 285, 290, 297*
Warhol, Andy, 57, *58*
Watson, Lee, *296*
Webb, John, 23
Wexler, Peter, 44, *108, 113, 285, 298, 299*
Whistler, Rex, 38
Wilde, Oscar, 32, 76, *271*
Wildinson, Norman, 32
Williams, Tennessee, 81
Willis, W. G., 270

Yale University Drama School, 37, 43–44
Yale University, 45

Zola, 79

dehmutt